Propaganda and the Cyprus Revolt

Propaganda and the Cyprus Revolt

Rebellion, Counter-insurgency and the Media, 1955–59

Maria Hadjiathanasiou

I.B. TAURIS

LONDON • NEW YORK • OXFORD • NEW DELHI • SYDNEY

I.B. TAURIS
Bloomsbury Publishing Plc
50 Bedford Square, London, WC1B 3DP, UK
1385 Broadway, New York, NY 10018, USA
29 Earlsfort Terrace, Dublin 2, Ireland

BLOOMSBURY, I.B. TAURIS and the I.B. Tauris logo are trademarks
of Bloomsbury Publishing Plc

First published in Great Britain 2020
This paperback edition published in 2021

Series design by Adriana Brioso
Cover image: A British soldier handing out documents while carrying
out interrogation work in Cyprus (© Bert Hardy / Stringer / Getty Images)

A catalogue record for this book is available from the British Library.

A catalogue record for this book is available from the Library of Congress.

ISBN: HB: 978-1-7883-1731-3
        PB: 978-0-7556-3754-6
      ePDF: 978-1-7867-3617-8
     eBook: 978-1-7867-2611-7

Typeset by Integra Software Services Pvt. Ltd.

To find out more about our authors and books visit www.bloomsbury.com
and sign up for our newsletters.

Contents

List of figures

Foreword

The conflict fought in Cyprus between Greek Cypriot fighters and British security forces is usually dated to the four years between 1955 and 1959. Most of the Island's Greek Cypriot majority wanted their colonial relationship with Britain to end; many favoured union (*Enosis*) with the Greek motherland, and some, particularly the young, were prepared to fight for these goals. Within the British Empire, Cyprus was something of an anomaly. A classic garrison colony, its shoreline nestling close to the Arab world, its base facilities and listening stations were becoming more, not less strategically significant over time. The violence in Cyprus, often depicted as an asymmetric war between local guerrillas, British soldiers and police, ran far deeper than this more limited contest suggests, leaving enduring legacies of sociocultural division, of communities and families torn apart. We now have abundant evidence – and, thanks to works like this one, more continues to emerge – of systematic rights abuses. Understandably perhaps, histories of these episodes, and of the conflict more generally, have tended to dwell longest on the conduct of the revolt and its suppression. But the contest to determine the future of Cyprus was not wholly a matter of bombs, bullets and beatings. Neither armed struggle nor the punitive restrictions of a four-year security clampdown definitively won out. Ultimately, it was the illegitimacy of Britain's colonial grip on Cyprus, as well as the methods employed to sustain it, that placed the island under hostile global scrutiny. This was a war of words and images. Sworn statements, photographs and news footage, grainy radio broadcasts heard on transistor radios, these were the audiovisual media of contested decolonization. The competing narratives about what was happening and why, the searing imagery of violence, much of it perpetrated against civilians and children, and the impassioned arguments – in pamphlets, in the press and in the courts – over rights claimed and rights denied: all of these things resonated locally and transnationally. In such volatile circumstances, the power, not just to coerce but to persuade, was what mattered most. It is this power that this book explores.

Maria Hadjiathanasiou's journey through the Cyprus revolt takes us to entirely new evidential and conceptual terrain as she charts the propaganda war fought between the British colonial authorities and their Greek Cypriot opponents in EOKA and other pro-*Enosis* groups. Advancing carefully, sometimes along, but frequently against, the archival grain, the book capitalizes on two bodies of evidence. Their contents tell very different stories – or, more often, the same stories very differently. First are the British Colonial Office files that formed part of the so-called Migrated Archive, a vast collection of records, much of it relating to colonial repression. Thanks to the efforts of historians David Anderson, Caroline Elkins, Huw Bennett and others, these materials have at last been made available to researchers. Second is the archive for the Historical Memory of the Struggle in Nicosia, a combination of Greek-language sources, locally retained colonial records and a panoply of EOKA materials. These records, some British, some Cypriot, certainly work to persuade. Their arguments come freighted with the cultural presumptions, the ideological claims and the policy objectives of their authors. Yet propaganda, as Hadjiathanasiou reminds us, is more than an effort of political persuasion. The evidence adduced to support it is selective. The mediums used to advance it are as varied as the recipients who read, hear or see it. To maximize their effectiveness, propagandist messages must be cut to the cloth of their audience. The most successful propaganda does not come off the peg; it is tailored. Its design may be simple; it may be sophisticated; to succeed, it must be relentless. Propagandists don't just relate information; they weaponize it: to convince others to do their bidding.

Finding an analytical path through such material is hard work. A great strength of this book lies in the care with which it triangulates opposing accounts of key episodes, landmark legal cases and mounting social protests as the Cyprus revolt developed. British propaganda efforts, sometimes half-hearted, often half-baked, were additionally hidebound by an institutional disdain for psychological warfare and the mind games such tactics implied. Britain's propaganda efforts seem, as a result, to have been a matter of catch-up, lagging hopelessly behind in trying to countermand the claims of the Orthodox Church, the Athens government, EOKA and its political wing, PEKA. More fundamentally perhaps, what emerges in the pages to follow is the dawning realization that the British simply lacked an authentic or persuasive propagandist message for the Greek Cypriot majority. Appeals to a safer political stewardship or a more stable economic future were hardly a match for the call to Hellenic ethno-religious unity and the attendant end of colonial oversight. If the effectiveness with which EOKA and its supporters pilloried British propagandist claims emerges powerfully, so do the attempts made by some unlikely British propagandists, among them the writer Lawrence Durrell, and the Director General of Information Services and psychological warfare in Cyprus Leslie Glass, to make the case for a British presence. It all makes for a fascinating study and a rewarding read.

Martin Thomas, Professor of Imperial History, University of Exeter

Abbreviations

AKEL	Progressive Party of Working People (*Anorthotiko Komma Ergazomenou Laou*)
AKOE	Anti-Killers Organisation of Expatriates (EOKA, reversed spelling)
ANE	Strong Youth of EOKA (*Alkimos Neolaia*)
BBC	British Broadcasting Corporation
BMEO	British Middle East Office
CBS	Cyprus Broadcasting Service
CIC	Cyprus Intelligence Committee
CID	Crime Investigation Department (Nicosia)
CIGS	Chief of the Imperial General Staff
CSA	Cyprus State Archives (Nicosia)
EOKA	National Organization of Cypriot Fighters (*Ethniki Organosis Kyprion Agoniston*)
GHQ	General Headquarters
IRU	Information Research Unit (Nicosia)
IWM	Imperial War Museum (London)
JIC	Joint Intelligence Committee (London)
MELF	Middle East Land Forces
MRLA	Malayan Races Liberation Army
NATO	North Atlantic Treaty Organization
OXEN	Christian Orthodox Youth Association (*Orthodoxi Christianiki Enosi Neon*)

PEKA   Political Committee of the Cypriot Struggle
            (*Politiki Epitroph Kypriakou Agonos*)

PEON   Pancyprian National Youth Organisation
            (*Pagkyprios Ethniki Organosis Neolaias*)

PIO   Press and Information Office (Nicosia)

RAF   Royal Air Force

SIG   Special Investigations Group (Nicosia)

SIMAE   Archive of the Council for the Historical Memory of the Struggle
            (*Symvoulio Istorikis Mnimis Agona EOKA*, Nicosia)

SEATO   Southeast Asia Treaty Organization

SOE   Special Operations Executive

S. of S.   Secretary of State for the Colonies

TNA   The National Archives (London)

UN   United Nations

Timeline of key events

1878	Britain occupies Cyprus. The island stays nominally under Ottoman sovereignty.
1914	Cyprus annexed by Britain after more than 300 years of Ottoman rule, in response to Turkey's alliance with Germany and Austro-Hungary in the First World War.
1925	Cyprus becomes a British Crown Colony.
1931	Cypriots protest against British rule. Government House is burned down. Martial law is declared. Decade of 'illiberal rule' follows under Governor Herbert Palmer.
1950	Makarios is elected Archbishop and *Ethnarch* of Cyprus. He becomes the leader of the campaign for *enosis* with the support of Greece.
1954	Robert Armitage becomes governor.
1955	General George Grivas and EOKA guerrilla organization begin an anti-colonial armed campaign on 1 April in pursuit of union with Greece. Field Marshal John Harding becomes governor and declares Cyprus in a state of emergency.
1956	Harding deports Makarios to the Seychelles after negotiations break down.
1957	Harding resigns and is replaced by diplomat Hugh Foot.
1958	Intercommunal conflicts between Turkish Cypriots and Greek Cypriots. British security forces intervene.
1959	Agreement signed between Britain, Turkey and Greece for Cyprus's independence.
	End of the emergency.
	Makarios returns to Cyprus.
1960	Cyprus gains independence. Treaty of Guarantee gives Britain, Greece and Turkey the right to intervene. Britain retains sovereignty over two military bases.

Introduction

This book reconstructs for the first time the history of propaganda in Cyprus at the end of empire, focusing on the years of the Greek Cypriot anti-colonial revolt against the British ruler between 1955 and 1959. It provides an original critical analysis of propaganda during the tumultuous 1950s, as used by the British and the Greek Cypriot/Greek sides, and it argues for propaganda's catalytic role in the development and final outcome of the revolt/emergency.[1]

The book adopts John M. MacKenzie's definition of propaganda:

> Propaganda can be defined as the transmission of ideas and values from one person, or groups of persons, to another, with the specific intention of influencing the recipients' attitudes in such a way that the interests of its authors will be enhanced. Although it may be veiled, seeking to influence thoughts, beliefs and actions by suggestion, it must be conscious and deliberate.[2]

This definition is used here alongside Simon J. Potter's argument on the boundaries of propaganda. According to Potter propaganda, information and education 'often blend into one another', as 'it is often in the interests of the propagandist consciously to blur the boundaries that separate them. Facts are seldom entirely uncooked.'[3] Next to the discussion on propaganda and information, a third term is added: 'psychological warfare'. The analysis of the archival material shows that during the Cyprus Emergency, British peacetime 'propaganda' was sometimes dubbed 'psychological warfare' often only to give the impression to those who were conducting it that they were engaged in a specialized form of counter-insurgency propaganda reserved for times of armed conflict.

In the existing historiography the significance of propaganda in the Cyprus revolt has not been given the attention that I argue here it deserves. British, Greek and Greek Cypriot propaganda had a radical effect on the development of events in Cyprus, significantly contributing to the island's independence in 1960. This argument is supported here using a variety of archival material, much of it unpublished and some of it recently declassified, accessed in the UK and Cyprus. It is demonstrated here that propaganda was a vital aspect of the insurgency and counter-insurgency campaigns during Cyprus's decolonization. Propaganda was an indispensable weapon of the insurgents and the counter-insurgents and an issue that constantly preoccupied the adversaries throughout the 1950s, before and during the armed conflict.

Simon J. Potter argues for propaganda's effectiveness when propaganda 'works with the grain of pre-existing ideas, beliefs and attitudes. If it is not to be rejected by its target audience, propaganda needs to chime with what people already think. It can seek to modify, augment, or reshape those preconceptions'.[4] It is argued here that British propaganda efforts in Cyprus were weak, disoriented and lacked a clear and consistent message. Various local but also international factors affected the ambitions and efforts of British propaganda about Cyprus, on the island and abroad. As I examine in the following chapters, arguably the most important factor was the lack of political direction coming from London regarding the future of Cyprus. This led to an ambiguous colonial policy on the ground. The lack of a clear plan for the future of the island made it impossible to weave an attractive story to tell and sell to the Greek Cypriots who, with the guidance of their religious and political leader Archbishop Makarios III, were asking for *enosis* (Cyprus's political union with Greece). The following chapters examine how the propaganda of the British colonial government failed to present the Greek Cypriots with a compelling, alternative future to *enosis*, even though it tried and even though it was a vital tool in British attempts in persuasion. As Lawrence Durrell elegantly phrased it, in Cyprus 'the stimulus of rhetoric' was not enough to stimulate the desired audience reaction.[5]

During the Cyprus revolt, services and servants of propaganda were responsible for producing and disseminating propaganda that, overtly or covertly, publicized and reinforced the positions of two rivals found in the island at the time: the British colonial government and the pro-*enosis* Cyprus *Ethnarchy* (i.e. Church of Cyprus leadership). Propagandists on the ground and elsewhere, in London, Athens, Ankara and Washington, often had the double role of recipient and supplier of propaganda, as they were exposed to propagandistic material coming from the opposing side. The effect and reach of propaganda upon its respective audiences, be that Greek Cypriot, British or international, arguably shaped the behaviour of these audiences. As the revolt progressed, propaganda not only influenced the behaviour of a respective interested party (UK, Greece, Turkey, Cyprus), but importantly, its goals and objectives in relation to Cyprus.

This book identifies and critically examines the propaganda tools of British, Greek Cypriot and Greek agencies acting in a formal and/or informal capacity on the part of their national (political, strategic and economic) interests during Cyprus's violent opposition to the British Empire. Research shows that propaganda in Cyprus was produced in and travelled through written, aural, oral and visual material, in the form of leaflets, radio and television broadcasts, newspapers and periodicals, cinema films, voice aircraft and, last but not least, word of mouth. Information and propaganda, psychological warfare, entertainment, public relations and cultural diplomacy were all called to arms. In order to comprehend how thoughts, ideas and worries on the issue of propaganda were translated into propaganda actions, I will pay special attention to key channels of propaganda for Cyprus: the media and their use by propagandists and their respective organizations in Cyprus and abroad (Cyprus Broadcasting Service [CBS], Athens Radio etc.).

On the issue of assessing the success or failure of the application of these 'tools', Erik Linstrum argues that in the case of the British Empire it was especially difficult to confirm that, for example, a propaganda pamphlet induced insurgents to surrender. 'So if imperial psychology was too big – in terms of the ambitions proclaimed by its champions – to ever fully succeed, it was also too big – too diffuse, too important to careers, and too entangled with endless other variables – to definitely fail. Its appeal resisted refutation.'[6] What I argue here is that in the episode of the Cyprus revolt, propaganda's 'appeal' on both sides 'resisted refutation', even though its results were diverse and not always successful.[7]

Focusing on propaganda's decision-making process and its application process has led to new information on the mode of interaction between competing propagandists. The research into the unpublished primary material, such as correspondence between the various interested parties on the 'future of Cyprus', a frequent topic for official musings, brings out the 'secret', 'personal' and 'confidential' (as these documents were originally classified) considerations of the 'official mind' regarding propaganda, information and psychological warfare. They also show what an important part of colonial governance these were. The significance of propaganda during the revolt is further highlighted in the personal reflections captured in the memoirs and letters produced by the protagonists of the revolt, including John Reddaway, head propagandist in the Cyprus colonial government, Governor Field Marshal John Harding and his successor, the last governor of Cyprus, Hugh Foot.

The available secondary material on the subject of propaganda in Cyprus after the end of the Second World War and until independence, with a focus on the revolt, is very limited. The existing historiography of Cyprus at the end of empire has focused, to a large extent, on the political dimensions that formed this episode of British decolonization in the eastern Mediterranean. Since the island's independence in 1960, the available primary material, largely drawn from British colonial archives with additional material scattered in state and private repositories around the world (UK, Cyprus, Greece, USA), allowed investigations in a variety of subjects related to the revolt and more broadly to British imperial policy after the end of the Second World War and until the end of British rule in Cyprus.

Popular themes examined so far are Britain's violent response to the Greek Cypriot anti-colonial revolt and struggle for *enosis* between 1955 and 1959, the United Nations international debates on the 'Cyprus problem', the Greek-Turkish conflict over Cyprus and Britain's role in this, the United States' and Russia's influence on British affairs during the Cold War and the formulation of British policy according to this, and the rise of Greek and Turkish nationalism among the Christian and Muslim population of Cyprus. Other explorative pathways in the process of Cyprus's opposition to the British Empire have been the island's strategic importance to Britain, growing significantly after 1945 in light of Britain's changing status in the world order, as well as the island's status as a diachronic 'peculiarity' (a term very much used in the primary material) among the British Empire's acquisitions. The military aspect of the 'Cyprus Emergency' is another preferred topic of research among some military historians, security and defence analysts alike. Other increasingly popular sub-topics of this investigative strand include the use of intelligence in Cyprus between 1945 and 1960 and the use of violence during the insurgency/counter-insurgency campaigns.

Nevertheless, end-of-empire propaganda in Cyprus remains a topic largely untapped, both in the Anglophone and Grecophone historiographies of the revolt. This book is the first attempt in connecting the dots of propaganda, with the aim to learn and comprehend what role propaganda played during the island's decolonization. No other study on the aspect of propaganda during the Cyprus revolt has been conducted so far, with the exception of a handful of short case studies in the last twenty years or so. For example, the first study, chronologically, was Susan Carruthers's book chapter '"Mischief in the Air": Cyprus: EOKA and the Struggle for Enosis, 1955–59' (1995) on British publicity policy for Cyprus and news management, on EOKA's 'smear campaign' and the themes of British propaganda for Cyprus.[8] Carruthers's research is a valuable starting point; her works, along with a handful of other studies on this subject, are examined in the following chapters.

The scarcity of research on the history of propaganda during the Cyprus revolt is further exemplified when the 'Cyprus Emergency' is juxtaposed to the amount and quality of research that has been conducted on the history of propaganda during other colonial emergencies at the end of empire, such as Malaya (1948–1960). Ian Cobain's conclusion therefore gains validity: since 1945, British forces have engaged 'in a series of small wars that were under-reported and now all but forgotten, or which were obscured, even as they were being fought, by more dramatic events elsewhere'.[9] One could argue that one of the reasons that the Malaya Emergency has traditionally enjoyed academic attention is because of its legacy as one of Britain's most successful counter-insurgency campaigns. Other smaller-scale colonial conflicts were relegated to the background. It is not an exaggeration to claim that up until this point, the case of Cyprus belongs to this group of somewhat 'lesser' emergencies, considered 'urgent', one could say, during the time they were taking place.

The significance of the role of propaganda in the Cyprus revolt makes both propaganda's and the Cyprus revolt's absence from the relevant historiography even more glaring; this is supported by one of this research's findings, namely that the British propaganda response to the Greek Cypriot insurgency was heavily based on the British response to other colonial emergencies, such as the Malaya and Kenya Emergencies. Some results are generated here that inform to an extent the history of other colonial emergencies at the end of empire. Cyprus government propagandists usually borrowed umbrella tactics from other emergencies during the British offensive in Cyprus. Some of them had field experience in other emergencies, such as Governor John Harding who was involved in the British counter-insurgency efforts in Malaya and Kenya. In this way, new information about the British response to the insurgency in Cyprus has wider implications, as it feeds into the pool of information on 'the British way in counter-insurgency' as David French put it.[10] It enhances our knowledge about decolonization in the British Empire and about the modern history of the twentieth-century nations that were formerly British colonies.

Failure in communication and 'disconnected' decolonization(s)

In order for propaganda to be relevant and effective in Cyprus it had to be supported by a clear political line and a vision for the future. Throughout the revolt, British propaganda for the Greek Cypriot audience lacked both.

Conversely, Greek and Greek Cypriot propaganda targeting the same audience offered both. Archbishop Makarios III, EOKA, and by extension, the Greek Cypriot public never became convinced about the prospect of resting their future in British hands. Was the British government planning to stay 'forever' in Cyprus? British propaganda did not say. Until late 1956 this seemed to be the case, yet still this was not clearly admitted. Scenarios changed in late 1956, and the British government considered alternative pathways for regional control, such as the partition of the island.

Disagreements and miscommunication among the various departments of the empire and beyond were significant reasons that led to unproductive efforts in British propaganda in Cyprus, the UK and abroad. As Robert Holland writes, 'At different times the task of finding a solution to the problem had oscillated like a game of "pass the parcel" – between the administration in Nicosia, the Colonial Office, the Foreign Office, the British Embassy in Athens, and 10 Downing Street.'[11] The myopia of the Cyprus colonial government on issues of colonial governance and the British government's bafflement regarding the future of the island were a source of ridicule and a target for enemy propaganda during the years of the revolt. EOKA and the *Ethnarchy* in Cyprus were extremely swift in picking on British propaganda tactics and rendering them ineffective, for example British propaganda based on propaganda themes used in Ireland during the 1920s, more than thirty years before the start of the Cyprus revolt. Andrew Mumford confirms this in his book *The Counter-insurgency Myth* (2012). 'Far from being the counter-insurgent exemplars that history has benevolently cast them, [the British] have in fact consistently proven to be slow learners and low strategic burners in the realm of counter-insurgency warfare.'[12] Mumford's argument is important here and is used extensively in the attempt to reconstruct the decision-making process of those responsible for propaganda including the Cyprus governor and the leader of EOKA, from the early 1950s to the end of the Cyprus revolt in March 1959.

Frustration was mounting when colonial officials on the ground, Colonial Office and Foreign Office officials in London, propaganda and psychological warfare experts at the British Middle East Office (BMEO) in Beirut, and British ambassadors in Athens, Ankara and Washington were trying to set their minds upon an agreed policy on propaganda for Cyprus, targeting local and international audiences.[13] In their attempted collaboration to tackle emergency conditions in Cyprus, and while having in mind the extensive repercussions this had on the international front, officials in Cyprus from early 1955 came to the realization that transplanting British counter-insurgency propaganda techniques from another theatre to Cyprus did not have the desirable result. The desirable result was to restore law and order in the colony, defeat EOKA and convince the Greek Cypriots of the benefits of 'the British connection'.[14]

I argue in this book that despite the current vogue for transnational history, analysis of the archival material has revealed clear limits on borrowing and flows of ideas between different colonial settings. Here I therefore attest that decolonization was less 'connected' than some of the recent historiography might lead us to believe.[15] Decolonization's 'disconnection' is not a shared perspective among historians of the British Empire; it is not a shared perspective in the primary material either. Not everyone agreed that many of propaganda's applications from elsewhere were applicable in Cyprus. Especially in the early days of the revolt, officials in the Foreign Office who had no personal experience of the situation on the ground, but who nevertheless had a strong opinion and definite say in the decision-making process, were usually pushing forward for more unrealistic plans and expectations, such as 'reorienting' the 'hearts and minds' of the Cypriots into making them faithful British subjects. However, what was desirable or what was envisaged by British propagandists on the ground was very often not achievable. This reflects a broader pattern, as Simon J. Potter writes, 'British policy in the colonies was often too inchoate to allow a really persuasive propaganda line to be developed, and the practical difficulties involved in targeting colonial subjects often seemed insurmountable.'[16]

In order to design and disseminate effective propaganda, in any terrain, understanding the target audience was a vital prerequisite and indeed a 'practical difficulty'. In the case of Cyprus, the reception of the success or failure of propaganda by diverse audiences, such as the Greek Cypriot audience, the British audience and 'international public opinion', significantly affected the progression of events, not only up until independence but also throughout Cyprus's post colonial history. The issue of audience understanding is explored here, and I argue that British propaganda in Cyprus was ineffective also because there was difficulty in understanding the psychology of the Greek Cypriot. Francis Noel-Baker, a Labour Party MP, wrote this to Lady Harding after the first round of negotiations between the governor and Archbishop Makarios broke down: 'Personally I am firmly convinced that the fundamental trouble was that *no-one* in authority, either in Nicosia or London, ever really understood the point of view and aims of the Archbishop or the feelings of most of the Greek Cypriots. To do that we must *know* the people concerned.'[17] This difficulty was largely due to the problematic racial stereotyping of the Greek Cypriot audience by the British propagandists. Preconceived ideas of who the Greek Cypriots were, what they aspired to and what they needed shaped propaganda in Cyprus but were not fit for purpose.

The British venture to project Britain's national image in Cyprus was arguably too little too late. From the early 1930s efforts were made through the fields of education, cultural policy, social welfare and public health to persuade the Cypriots of the importance of the British connection and its material benefits.[18] As Andrew Mumford argues, the British and colonial governments employed economic and social measures to regain control in the territory and at the same time to impose legal measures in an effort to win popular support and loyalty for the government and discourage sympathy and help for the insurgents.[19]

Erik Linstrum, in his book *Ruling Minds: Psychology in the British Empire* (2016), challenges the traditional view that up until recently saw techniques in psychology being accepted as 'reliable and useful sources of knowledge about the inner lives of people living in what was then the world's biggest and most diverse political system', the British Empire.[20] Linstrum proposes that the 'science of the mind' as he called it offered new ways to 'expose pathologies at the root of the relationship between colonizer and colonized'.[21] 'In the colonies, psychology has appeared as another building block in the edifice of domination that branded whole populations as irrational and inferior.'[22] This perception of the colonized subject's irrationality is examined in the course of the book. Racial stereotyping of the Greek Cypriot was common practice for the designing of colonial policy and governance. Linstrum supports the view that the relationship between science and empire was a tenuous collaboration marked by tensions and 'misunderstandings', a word that Robert Holland and Diana Markides also used in their work on Anglo-Cypriot relations.[23]

Linstrum writes that the Second World War was a turning point for the instrumentalization of psychology, arguing that from this point onwards colonial and imperial officials aimed at the psychological origins of anti-colonial movements. In peacetime, this was exemplified through the designing of education programmes to discipline emotions and reshape attitudes.[24] During armed conflict, in counter-insurgency campaigns, it meant developing propaganda tactics and justifying brutal practices of interrogations.[25] I investigate here Linstrum's argument with reference to the Cyprus revolt and show how experts in psychological warfare and propaganda were assigned to design a psychological approach towards the Greek Cypriot audience in order to win its support for colonial rule while concurrently disengaging them from EOKA. Terminology will prove important. As the revolt progressed 'propaganda' was to be called 'psychological warfare', where sometimes it was even called 'psychological support' for the Greek Cypriot population.

Linstrum, echoing Mumford and Potter, concludes:

> The people involved in imperial psychology – belonging to many different professions and working in many different places – were so dispersed, an ambiguous or disappointing outcome in one case did not always prevent others from trying the same methods elsewhere. Then, too, experts who invented new tools or turned them to a novel purpose had a vested interest in declaring their success.[26]

These 'vested interest(s)' are examined here through the study of archival material, and new evidence that enlightens and enriches the limited debates on British failed efforts in propaganda for Cyprus is brought to light. These failed efforts also provide an explanation as to why Cyprus, as a 'small-war' case study, has been neglected so far, whereas, for example, the Malaya Emergency, remembered until today for its success as a counter-insurgency campaign that included an effective propaganda offensive, has been given extensive academic attention.

British belated attempts in propaganda in Cyprus were largely futile because of an arguably misconceived, spasmodic and underfunded post–Second World War British (propaganda) policy, but also for a combination of other, arguably equally important reasons. The most significant of these reasons were the Cypriots' long absence from training 'in all things British', the zealous overstimulation of a Greek nationalist feeling propagated by Archbishop Makarios and his collaborators, and at the same time the boycotting of the British attempts in propaganda 'by order of the ecclesiastical authorities'.[27] Finally but crucially, the explosive climate in international affairs after the Second World War was influenced by a pervasive sense of the threat of communism, nationalism and anti-colonialism, those fearful-isms, the nightmares of an empire in retreat.

Diana Markides, in her article 'Britain's "New Look" Policy for Cyprus and the Makarios–Harding Talks, January 1955–March 1956' (1995), explores the circumstances in which the British government, upon the commencement of the revolt, attempted to accommodate the pressures created by internal agitation and the new international climate.[28] Markides argues that 'the failure in communication, even a certain unwillingness to communicate' prevented the successful outcome of the negotiations between Archbishop Makarios and Governor John Harding.[29] This argument is expanded here, along with Rory Cormac's argument on the evolving impact of strategic intelligence upon British government understandings of, and policy responses to, insurgent threats and how intelligence agencies in fact (mis)understood the complex relationship between the Cold War, nationalism and decolonization.[30] As Cormac writes in his book *Disrupt and Deny: Spies, Special Forces, and the Secret Pursuit of British Foreign Policy* (2018), 'Britain's colonial rule was built on information management and it is no exaggeration to describe the British Empire as an "empire of intelligence".'[31] 'Waged under the shadow of Nasser and fear of British decline, covert action experienced a high point in the early 1950s. It became almost mainstream.'[32]

Evanthis Hatzivassiliou, who has researched the political and constitutional aspects of the Cyprus crisis, in his article 'Cold War Pressures, Regional Strategies, and Relative Decline: British Military and Strategic Planning for Cyprus, 1950–1960' (2009), convincingly argues that strategic and military needs in Cyprus, as these were perceived by Whitehall in the 1950s, were 'a crucial factor in British decision-making on Cyprus' in regard to Britain's Middle Eastern position.[33] Hatzivassiliou's argument is further supported here and shows how British propaganda policy intended to facilitate Britain's strategic ambitions, by downplaying them while bringing to the foreground specific propaganda themes. These propaganda themes meant to divert local Greek Cypriot/Greek and international attention from these ambitions.

Reactive propaganda, violence and a 'crisis of trust'

The lack of a British plan for Cyprus and a failure in communication between the parties involved in the decision-making process for an action plan to deal with the 'Cyprus problem' were not the only reasons why the colonial government was left severely behind in the propaganda race. Aggressive Greek Cypriot/Greek propaganda in combination with the legitimacy of the Greek Cypriot demands, as these were supported by international current affairs namely the wave of anti-colonialism and decolonization during the end of empire, were another significant reason for British propaganda's weak impact in Cyprus and, to an extent, abroad. The Greek Cypriot and Greek propagandists amply exploited and ridiculed British propaganda on the one hand and gave particular importance to the designing and use of their own propaganda on the other.

Although the available archival material on EOKA's propaganda is considerably less, as no EOKA archive was salvaged and Archbishop Makarios's archive has not yet been declassified, from what could be retrieved from published sources, propaganda seems to have been a vital part of the policies designed by EOKA's leader General Grivas, by the Greek government and by Archbishop Makarios. Panagiotis Dimitrakis, in his book *Military Intelligence in Cyprus: From the Great War to Middle East Crises* (2010), argues that General Grivas proved to have a very good understanding of tactics and made excellent use of propaganda during the critical four-year period.[34] Dimitrakis, in his article 'The Special Operations Executive and Cyprus in the Second World War' (2009), uncovers important information on British propaganda methods. I argue in later chapters that these methods continued to be in use after the end of the Second World War, throughout the 1950s and at least until the island's independence.[35] Below I identify and classify in short propaganda's diverse results; they are to be examined in more detail and with the use of examples in the following chapters.

During the 1950s, especially after EOKA began its campaign in April 1955, British propaganda for Cyprus in Cyprus could be characterized as reactive and eventually (if not 'therefore') weak. The investigation into the official considerations surrounding the production and use of propaganda reveals that discussions on the issue did not always lead to successful actions and assertive strategies. The Greek and Greek Cypriot propaganda offensive led the propaganda war. The colonial government was usually 'on the defensive', as colonial officials often complained in 'secret and confidential' correspondence.[36] For example, during the 1950s, Athens Radio, the most significant media outlet for Greek propaganda broadcasting in Cyprus, vigorously supported the Cypriot cause for liberation from British rule and *enosis* with Greece. The Greek Cypriots listened to it assiduously. Conversely, CBS reacted to this propaganda offensive by attempting to discredit the *enosis* demand, accusing the Church of Cyprus of condoning violence and inciting the Greek Cypriot public. Going against the Church was arguably the wrong way of approaching the Greek Cypriot masses who most of them were pious peasants.

At other times, official discussions about propaganda merely led to inaction. Waiting for what the Greeks were going to do next was a common practice of the colonial government that rarely took the initiative, even though it was always discussing the possibility of a renewed propaganda offensive against EOKA. Furthermore, there were times when policy did not always lead to the appropriate use of propaganda. In fact, it seldom had the intended outcomes. For example, the most evident result of British propaganda's failed techniques in Cyprus was a 'crisis of trust', to use Robert Holland's phrase, between the British in Cyprus and the Greek Cypriot people. There was also the result of ineffective propaganda, when propaganda media were having no effect on their target. Counter-propaganda coming from the enemy side contributed considerably to some of these possible results.

Importantly, British propaganda during the Cyprus revolt was also directly affected by the simultaneous use of violence and coercion. One cannot study the one without taking into account the other. The use of coercive measures, primarily under Governor Harding's regime, and also EOKA's violent and intimidation tactics, had a fair amount of responsibility in the forming of Greek Cypriot psychology. As the revolt progressed, propaganda designed by the British and Greek Cypriot sides was backed up and at various instances overshadowed by the simultaneous use of violence and coercion. At the same time, propaganda also became more aggressive, categorical and inciting; for example, Cypriot insurgents were branded 'terrorists' by the British and colonial governments' media outlets. On the other hand, Governor Harding was called 'Gauleiter' and 'satrap' in PEKA's (Political Committee of the Cypriot Struggle) leaflets, cordons were 'concentration camps', British security forces were 'Insecurity Forces', while Harding's soldiers of the Special Branch persecuting EOKA were called 'antichrists'.[37]

Robert Holland convincingly argues for 'a crisis of trust' between the British and the Greek Cypriots during the revolt.[38] His book *Britain and the Revolt in Cyprus, 1954–59* (1998) reconstructs the 'inner history' of the revolt, masterfully providing a case study on this violent episode of this 'special and mangled form of British decolonisation', while considering the effects of the Greek Cypriot insurgency and the British counter-insurgency on the politics of the surrounding region, particularly in relation to the emerging ethnic struggle between Greeks and Turks.[39] This book uses extensively Holland's argument on the 'crisis of trust' between the British administration and the Greek Cypriot people.[40] Some of the primary material Holland uses here includes reports by John Reddaway, the Cyprus colonial government's head propagandist, and by Leslie Glass, Director General of Information Services and psychological warfare in Cyprus. During my research I discovered that Glass in fact invented the term 'splitting of sympathy' to express the violent rift created between the British administration and the Greek Cypriots. The term is used extensively here. Although Glass warned against the splitting of sympathy in 1956, I argue that due to Governor Harding's violent and coercive methods this could not be prevented. Aaron Edwards paraphrases Holland, Harding's '"honest but doomed integrity" placed him at a disadvantage, especially as he clumsily put in place a template designed more for Asian and African climes than more urbane Mediterranean sensibilities'.[41]

Evanthis Hatzivassiliou in his book *Strategies of the Cypriot Struggle: The 1950s* (2004) convincingly argues that during the revolt, several incidents took place leading to the transition of the Greek Cypriots from intentional disobedience to the British colonial government to open hostility against it.[42] Two of these incidents were in fact decisions taken by Harding: the first was Archbishop Makarios's exile to the Seychelles in March 1956 after negotiations between the two figures of authority broke down, and the second was the execution by hanging of nine EOKA members, including an 18-year-old boy. Going a step further, although historical research attributes the splitting of sympathy to a number of coercive measures imposed on the Greek Cypriot population during the emergency years, in this book I refocus this point by arguing that propaganda and, its more aggressive form in times of conflict, psychological warfare were also a significant factor adjunct to coercion. Coercion and propaganda jointly contributed to the Greek Cypriots' mounting feeling of dissatisfaction and frustration against the colonial government and especially its security forces. Propaganda therefore was counterproductive. Dissatisfaction eventually led to open hostility against the British in Cyprus and open support for EOKA.

In the last twenty years or so a shift is noted in the topics that interest researchers of the British Empire and the empire's relationship to its colonial subjects. Recently research has predominantly focused on the issue of violence during encounters between colonizer and colonized during decolonization. With this in mind, much academic revisionist research is conducted on the use of coercion during the British Empire's small wars. Much of this research deconstructs the myth of the 'hearts and minds' doctrine, popular in the primary, official accounts of the various campaigns and in the secondary literature up until the early 2000s. Until then, this doctrine seemed to monopolize academic discussions on the effectiveness of propaganda during the empire's emergencies. It is only recently that historians have proposed a new argument that coercion in the form of violence, and not persuasion through propaganda, was the default method of the British counter-insurgency campaigns during colonial uprisings. Indeed, remarkable research, such as Caroline Elkins and David Anderson's on the Mau Mau Rebellion and the British counter-insurgency campaign, reveals the brutal approach of British counter-insurgency campaigns. Their work has arguably liberated the conceptual approach on the topic and has encouraged other researchers to undertake similar investigations placing violence as their focus.

This book takes the less-travelled pathway of propaganda, although the theme of violence is indeed a resonant one. As I demonstrate in this book, violence directly informs (the study of) propaganda. During the 1950s the war of propaganda in Cyprus preceded the recourse to violence. I chose propaganda as my focus exactly because propaganda was in fact the opening chorus that remained on stage throughout the conflict. Although research on the violent aspect of the Cyprus revolt should certainly continue, research into the aspect of propaganda arguably should come first as propaganda precedes violence chronologically, and propaganda's study places violence in a more informed context. Martin Thomas in his book *Fight or Flight: Britain, France, and Their Roads from Empire* (2014) writes that Cyprus for Britain was a 'less blood-soaked conflict'; however it proved to be 'even more intractable'.[43] I argue in this book that propaganda was a significant reason leading to this intractability, complicating considerably the mode of interaction between the competing agencies.

The results of this research show propaganda as violence's faithful companion, even though the one is diametrically different in temperament, mood and expression from the other. It is worth noting here that attention is also given to propaganda intended *to provoke* violence. Violence arguably always steals the show due to its obvious impact. Yet the two maintain a strong and lasting relationship. When violence finally erupted on a large scale with the beginning of the EOKA armed campaign on 1 April 1955, and with the implementation of emergency regulations on 26 November 1955 by Governor Harding, attempts in propaganda also intensified, making violence and propaganda the joint protagonists of this episode. I argue here that in Cyprus 'hearts and minds' were being coerced as much as they were being courted. This discovery further challenges the pervasiveness of the 'winning hearts and minds' doctrine and further de-mythologizes it.

In the field of historical research on the military aspect of the Cyprus revolt, or the 'Cyprus Emergency' as it is usually called in military studies, David French's work is arguably at the forefront. His book *Fighting EOKA: The British Counter-insurgency Campaign on Cyprus, 1955–59* (2015) is the first book about the revolt to make use of the recently declassified British colonial material on the history of the empire's colonies, including Cyprus, which may now be accessed at the National Archives in London (Migrated Archives, 2012). French's book has been a most valuable addition to the field of counter-insurgency studies, one that largely informs the unknown history of the British counter-insurgency in Cyprus. Next to this book is French's article 'Nasty Not Nice: British Counter-insurgency Doctrine and Practice, 1945–1967' (2012) where he examines the extent to which the British attempted to apply the up-until-recently popular notion of 'winning hearts and minds' to the Greek Cypriots, but also to the people of Palestine, Malaya, the Suez Canal Zone, Kenya, British Guiana, Oman, Nyasaland, Borneo and Aden, during their counter-insurgency operations. In alignment with the issues raised by historians where they reassess the post-1945 way of British counter-insurgency, French uses a plethora of previously inaccessible historical evidence in order to prove that the real foundation of British counter-insurgency doctrine and practice was not the quest to win 'hearts and minds' of colonial populations, but rather the application of 'wholesale coercion' to safeguard British interests.[44]

In support of David French's argument, David M. Anderson endorses the view that even though the British had previous knowledge from their cumulative experience of colonial counter-insurgency campaigning in the 1940s and 1950s, for example in Palestine, Malaya and Kenya, in fact little of this could be used by the colonial police in Cyprus in order to

> reconcile the contradictions between maintaining control against a terrorist insurgency and keeping faith with the professed aim of moving the colonial police away from methods of coercion and towards policing by consent. [...] As a quasi-military force, perceived as the principal arm of state coercion, the police had been placed in the front line of the struggle against EOKA.[45]

Consequently, although the colonial police managed to establish some control over the situation, it was at the expense of their legitimacy in the eyes of the majority of the people as an impartial civil authority. This point is developed in the course of this book, arguing that with the use of coercive measures under Governor Harding's regime soon came a 'splitting of sympathy' between the Greek Cypriot public and the British in Cyprus. Andrew R. Novo, in his article 'Friend or Foe? The Cyprus Police Force and the EOKA insurgency' (2012), reaffirms French's and Anderson's position and writes that 'by virtue of the situation, British policymakers had trouble implementing the strategy their experience and philosophy taught them would be ideal – the primary reliance on the police for law and order during an insurgency'.[46]

In Cyprus, a police force depending on Greek Cypriot officers for its security operations proved ineffective. This was because EOKA targeted Greek Cypriot policemen, thus making them desert the force and virtually run for their lives, afraid of being labelled as 'traitors', with the lethal implications this entailed. Others who stayed were often EOKA operatives assisting the struggle. It did not take long for the British to turn to Turkish Cypriots to man the force, even though that the political cost of this was high. This last point gives cogency to numerous claims about the increased use of the Turkish community by the

British, 'in an unacknowledged divide and rule policy', as Michael Crawshaw called it in *The Evolution of British COIN* (2012).[47]

Andrew Mumford argues that the theoretical construct of British counter-insurgency thinking 'continuously deviated' in practice and in reality.[48] This book further supports and expands on this claim. As one discerns from the above example on Cyprus's colonial police force during the revolt, 'the ideal' during emergency conditions essentially differed from 'the real'. In the following chapters, I argue that although discussions on the use of propaganda and psychological warfare in the Cyprus revolt were constantly taking place between colonial and other officials (in London, Athens, Ankara, Washington) with the purpose of redesigning the colonial government's propaganda policy, and although the theoretical approach of such a policy was constantly being debated, in reality counter-insurgency propaganda methods 'continuously deviated' from the ideal and were doomed to adjust to reality, leading more often than not to the use of coercion. As Martin Thomas aptly writes: 'Between 1954 and 1959 increasing numbers of British troops were used to lock down the island through curfews, searches, collective punishments, and targeted operations. As a result, the garrison island of Cyprus [...] became the unlikely setting for some of the severest restrictions anywhere in the British Empire.'[49]

I give emphasis to an important finding of this research here: David French's argument on the use of 'wholesale coercion' instead of 'hearts and minds' during the British counter-insurgency campaign pre-exists in the Cypriot and Greek primary and secondary source material in the Greek language. This material in Greek is largely missing from the historiography on the topic in English due to language barriers in the research process. The Migrated Archives, which include previously inaccessible material in English, have brought Anglophone historiography closer to the Greek/Greek Cypriot historiography. Therefore, French's presentation of this colonial material is indeed new and original to the non-Greek-speaking, Anglophone audience. As French himself aptly writes, 'Historians in the past have been handicapped by the fact that, unbeknownst to them, the British government had retained a number of files [...], files that were part of the Foreign and Commonwealth Office's "migrated archive".'[50] Access to this material in English, therefore, has significantly enlightened academic research on the topic. However, primary and secondary material produced in the Greek language remains untranslated and is still largely missing from the Anglophone historiography.

What this book argues is that although the 'wholesale coercion instead of hearts and minds' argument currently gains validity due to the amount of historical research being conducted on the empire's 'small-wars', the realization that British officials were unable to understand the nature of the majority of the Greek Cypriots supporting EOKA, actually permeated Greek Cypriot mainstream consciousness since the time of the revolt. This has so far failed to become an argument in the Anglophone historiography because of the respective language barriers or 'a failure in communication', to use a familiar phrase. In a similar manner, although the failure and inefficiency of British propaganda was acknowledged by the colonial government's propagandists throughout the counter-insurgency campaign, research into Greek Cypriot material has revealed that this understanding was also shared by the Greek Cypriot audience since the early years of the revolt. Even though under Governor Hugh Foot, the colonial government did try to revise its propaganda policy, in order to improve its image which had been heavily tarnished in front of local and international public opinion by Harding's coercive regime, it mostly merely pondered on the possibility. Thus, the government finally failed to mount an effective propaganda assault against Greek and Greek Cypriot propaganda agencies. The following excerpt from a note on propaganda is revealing:

> Having being heavily indoctrinated, by Athens Radio and the Greek Orthodox priesthood in particular, into a state of mind which rejected any British statements and accepted as gospel the Greek/Makarios/EOKA line, the Greek Cypriot has scarcely been amenable to 'propaganda' put out by the Cyprus government.[51]

The study of the archival material reveals yet another reason limiting British propaganda's reach: 'The gimmicks of what is termed psychological warfare are ineffective against a people which is well accustomed to conventional mass communications media and which in any case has already decided what it wants and what it wants to know.'[52] Although a predominantly peasant population, Greek Cypriots were used to (and eager learners of) a range of modern mass media. As I examine in the following chapters, British propaganda for Cyprus aiming at international audiences was arguably more focused, more honestly and confidently ambitious than the propaganda targeting the Greek Cypriots ever was. British propagandists believed that they could affect and gear 'international public opinion' much more easily than the local Greek Cypriot which was believed to be 'fixed', if not fixated. 'More important than an unavailing attempt to change local thinking and fixed ideas has been publicity material for overseas use,' one colonial official evidently wrote.[53]

Although coercion was used quite extensively during the British counter-insurgency in Cyprus, I argue here that it was not 'wholesale coercion' as

David French and other historians have recently argued. I give below French's conclusion before offering a revised view:

> Coercion was always the basis of British counter-insurgency campaigns. Whatever forms it took, be it cordon and search operations, collective punishments, or forcible population resettlement, it was never something that was welcomed by the people on the receiving end. At the very least what the security forces were doing was likely to offend their dignity. At the very worst it might threaten their physical well-being and even their lives. The rhetoric of 'hearts and minds' suggests that the British must have gone out of their way to counterbalance these policies with other more benign ones in an effort to gain the active cooperation of the population. But in reality conciliation, whether it took the form of a deliberate policy of carefully calculated political concessions, or of buying support through investment in development projects to raise living standards, was something that the British usually practised on only a limited scale.[54]

Contrastingly to David French's conclusion, this book argues that propaganda was a significant aspect of the British counter-insurgency campaign. Analysis of newly accessible archival material allows for this argument. Although coercion was certainly a prominent aspect of the British offensive against EOKA, and – as collateral damage – against a very large percentage of the Greek Cypriot population who supported EOKA, nevertheless it was not used on its own. Furthermore, evidence shows that propaganda was an equally, if not more, significant aspect of the pro-*enosis* coalition between EOKA, Archbishop Makarios and Greece. It is therefore misleading to underplay the influence that is attached to propaganda in the Cyprus revolt.

From a British experience to bilateral uses of propaganda

David French continues an established trend in the historiography of the British counter-insurgency campaigns at the end of empire by focusing on the British experience of the emergency. This book argues that a connected history of the British and Cypriot experiences is still needed. More significantly, existing accounts usually fail to acknowledge the existence of an alternative experience to the British one or rush to unsubstantiated assumptions on the experience about the colonized. When they *do* attempt to comment on the Cypriot experience they appear uninformed in the eyes of a reader who is aware of some of the primary and secondary material in the Greek language. For example, in

French's *The British Way in Counter-insurgency, 1945–1967* (2012), at the end of his chapter on 'Winning Hearts and Minds', the author concludes:

> Almost everywhere attempts to buy support for the colonial regime by promoting investment in economic development foundered on the shortages of money and the reluctance of the Treasury to provide more than the bare minimum of funding. Buying 'hearts and minds' was never a real possibility. The British could not afford the down payments.[55]

Even though French adds that this is in fact 'a moot point', since it is questionable whether it would have made 'much difference' to invest more into economic development programmes, the fact that he seems to suggest that every man has his price actually undermines his insightful writing. This approach is juxtaposed for example to Martin Thomas's argument that corresponds more closely to the primary and secondary material in Greek. For example, Thomas writes: 'The depth of national sentiment shared by Greek Cypriots and their mainland brethren was mistakenly read as illicit complicity, not fellow feeling.'[56]

The essence of Greek Cypriot irredentism was arguably based on a shared cultural consciousness with the Greek people and not on financial merits. This point is supported in this book through the use of archival material, from Greek, Greek Cypriot and British sources which express the view that in Cyprus, it was not because hearts and minds could not be bought into supporting the colonial regime, but because they could not be influenced or persuaded into supporting it. As Freya Stark aptly put it, as early as 1952 in one of her visits to Cyprus, this was because 'the spiritual force [was] all on the other side [Greek]', 'even a casual glance at Cyprus shows that there is one thing that is really important to a Cypriot [...] – and that is his Church; so obviously we must either be working with this Church or, eventually, fail [...] How silly governments are!'.[57]

During British rule in Cyprus, the Greek Cypriot man in the street knew very well that Greece was not to be looked upon for its non-existent financial allurements. However, the consensus among the people was that a poor mother was far better than a parasitical, and at times, very cruel stepmother. French's 'misunderstandings and contempts [*sic*] impregnating race relations', to use a phrase by Robert Holland, are partly justified as most of his source material comes from British secondary sources and British colonial archives.[58] As we will see in more detail in the following chapters, in the Greek and Cypriot academic and popular literature dating to the 1950s and early 1960s (and even later than that), it is no news that the British counter-insurgents not only 'frequently misunderstood the real nature of their opponents' as David French aptly wrote, but also misunderstood the people's mass psychology on an island-wide scale.[59]

Where this study claims originality, apart from the fact that to a large extent it uses previously unpublished material, is the comparative and interactive approach it takes towards bilateral uses of propaganda during the revolt, developed by Greek and British agencies in Cyprus and abroad. Andrew Mumford argues:

> An analytical propensity to focus solely on counter-insurgency as a one-way process, analysing just actions of the state army and security forces. The failure to interpret counter-insurgency as an interactive process between insurgent and counter-insurgent, where the strategy, tactics and resourcefulness of the former are as important to the outcome of an insurgency as that of the latter, has revealed that counter-insurgency is suffering from a paucity of analytical understanding.[60]

By focusing on this 'interactive process', this book examines Mumford's argument and adds another dimension to it, namely that propaganda was also 'as important to the outcome' of the conflict. Taking on a comparative direction, it supports the view that the comparison is arguably mandatory for any researcher who aspires to see both sides of the coin. This is not to perpetuate the dichotomy between 'insurgents' and 'counterinsurgents', 'terrorists' and 'state soldiers', 'freedom fighters' and 'colonial rulers', or indeed any other mutually exclusive persona described and stereotyped in contrasting national(ist) historiographies, be that British or Greek Cypriot and Greek. I contend that it should have been self-evident that a counter-insurgency study cannot exist without the simultaneous study of the insurgency that instigated it from the insurgent's point of view. There have been, and are still being, produced several studies on the British Empire's small wars that disregard this. In this light, French's title *Fighting EOKA: The British Counter-insurgency Campaign on Cyprus, 1955–59* is very fair and accurate, as it captures the essence of his book, which is the British response to EOKA, not EOKA's and the Greek Cypriots' response to the British counter-insurgency. What this book argues for is for a combined perspective that brings together the two responses to the emergency/revolt.

A historian who has been using this methodological approach in his work is Andreas Karyos. Focusing mainly on the revolt years, Karyos explores various aspects of it. He has produced focused studies on the nature of the emergency, particularly the military aspects of the revolt and EOKA's strategic rationale, using primary material in both the English and Greek languages, for example, his article 'EOKA and Enosis in 1955–59: Motive and Aspiration Reconsidered'

(2009). In his book chapter 'Britain and Cyprus, 1955–1959: Key Themes on the Counter-insurgency Aspects of the Cyprus Revolt' in the collected volume *Great Power Politics in Cyprus: Foreign Interventions and Domestic Perceptions* (2014), he looks at the emergency regulations imposed by the colonial government on the Greek Cypriot public, the synthesis and activities of the Cyprus Police Force during the revolt, security intelligence in the island, the use of the British Army and Navy during the counter-insurgency and others.[61] In this way he successfully demonstrates how the study of specialized aspects of the various methods used by the British in Cyprus provides proof for the failure of their counter-insurgency effort. In turn, this adds to the argument that the Greek Cypriot population was alienated from the colonial administration during the period in question.[62]

Karyos has also touched upon the topic of propaganda in Cyprus during the revolt. His article 'The Political Committee of the Cypriot Struggle (PEKA), 1956–1959: An Introductory Approach' (2014, in Greek) focuses on PEKA's role in cultivating the Greek Cypriots popular support to EOKA's activities, the reasons that led to the foundation of PEKA, the organization's structure and its 'acting method'.[63] He convincingly argues how PEKA's establishment reflected EOKA's need to secure the support and guidance of the Greek Cypriot public, leading for example to the mass movement of passive resistance in late 1957.[64] His methodology is particularly useful. Apart from using written archival material in Greek and English, he has conducted oral history interviews, for example with Greek Cypriot EOKA fighters.[65] One severe limitation to the accessibility of Karyos's research is the fact that a considerable part of it is in Greek and currently untranslated, therefore not reaching a non-Greek-speaking public.

Propaganda to 'divide and rule' and partition 'as last resort solution'

Regarding the issue of the misunderstanding the Cypriot audience, another dimension to it will be added here. Rather than 'misunderstanding', it will be argued that the British and colonial governments in fact 'understood' (as in 'envisaged') a different future for the Cypriots. They envisaged a future where Britain would continue having a say in internal affairs even after decolonization. Arguably, in order to achieve this, the infamous 'divide and rule' strategy was put into practice. Although suggesting that the 'divide and rule' strategy was implemented in Cyprus is not really an original idea, what *it is* original is to argue that propaganda were a significant means through which this strategy was implemented.

In the fascinating collaborative article co-authored by Robert Holland, Carl Bridge and H. V. Brasted, titled 'Counsels of Despair or Withdrawals with Honour? Partitioning in Ireland, India, Palestine and Cyprus, 1920–1960' (1997), the authors dared to touch the much-contested topic of imperial Britain's 'divide and rule' strategy. The 'divide and rule' argument has been used extensively by non-British historians of 'the periphery', as they have been most commonly called in the British historiography. Their interpretation of history has been often called by imperial historians a 'nationalist interpretation'. However, in the same way that a country's national history may be branded as 'nationalist', 'Imperial history becomes imperialist history when it uncritically accepts the stories contemporaries told about themselves and their actions', as Erik Linstrum very aptly writes.[66] It could be argued that calling the supposed policy of 'divide and rule' a 'conspiracy theory' is just irresponsible as presenting it as fact.

Although the authors of 'Counsels of Despair…' do not go as far as agreeing with several non-Anglocentric historians, such as Hubert Faustmann, that the 'divide and rule' strategy was indeed implemented during decolonization, they lay out the possibility that 'if "divide and rule" existed in these places it was not mediated through formal politics'.[67] Hubert Faustmann in his book *Divide and Quit? British Colonial Policy in Cyprus 1878 – 1960* (1999) takes the debate one step further, arguing that 'divide-and-rule mechanisms were consistently and consciously applied during most but not all parts of British rule' in Cyprus even though there was 'a direct link between the degree of a challenge to British rule and the extent to and intensity with which the British applied divide and rule'.[68] The 'divide and rule' argument, although not the focus of this research, will be tested to some extent in the following chapters where methods of implementation of an informal, secret 'divide and rule' strategy through the field of propaganda will be examined.[69]

As a consequence of these findings, this book agrees with Faustmann's argument which supports the idea that following the end of the Second World War until Cyprus's independence, the British reply to the escalation of nationalist pressure was a corresponding escalation of divide-and-rule policy by involving Turkey.[70] This is a claim seen in other historians' work as well, for example Diana Markides's argument about Turkey's involvement in the debates on the future of Cyprus by Britain, after the London conference in December 1955. Markides writes that 'Turkey had been introduced as an interested party, a role she undertook with increasing zeal, and the first criterion for a settlement became agreement between Greece and Turkey'.[71] Faustmann argues for a British 'readiness' to bring the mother countries, Greece and Turkey, as well as both communities, the Greek Cypriots and the Turkish Cypriots, 'at each other's throats', in circumstances such as the London conference in 1955. With a touch of irony and with raised eyebrow he concludes that 'it seems naive to assume that the British did not know what the result of their actions would be'.[72]

In their insightful comparative study 'Counsels of Despair...' Holland et al. investigate partition, as a policy adopted by British policy-makers during decolonization. This infamous British imperial policy, the authors write, was used in 'extreme circumstances', where populations of emerging nations were viewed as 'irreconcilably divided', in territories that proved for the British and colonial governments particularly difficult to handle.[73] The authors argue that even though partition was an unattractive choice, it was nevertheless a 'last resort' solution, used when all other means of stabilization in the respective colony had failed and while they were confronted with a situation of 'mounting chaos'.[74]

Holland et al. put forward the proposition that it should be reconsidered whether, in deciding to partition, the British were on the point of collapse, hurrying to leave due to 'failure of will' and 'too early', as it has been suggested by some historians. The, now accepted as weak, 'failure of will' argument has famously been debated by Ronald Hyam in his acclaimed comprehensive overview on *Britain's Declining Empire: The Road to Decolonisation 1918–1968* (2006) as one of the four reasons for the end of empire.[75] The idea of 'mounting chaos' will be explored in this book and it will be argued that on the one hand British propaganda methods and on the other hand a powerful combined propaganda campaign coming from the *Ethnarchy*, EOKA and Greece, both targeting the Greek Cypriots, considerably contributed towards this.

Evanthis Hatzivassiliou in his article 'Blocking Enosis: Britain and the Cyprus Question, March–December 1956' (1991) examined a ten-month period, starting with Archbishop Makarios's deportation and finishing with the British acceptance of the possibility of partitioning the island between the Greeks (80% of the population) and the Turks (18% of the population), by giving each a separate right of self-determination.[76] Hatzivassiliou's article is a scrupulous reconstruction of the events and factors that formulated British policy on Cyprus's future status during that period, 'the history of British dilemma' as he named the short period starting with Archbishop Makarios's deportation and during British attempts to reach an agreement with Greece and Turkey. As Martin Thomas explains, Harding 'never claimed to have a particular political solution in mind, but he held stronger views about the heightened security measures necessary to avert another Palestine-type humiliation'.[77] In this book, this dilemma and/or indecisiveness will also be examined through official debates on the issue of propaganda, further expanding on Hatzivassiliou and Thomas's arguments.[78]

The British government moved gradually towards the idea of partition between June and December 1956. Partition, it has been argued, would serve the main objective of the British official mind, which was to transfer power to viable successors, the 'moderates' as they were called, while safeguarding British interests in the region, eventually by acquiring two British sovereign bases on the island. The colonial government's attempts to influence and use Cypriot 'moderates' to serve Britain's interests are going to be examined in the following chapters.

However, physical partition was not the only form of partition to be tried out in Cyprus. A metaphorical partition of the Greek Cypriots and the Turkish Cypriots, under the guidance and watchful eye of the colonial government, was arguably taking place since the beginning of colonial rule on the island. Rebecca Bryant's work on nationalism in Cyprus is particularly relevant to this argument. For example, in her book *Imagining the Modern: The Cultures of Nationalism in Cyprus* (2004) she demonstrates how Muslims and Christians in Cyprus were transformed into Turks and Greeks (echoing Robert Holland and Diana Markides) and how these two conflicting styles of nationalist imagination emerged through the Cypriots' encounters with modernity under British colonialism and through a consequent re-imagining of the body politic in a new world in which Cypriots were defined as part of a European periphery. Her article 'An Aesthetics of Self: Moral Remaking and Cypriot Education' (2001) is concerned with education as the main motor of nationalism and the source of patriotic allegiance and its role in Cypriot conflict. Her argument that the advent of Greek and Turkish nationalisms in Cyprus and the divisiveness that they entailed 'did not represent a radical disjuncture but rather the elaboration of goods and goals that had historically defined the order of each community' is particularly convincing.[79]

Elements of how Greek education in Cyprus influenced the Greek Cypriots, especially the youth, into participating not only willingly but arguably enthusiastically into a collective struggle against the colonial power will be explored here. The book therefore is in agreement with Bryant's argument that 'education easily elides with experience, propaganda with patriotism, symbol with sensation'.[80] It also agrees with her conclusion that for Cypriots who defined a good life in ethnic or national terms, 'education became a moral enterprise, since through it they could fashion themselves into persons better capable of realizing those ideals'.[81] It could be argued that the divide-and-rule strategy was one of the few British propaganda ventures that could be characterized as successful. However, in order to elaborate on this claim this research would have to expand into the 1960s and 1970s in order to examine the effects of this method.

An intervention is attempted to be made in this book on debates about the Cyprus revolt, about imperial history and emerging nationalisms more widely. The argument about bilateral uses of propaganda during the Cyprus revolt brings new insight into British imperialist tactics and also draws attention to the ways in which those tactics were successfully undermined by the other side but, even more interestingly, unintentionally by the British themselves. For its site-specific but also its wider implications the study of propaganda during colonial insurgencies and counter-insurgencies needs to be addressed, investigated and brought to the foreground.

The following chapter of this book looks at the initial considerations of the British and Greek sides on the issue and use of propaganda. This chapter is a prelude to the study which follows on the propaganda war raging between 1955 and 1959, during the years of the Cyprus revolt. Chapter 3 investigates Field Marshal Harding's propaganda plans for Cyprus upon taking the governorship of the island. His close collaborators are identified and their role in the propaganda process is reconstructed and analysed, along with an examination on the importance of 'public opinion' and a 'crisis of trust' on the domestic (Greek Cypriot) front. Chapter 4 focuses on three case studies on different media used for propaganda purposes throughout the 1950s: Sound (radio, voice aircraft), Print (newspapers, publications, leaflets) and Vision (television, cinema). Finally, Chapter 5 looks at Cyprus's last governor Hugh Foot's rule, in the midst of collective Greek Cypriot passive resistance and EOKA's smear campaign against the British, and clandestine propaganda from both sides. This chapter ends by looking at the intention of the colonial government to redesign psychological warfare for Cyprus, before this plan was cut short by the end of the emergency and a political agreement on the future of Cyprus.

Sources and limitations

The reconstruction of the history of propaganda in Cyprus for the purpose of this book has not been without its challenges. Archival material accessed was mostly fragmentary, kept in a variety of repositories and files, thus being stripped of chronological progression. This book is principally based on primary, unpublished, material retrieved from a variety of archives, pertaining to the crucial decade of the 1950s, before and during the Cyprus revolt. The bulk of the primary colonial material analysed here was accessed at the British National Archives in London. Much of this has been declassified, gradually becoming publicly accessible between 2012 and 2013, the 'Migrated Archives' of the Foreign and Commonwealth Office as they are often called. Their disclosure has made possible this research on the use of propaganda during the Cyprus revolt, significantly expanding the limited academic research on this topic.

A one-year field trip to Cyprus was an invaluable opportunity to access otherwise inaccessible primary and secondary material. Research in Cyprus was mostly conducted at the Cyprus State Archives (CSA) in Nicosia. The records stored at CSA amount to 13,187 linear kilometres of shelving and a large part of the collection is the colonial governors' Archives and the Secretariat Archives dating from 1878 to 1960, as well as other groups of colonial records. The archives remain un-digitized and inefficiently catalogued; therefore the author had to spend hours there, manually researching several indexes in order to choose what files she wanted to access. In order for these files to be seen, one has to order them and they will become available for viewing in two to three days' time.

The Cyprus Library in Nicosia and Limassol's Municipal Library were also important sources of information, as primary and secondary material in the Greek language was retrieved and accessed there. For example, first and rare editions of biographical accounts and diaries of Cypriots who lived and/or fought during the revolt, and literary novels about the struggle, such as Costas Montis's *Closed Doors* (1964) and Rodis Roufos's *The Age of Bronze* (1960). Excerpts from these are translated for the first time to English by the author, thus bringing fascinating, and otherwise inaccessible, material to the attention of an English-speaking audience. Through the selection, translation, analysis and dissemination of this primary material, the limited academic literature on the Greek Cypriot response to the British campaign is considerably enriched. Furthermore, primary and secondary material in the Greek language was accessed at other local repositories such as the Archbishop Makarios III Cultural Centre and Library, the Press and Information Office, the Archive of the Council for the Historical Memory of EOKA's Struggle, the Centre of Visual Arts and Research (CVAR), all in Nicosia. Newspapers published during the 1950s were accessed at the Newspaper Archive of the Limassol Historical Archive.

Furthermore, primary material such as biographies, novels and diaries of British 'men on the spot' who served in Cyprus during the 1950s was accessed at the British Library, the Cambridge University Library, the Bristol University Library and other UK university libraries. Last but not least, digital resources have been a very useful source for this book. Online articles such as Sergeant Major Friedman's 'Cyprus 1954–1959', and databases such as the Oxford Dictionary of National Biography and the British Pathé for videos covering Cyprus in the 1950s, and especially obituaries for the empire's servants who were in Cyprus at some point during the revolt have all been a treasure of information.

A significant limitation to this research is the lack of an EOKA archive. Petros Papapolyviou argued that the nature of the Cypriot revolt 'did not even remotely allow for the creation and preservation of an archive'.[82] Total secrecy and confidentiality were vital prerequisites for the continuation of the struggle; therefore keeping an archive was forbidden. In an attempt to make up for this loss, this research draws evidence about how EOKA thought and behaved from other primary material, such as memoirs, accounts and testimonies of members of the organization, as well as of members of the Greek Cypriot public who assisted in many ways EOKA's campaign. Furthermore, the Archbishop Makarios III archive remains closed to the public and has been in the process of being catalogued for years now with no prospective opening date.[83] Another source that, at the time of writing this book, remains inaccessible is the archives of the Greek Ministry of Foreign Affairs covering the Cypriot struggle: these remain closed, and it is not known when they will become available to researchers and what they will contain. Research into Turkish archives was not possible because of the lack of knowledge of the Turkish language. The book only deals with propaganda targeting the Turkish Cypriot community to a limited extent, as the focus of this project was on propaganda between the British and Greek sides.

2

'A task of first-rate importance': Planning propaganda for Cyprus

Introduction

Shortly before the beginning of EOKA's anti-colonial revolt, British officials in the field came to the conclusion that propaganda had to be used as a blatant instrument of policy in Cyprus in order to shape the island's future according to the British government's aspirations. With EOKA's campaign already in action, members of the colonial government were forced to realize that propaganda at that point could only be used as a weapon in combination with the use of armed force in order to restore law and order in Cyprus but also to persuade the Cypriots that their future lay with Britain and not with Greece. Before Field Marshal John Harding arrived in Cyprus to take governorship, Governor Robert Armitage attempted to design, or at least was interested in designing, a propaganda strategy targeting the Cypriot people. According to his judgement, the 'need to make a start on carrying out this new policy of Government propaganda is [...] urgent and important'.[1]

This chapter explores the start of this 'new policy of Government propaganda' in an attempt to understand just how 'urgent and important' this was, *why* it was important and *how* it was meant to contribute to the British counter-insurgency campaign in Cyprus. It is argued that these first steps set the tone for the colonial government's later efforts in propaganda during the revolt in Cyprus. The official discussions around the design and use of propaganda highlight some persistent considerations that preoccupied the minds of propaganda experts and non-experts dealing with propaganda issues about Cyprus up until the end of the emergency. At the same time the methods of the two primary propagandists of the Greek Cypriot side, the political and military leaders of the struggle, Archbishop Makarios III and General Grivas, are to be explored. In this way, a comparative study of propaganda emerges on the years preluding the Cyprus revolt and of its early stages.

'Seditious utterances': Archbishop Makarios, the *Ethnarchy* of Cyprus and the Church of Greece

With the end of the Second World War the Cyprus colonial governments gradually became obliged to admit that the Greek Cypriot demand for *enosis* was not merely the advent of post-war nationalism and anti-colonialism, and neither was the Church's preoccupation with local politics. During the early 1950s Makarios III, the Archbishop and *Ethnarch* of Cyprus, began developing such a powerful island-wide propaganda campaign that by the time EOKA's armed campaign commenced on 1 April 1955, the majority of the Greek Cypriot public was ready to support the national, anti-colonial effort for liberation from British rule.[2]

The idea of *enosis*, romantic and platonic as it may have been up until that point, was to become an ambition for which the majority of the Greek Cypriots were to fight for, in one way or another, during the years of the revolt. In the referendum held in January 1950 by the Church of Cyprus, before Makarios's election as Archbishop in September of the same year, signature books were provided in churches. The referendum, which was about a prospective union with Greece, attracted 96 per cent of the Greek Cypriot support in voting.

In a June 1955 Top Secret report by the Cyprus Intelligence Committee (CIC), titled 'The Application of Psychological Warfare to the Cyprus Question', one finds the committee's interpretation of the plebiscite.

> In 1950, when the Church sponsored an 'Enosis' plebiscite in Cyprus, Greek Cypriots felt able to save face for the present by voting in favour of 'Enosis', well knowing that even an overwhelming majority would still in no way effect a change of sovereignty. Subsequent events have all tended to isolate the waverers and opponents of 'Enosis'. The belief which many Cypriots now hold [is] that, whether they like it or not, 'Enosis' is approaching.[3]

In the years to follow until Cyprus was granted independence, this referendum was to be used by the Greek Cypriot representatives and the Greek supporters as leverage against British plans for staying on the island.

The spearhead of the political struggle was to be Archbishop Makarios III, a passionate supporter of *enosis*. A priest before ascending the Archiepiscopal throne at the young age of 37, he had previously received a World Council of Churches scholarship to undertake study at Boston University in Massachusetts, USA. He was well educated, well travelled with a good command of the English language. In his highly influential role as the Archbishop and *Ethnarch*, he was the national and religious leader of the Greek Cypriots. In this capacity, he was able to rouse from the pulpit the people's support for the national cause and excite their national feeling.

In the colonial government's understanding, Makarios was achieving this through church blackmail, threats, seditious sermons and intimidation.[4] According to British intelligence, churches were being used by priests to repeat the political rhetoric of the Archbishop. At the other end, as will be examined in later chapters, Greek Cypriots were also being insidiously incited through the political rhetoric of Athens Radio broadcasting from Athens and through the local press. Although the colonial government could and did fight back against radio and print propaganda, it found it particularly puzzling, deeply unsettling and extremely difficult, if not impossible, to counter and compete with the religious aspect of the Greek and Greek Cypriot propaganda campaign. This was for the simple reason that British rule in Cyprus could not offer a religious alternative as England was a secular state. As Freya Stark commented as early as 1952 in one of her visits in Cyprus, 'the spiritual force' was all on the Greek side.[5]

Archbishop Makarios's speeches were an attractive, persuasive, political rhetoric that bound God and motherland together, making the belief in these two sacred and inseparable. As Harding had factually described, Makarios was a figure of the Eastern Orthodox tradition, who had a tremendous appeal to his flock. In a previous report, the Cyprus Director of Education wrote, 'Nationality in the East is largely a matter of religion'.[6] He was right. The Autocephalus Christian Orthodox Church of Cyprus, founded on the Byzantine traditions of the East, and led in the 1950s by a charismatic inheritor of that tradition, had been transformed after the end of the Second World War into a militant, cultural institution, acting as a public body and represented by a compelling leader. A practical example of the amalgamation of religion and motherland in Cyprus in the age of nationalism could be found in EOKA's oath, taken before a priest, and declaring blind faith in the sacredness of the cause.[7] The oath essentially gave religious sanction to the national cause.

However, a more sinister aspect to the Church's campaign for *enosis* also exists. Those Greek Cypriots who were not willing to support the cause were harassed and intimidated by the Church and its representatives. This is evident, for example, in the following letter sent to the governor in June 1953:

> I am a Cypriot and ex-Serviceman and served in the British Army from 1941 to 1943 during which time I was wounded. I am a loyal British subject and as such I decorated my stall in the market in honour of Her Majesty the Queen's Coronation. I received first prize in the competition for the best decorated shop.

The Bishop of Kyrenia sent for me and informed me that should I get married and have any children, he would not baptise them nor would he bury any of my family. He has also given instructions that Cypriots are not to trade with me at my stall. I wish to protest strongly against the conduct of the Bishop and to request that His Excellency will take the necessary steps to protect a patriotic British subject from such persecution. (Sigd.) Savvas N. Rialas[8]

This letter, if authentic, is extraordinary. It reveals an aspect of the *enosis* campaign pursued by the Church of Cyprus, which up until this day remains relatively unknown and it is absent from the historiography of the Cyprus revolt. Although violence, intimidation and psychological warfare on the part of EOKA targeting Greek Cypriots who were not conforming to the organization's orders and demands have been recorded and discussed in the relevant historiography, psychological warfare by the Church against the people has not yet been examined in the secondary literature. The above letter therefore offers a gateway into an aspect of the Church's methods that is particularly intriguing.

Furthermore, lobbying was a crucial part of the *enosis* campaign in order to achieve international support for the Greek Cypriot cause. With several newly established African states joining the UN during the 1950s, the organization was rapidly becoming much more diverse in identity, and ample support was found for an anti-colonial struggle against a declining empire whose time seemed to be up. Archbishop Makarios himself was doing propaganda through local and international tours, preaching the gospel of *enosis*. His 'enlightenment campaign' outside Cyprus targeted public opinion where support was needed, most importantly in the United States and UK.[9]

For example, as early as October 1952, the Archbishop travelled to the United States where he performed a three-month campaign on the Cyprus question. There he met with and informed politicians and representatives of Greek community organizations. He gave radio and television speeches. He formed a liaison committee called 'Justice in Cyprus', with the support of wealthy Greeks and Americans. In their article 'Cyprus 1954–1959', the authors SGM Herbert A. Friedman (Ret.) and Brigadier General Ioannis Paschalidis, commenting on Makarios's tour, called this 'Intelligence Preparation of the Battlefield'. 'He was setting up the world public to recognize the legitimacy of the insurrection that he knew was coming.'[10] As will be examined later on, this was arguably true.

Imposing as Archbishop Makarios was, not only due to his persuasive rhetoric, but also due to his physical appearance in his all-black clerical clothing of the Eastern Orthodoxy, he was the face of the struggle for *enosis*. However, there was a whole apparatus behind him in Cyprus, in Greece, in London and abroad that supported him and whose work was indispensable to the anti-colonial effort. In Cyprus, a corpus of subsidiary Church organizations, as well as other bodies and individuals loyal to Makarios and his ambitions, had their fair share of public influence. In Cyprus, the *Ethnarchy* was a source of concern for the colonial government. This concern was to be heightened during the insurgency and counter-insurgency campaigns.

Research has shown that the activities of the *Ethnarchy* were known to the colonial government through Intelligence and the Police, even before the beginning of EOKA's campaign. For example, on 28 October 1954 the Superintendent of Police of the Special Branch, in Nicosia, sent a secret report to the Senior Assistant Secretary, six months before the beginning of EOKA's liberation campaign. In this he was informing him of the nature of the 'Ethnarchy Organisation' and the functions and structure of its various bodies: the *Ethnarchy*, the *Ethnarchy* Bureau, the *Ethnarchy* Council, the National Assembly, the *Ethnarchy* Education Council and the Councillors in Athens.[11] Information was said to come from 'a reliable and delicate source', perhaps hinting at the existence of informers close to the *Ethnarchy*, for example British people who had a personal relationship with members of the *Ethnarchy*, such as Lawrence Durrell who is to be studied later on. It is interesting to observe in the extract below, the superintendent's use of analogy in his attempt to comprehend the *Ethnarchy*'s structure by comparing it with the structure of a more familiar setting such as the British Cabinet.

> The *Ethnarchy*: This is simply the national leadership. The *Ethnarchy* Bureau: [...] advisory and policy making body. The *Ethnarchy* Council: Its duties are to discuss the national struggle, advise the *Ethnarchy* [...] It is not composed entirely of yes-men and individual disagreements do sometimes occur. [...] In a sense it is the Archbishop's 'cabinet' in that it consists of zealous nationalists whose specialised professional activities embrace the press, the law, education, literature and the nationalist trade and rural unions. [...] The National Assembly: [...] an enlargement of the *Ethnarchy* Council [...] its sole purpose is to give the appearance of a general representation of the national struggle [...] members are all 'loyal' nationalists. The *Ethnarchy* Education Council: [...] the duties of this body are to consider the matter of Greek education in the Colony in relation to the national struggle. The Councillors in Athens: [...] Their duties are to keep *enosis* agitation alive in Greece [...] individuals approved by the Archbishop to keep agitation going in Greece on his behalf.[12]

In London, Zenon Rossides, a member of the *Ethnarchy* Bureau, was the man behind a number of articles populating Britain's press columns with the

Greek Cypriot point of view of the Cyprus issue. This was being performed in an 'assiduous and systematic way' as Governor Harding had characteristically said, thus influencing public opinion in Britain and elsewhere.[13] In Greece, the Church which aligned with the Church of Cyprus furthered the cause through whatever means possible. This was known to the British administration. In a personal and confidential letter to W. Hilary Young of the Foreign Office in November 1954, Charles Peake, the British Ambassador to Athens, observed that the Orthodox Hierarchy in Greece was 'implacable, possessed of great political power and utterly unscrupulous', doing anything in its power to 'prevent agitation dying down and to add fresh fuel to the flames'.[14]

When under Governor Harding's command the Archbishopric in Nicosia was raided, several documents were confiscated which proved Makarios and the Church's support of the EOKA campaign; this was labelled 'complicity in terrorism'.[15] The documents were said to prove that the Archbishop was 'up to his neck with terrorism', as one official wrote.[16] In an official translation of a carbon copy of a letter written by Makarios to the Archbishop of Athens and Primate of all Greece, Spyridon, on 19 January 1956, Makarios was thanking him 'for all you've done on behalf of the common cause'.[17]

What arises from the above discussion is that the Cyprus government was aware of the 'subversive' activity taking place under the *Ethnarchy*'s roof before the beginning of EOKA's campaign. The colonial government had intelligence, as the report seen above proves, and therefore knew about the apparatus and human resources the *Ethnarchy* was in possession of in order to further its national cause in Cyprus and in Greece. This piece of information will be explored in the following sections of this chapter as it is important, since it explains why the colonial government sought expert advice on propaganda that would target the Greek Cypriot local audience, before the beginning of the revolt.

General Grivas and the methods of EOKA

As skilful as Archbishop Makarios's political rhetoric was in his struggle to liberate and unite Cyprus, General Grivas Dighenis, EOKA's leader and the military arm of the struggle, had an equally decisive role in the Greek Cypriot propaganda effort. General Grivas's published *Memoirs* (1964) is an enlightening source of information as it reveals the significance Grivas gave to propaganda, at least in hindsight.[18] General Grivas believed that propaganda was a means of sustaining the Greek Cypriot people's faith in the struggle, of providing assistance and support to Archbishop Makarios's negotiations and political struggle, and of informing and influencing the press and therefore international opinion about what was happening in a small British colony in the eastern Mediterranean. With his *Memoirs* having been translated into English and published as early as 1964 it makes one wonder how the propaganda aspect of the Cyprus Emergency has been up until this point significantly neglected and overshadowed by other aspects of the insurgency and counter-insurgency campaigns.

General Grivas designed his preparatory plan for EOKA's anti-colonial campaign in 1952, three years before the start of the Cyprus revolt, while he was still in Athens. There he defined EOKA's objective:

> To arouse international public opinion, especially among the allies of Greece, by deeds of heroism and self-sacrifice which will focus attention on Cyprus until our aims are achieved. The British must be continuously harried and beset until they are obliged by international diplomacy exercised through the United Nations to examine the Cyprus problem and settle it in accordance with the desires of the Cypriot people and the whole Greek nation.[19]

It is interesting to see here that the first goal of Grivas was for EOKA 'to arouse international public opinion'.[20] Even though 'deeds of heroism and self-sacrifices' were to contribute to 'settling' the problem and achieve *enosis*, Grivas's first objective was to incite international public opinion to turn its sympathetic gaze on Cyprus. Grivas would carry out EOKA's campaign in three fronts: sabotage against the colonial government's installation and military posts, attacks on British forces by armed fighting groups (guerrillas) and the organization of passive resistance by the population. It was envisaged that as the campaign proceeded, any response on the part of British agents would be countered and neutralized by EOKA. Importantly, 'any Cypriots who work for the enemy or act against our interests' would be 'punish[ed] severely'.[21] This brings to mind Savvas N. Rialas's complaint against the Church examined above.[22]

A crucial prerequisite for the successful progression of EOKA's campaign, as estimated by Grivas, was the moral support 'of the whole Greek nation'.[23] Grivas's message was that 'the people of Greece are behind the Cypriots to a man' and this 'should be made clear to the world'.[24] Support was to be displayed through demonstrations in all Greek cities, public applause for EOKA's campaign as soon as it began, and denunciations of the violence and pressure used by the British against an unarmed people. 'Propaganda through newspapers, leaflets etc. must be used to enlighten public opinion in Greece'.[25] PEKA, the Political Committee of the Cypriot Struggle, was also included in Grivas's preparatory plan. The committee, which was to be formed in Athens, was to be responsible for all preparations for the delivery of the above plan at the proper time. The main axis of the campaign would be sabotage.

Crucially, the preparatory plan clarified that by the above means EOKA was not expected to impose a total material defeat on the British forces in Cyprus. On the contrary, its purpose was to bring about a moral defeat by keeping up the offensive until the objectives of the Greek Cypriot side were realized.[26] General Grivas clarified that EOKA's intention 'was to focus the eyes of the world on Cyprus and force the British to fulfil their promises'.[27] Sabotage against the colonial government's installations and military posts and attacks on British forces were to be mostly executed by the EOKA guerrillas, often with active or passive help of members of the Greek Cypriot public (this often meant their silence).

The third front of the campaign, 'organisation of passive resistance by the population', upon which there is currently very little research being done, is explored in this book. This research into archival material showed that Greek Cypriot and Greek propaganda organizations worked tirelessly during the four-year struggle to maintain a strong propaganda front. Their diverse media and tactics were used to achieve a moral defeat over the enemy, the British colonial government and its emergency apparatus (Special Branch, Police, Intelligence etc.). Archbishop Makarios was central to General Grivas's propaganda plan.

The Archbishop, an undoubtedly influential figure, guided and 'enlightened' the common effort, inside and outside the geographical boundaries of Cyprus. General Grivas felt entitled to assume that EOKA's military successes would be exploited internationally by Makarios, winning support for EOKA not only in Cyprus, but most importantly in Britain, America and the UN.[28] However, it would be reasonable to argue that, without General Grivas's planning of EOKA's campaign, and the collaborative effort between him and the Archbishop, none of their aspirations would have materialized. With Archbishop Makarios and General Grivas leading the revolt, the 'saint' and the soldier, the Greek Cypriots had gained not one, but two leaders whose promise entailed liberating a suppressed people from British imperial rule and uniting them with their chosen motherland Greece. Propaganda therefore, that third front, was a priority for both Grivas and Makarios. They were not alone in their struggle. They had the support of the Church of Greece, the Greek people, and previously colonized nations. The time was right and it was on their side. The British colonial government knew this and intended to reverse this course of action.

Cyprus government: In search of a 'new policy' for 'straight forward political propaganda'

Propaganda for Cyprus did not start concurrently with the beginning of the Cyprus revolt in April 1955, nor did it start when Governor Harding declared the island in a state of emergency in November of the same year. Research into the Migrated Archives has revealed secret correspondence between the pre-Harding colonial administration under Governor Robert Armitage and officials of the British Middle East Office (BMEO) in Beirut. The leading figure in these conversations on propaganda and psychological warfare was Leslie Glass, Head of Information Department, BMEO. Glass plays an important role here, as the propaganda/psychological warfare policy for Cyprus was largely designed by him during the period of the Cyprus Emergency.

Glass had served as the head of psychological warfare in the Far East during the Second World War and of the Information Division of the British Middle East Office.[29] His expert advice had been also requested in October 1954 when he was asked to visit Cyprus to discuss with the governor 'publicity questions' regarding *enosis*.[30] In June 1955, three months into the insurgency, he was again requested to visit the island as soon as possible in order 'to discuss and advise on propaganda problems in the current situation'.[31] 'We had been thinking about psychological warfare', 'we have been considering what the next step should be, and the difficulty is that we have no expert here to consult', wrote J. W. Sykes, Cyprus Acting Colonial Secretary to J. H. Peck, Head of Political Division, BMEO, on 27 June 1955.[32] Leslie Glass was to be this expert and his consultations were to play a leading role in the game of propaganda and psychological warfare for Cyprus.

At a meeting taking place in July 1955, between Sykes, Glass and Peck, Glass offered his expert advice on the issue of psychological warfare for Cyprus. Glass's advice was put down on paper by Sykes who then informed the Cyprus Acting Colonial Secretary. Glass advised that the Cyprus colonial government

> ought to be on our guard against being misled by the term 'psychological warfare'. For most people this conjured up ideas of a highly specialised, esoteric technique which was no part of the equipment of the ordinary administrator or political officer. The truth was that nine tenths of 'psychological warfare' was simply straightforward propaganda which required specialised knowledge of the political problems involved and a high degree of political savoir faire rather than any close acquaintance with the 'underhand' techniques developed during and after the last war. The latter were certainly important but they would necessarily provide the medium for only a small part of the total activity.[33]

Glass also advised that to conduct psychological warfare consistently and effectively would cost money, and it was 'better [...] to leave it alone if we were not prepared to spend liberally on it'.[34]

After this meeting a preliminary secret note was produced 'on the general question of political propaganda', titled 'Publicity and Propaganda on the Cyprus Problem' (dated 16 July 1955).[35] This original finding is arguably the first note considering in general lines the strategic planning of propaganda on Cyprus during the revolt and drawing from 'the usual pattern of a publicity and propaganda organisation'.[36] It should be mentioned here that this note was found in a file titled 'Cyprus: Application of psychological warfare to the Cyprus question', further confirming what has been implied so far: the overlapping of 'propaganda' and 'psychological warfare' in the case of the Cyprus Emergency.[37]

The note called for a head of the propaganda organization who would be in daily and close contact with the executive political head, the Colonial Secretary. Glass, judging by his own experience, emphasized the fact that if psychological warfare was to be performed 'seriously' in Cyprus, all the island's organs of publicity, propaganda and public information had to be placed in the charge of an experienced, senior political officer, preferably within the ranks of the island's government service. This officer would have to have the governor's trust, he would have to be well acquainted with government policy and he would have to be given the freedom to act more or less alone, without constant supervision and prodding.[38] The Head of Propaganda was to be responsible for three main sections of propaganda: '(i) publicity intelligence; (ii) plans; and (iii) production and dissemination'.[39]

A small committee of three including the head of propaganda and the heads of publicity and intelligence and production section would be concerned with the organization and planning, themes, channels and targets of propaganda. The head of propaganda would attend policy meetings and discussions and would sit in as a member of the Cyprus Intelligence Committee (CIC), recommended to established in 1954 by the Colonial Office and MI5.[40] His function within the committee would be to ensure for the declassification and release for publicity purposes of intelligence material which he deemed worthy of publication and propaganda and, at the same time, to feed into the intelligence machine information obtained by his organization from overt sources.

The head of publicity and propaganda was to prepare analyses of 'unfriendly' propaganda based mainly on overt material, in other words radio monitoring reports and the press, and the collection of suitable material for use in the counter-propaganda effort. The propaganda planning committee would have to meet regularly and they would need to co-opt outside advice from interested parties such as representatives of the British Middle East Office and Public Relations Officers. They would also need to keep close contact with the British Embassies in Athens and Ankara as well as with London. This was in order to channel publicity and propaganda material destined for wide dissemination outside Cyprus, in their attempt to influence positively international public opinion.[41]

Around the same time, in mid-July, the then CIGS (Chief of the Imperial General Staff) Field-Marshal Sir John Harding visited Cyprus to review the situation. His visit ended in recommending to London that further reinforcements be send to Cyprus to bolster the security forces. This suggestion materialized only later that year, when the War Office sent to the island two Royal Marine Commando units and two infantry battalions. Until then, as Aaron Edwards writes, 'The security forces were losing momentum, in large part because of the almost total lack of intelligence on the enemy they faced.'[42]

A three-power conference between Britain, Turkey and Greece was to take place in late August 1955 in London 'on Cyprus and Eastern Mediterranean problems'.[43] In this conference 'the British Government will once again be faced with the task of making up its mind about what to do with the beautiful, arid, poverty-stricken island', as it was quite haughtily and with a familiar patronizing tone phrased by a reporter in the conservative *Spectator*.[44] The colonial government, after receiving advice from the expert team at the British Middle East Office, immediately got into action, devising a propaganda programme for Cyprus. First and foremost, the governor and his team, including the Director of the Intelligence Service and the Controller of the Cyprus Broadcasting Service, had to consider 'the radio voice, the written word and also the spoken word', as well as the aspect of intelligence organization by putting out 'faked pamphlets and inspire leakages of information'.[45]

> We have already decided on an aggressive policy and after the London conference is finished we have got to move more actively into the attack. This will be so whether the talks break down or whether they are successful. We must, therefore, have – (a) a Government directive to those concerned with this propaganda and (b) the organisation to carry it out. There will have to be a clear understanding of what exactly we are aiming at [...]. I am acting on the assumption that the policy which we shall have to follow will be that at some indeterminate date in the future, which will be not less than 10 years from now, the people of Cyprus will be entitled to discuss with H.M.G. whether there should be any change in their status. This interim period should see the setting up of a Legislature and an Executive Council which would progress steadily towards full internal self-government.[46]

It was expected that 'there will certainly be a continuing need for several years for political propaganda'.[47] At the same time and importantly, it was believed that 'the extent to which the Archbishop and/or the communists accept the type of constitution offered will affect the type and amount of propaganda'.[48] It therefore becomes evident how significant the idea of propaganda was to the British and colonial governments. At the same time, the fact that propaganda has not been extensively researched and analysed, and it has not even been acknowledged as a crucial aspect of the Cyprus revolt, is particularly problematic.

Based on the above premise, in the interim period government propaganda had to focus on the advantages to be gained by 'the merits of democratic Government', which would see the introduction of a Legislature and the Executive Council extensively altered, curbing the power of the *Ethnarchy*. As a start, 'the facts of Cypriot life' had to be explained to the Cypriots.[49] It was estimated that this task would not be without hostile interference. Although the note does not refer specifically to which hostile quarters, it is arguably safe to assume that at this point it meant the *enotists*, the communists, and even anti-colonial quarters from Greece and Turkey.[50] Importantly, it was stated that in order to counter these hostile pressures the colonial government was to 'employ every type of propaganda, both white and black'.[51]

White propaganda's themes were to be 'the present economic and financial stability, the likelihood of large sums of money being spent in the Island for defence purposes, the assistance that is given through Imperial preference and the advantages of belonging in the sterling area; the avoidance of military service and any burden of defence commitments, the prospect of grants and loans from the U.K.'[52] On the other hand, black propaganda was to include refuting Greece's allegations that it wanted Cyprus only for sentimental and not for economic reasons and that Greece would financially help Cyprus more than the British government. Black propaganda was also going to explain that the Commonwealth connection would be lost if Cyprus united with Greece. Not only that, but that being in the Greek orbit Cyprus would suffer from heavy taxation, especially for defence, the liability of national service, the danger of jobs being taken by Greeks, particularly in the civil service, loss of trading agencies to Greek firms, and being financially linked with the weak drachma.

As seen above, the themes of propaganda were all set. Nevertheless, there were practical issues regarding the application of propaganda that had to be urgently addressed. Namely, neither the future Head of Propaganda, nor the Director of Intelligence, nor the Cyprus Broadcasting Service Controller was able to cover the above needs due to their very busy schedules. At the same time, propaganda from the other side was coming out loud and clear through various sources and media, through Archbishop Makarios and his collaborators, and through Greece's press and radio propaganda. The colonial government could not afford stalling any longer. In late July 1955, experts at the British Middle East Office were therefore pushing for the newly founded Cyprus propaganda organization to make a start on 'really effective counter propaganda to Radio Athens and the Nationalist Press'.[53] It was expected that the Greek propaganda campaign would step up as the London three-power conference approached and, if they failed, as the Greek appeal went to the UN.[54]

They arrived at the conclusion that another officer had to be put in charge of 'the single-minded pursuit of the propaganda programme'.[55] In one of his Minutes to the Cyprus governor, the Acting Colonial Secretary tellingly wrote that 'until we can get a man to control the [propaganda] apparatus we are not going to get very far'.[56] Someone 'should start the ball rolling [...] to see if they could pull somebody out of the hat'.[57] That someone had to be an officer 'with a real political flair' and of 'sufficient seniority', to have 'a good knowledge and experience of Cyprus and of the Cypriots', someone with not necessarily an expert knowledge of '"psychological warfare"' as there was 'no particular magic about that' and since the British Middle East Office was more than willing to offer the necessary advice needed. Where this officer should focus on was in doing 'predominantly a straight forward political propaganda'.[58]

Determined to pass on to the next phase, Governor Armitage wrote to the Secretary of State for the Colonies, asking for his urgent approval of the general policy of propaganda set out for Cyprus. According to Armitage, the planning and direction of propaganda, publicity and information for Cyprus was from now onwards 'a task of first-rate importance'.[59] In order to persuade the secretary, Armitage highlighted the apparent change that he had perceived taking place within less than a year in Cypriot public opinion regarding British rule in the island.[60] For this he blamed Athens Radio 'and the rising tide of calumny, misrepresentation and intimidation in the local Press'.[61] The result of their activities was 'to undermine the confidence of the Cypriot public in the stability, integrity and efficiency of the British Administration'.[62]

The Governor was categorical in his estimation; one could argue that he sounded insulted, if not a little hurt, by the Greek Cypriots' behaviour: 'There is no doubt in my mind [...] that we can no longer afford to count on the Greek Cypriots' appreciation, even tacit and grudging, of the benefits of the British rule, much less of self-governing independence'.[63] He also sounded annoyed by the culprits, Greece and the *Ethnarchy* of Cyprus, who 'would have the people of

Cyprus take in blindness and ignorance' a decision guided by their own ambitions. In stressing the importance of propaganda to the Secretary of State, Armitage was surely aware of the innate distaste for the word ('propaganda') among the officials of the British government. He also stressed the fact that from now onwards the Cyprus colonial government would have to speed up its propaganda and publicity efforts by telling 'the truth' in a louder manner, in order to refute, patiently and tirelessly, 'the damaging accusations of Athens Radio and the local Press'.[64] Ironically, he also stressed the necessity for clandestine propaganda in Cyprus, but he did not expand on this, as it would arguably have undermined his somewhat self-righteous statement on telling 'the truth'. Rory Cormac, in his book *Disrupt and Deny: Spies, Special Forces, and the Secret Pursuit of British Foreign Policy* (2018) explains how by the mid-1950s Britain's counter-insurgency campaigns relied on covert operations, involving black propaganda and deception, in Palestine, Malaya, Cyprus and Kenya. Covert action was meant to supplement conventional political and military counter-insurgency techniques.[65] Examples of this for the case of Cyprus will be studied later on.

John Reddaway in charge and the first 'General Directive for Propaganda Services'

The man who was to take upon his shoulders the cumbersome and challenging task of propaganda for Cyprus was A. F. J. Reddaway, who in mid-1955 was acting as Secretary for Communications and Works and Deputy Colonial Secretary. 'A local man', with long experience of Cyprus in a wide variety of administrative posts, with excellent command of Greek and a good knowledge of Turkish, he was thought to have 'many useful contacts among the local people' that would prove beneficial for this task. He had also spent a year at the Imperial Defence College and this, importantly, would facilitate in dealing with the international aspect of the Cyprus issue and communicating with officers at the British Middle East Office.[66]

In a confidential minute to Governor Armitage, the Acting Colonial Secretary wrote that Reddaway could 'fill the bill admirably' as he had 'all the qualities required' for this position.[67] Reddaway was therefore to be relieved of his other duties immediately to concentrate entirely on propaganda work. It was envisaged that, due to the urgency of the situation, the government's new policy on propaganda would be established and put in operation before the London talks. However, local attention need not to be drawn to this effort and Reddaway, although his duties were to be delegated to other officials, was to retain his previous title as Deputy Colonial Secretary.

Upon being assigned the job, Reddaway, perhaps overwhelmed by this new task of which he had no previous experience, immediately wrote to the Colonial Secretary a concise letter. In this letter, he put on record some serious considerations regarding the government's new policy on propaganda for Cyprus.[68] Evidently, he was worried. He shared his distress with the governor and with the Colonial Secretary who 'entirely agree[d] throughout'.[69] The letter is a crucial piece of evidence which reveals the genuine feelings and reservations of the highest-ranked administrators of the Cyprus government on the issue of propaganda. Reddaway's pessimism is unmistakeable and his admittedly defeatist approach arguably sheds light on the government's future efforts during the years of the Cyprus Emergency. It is worth quoting here in full his three main considerations:

(i)   it is now very late to begin trying to undo the cumulative harm which we have suffered over the past ten years or so by reason of our failure to tackle effectively the vital task of influencing in a positive manner Cypriot public opinion. It is going to be a long and up-hill struggle;

(ii) attitudes which have hardened over the years cannot be changed overnight. We must not expect quick results from our new policy. As H.E. has said, throughout our propaganda there must run a thread, 'never ending, ever spinning, refuting Athens, carefully, moderately boosting Cyprus equally.'; this requires time;

(iii) propaganda can never be more than a useful adjunct of policy. In Cyprus it will not by itself suffice to persuade moderate sensible people to come forward and make heard the authentic voice of Cyprus. Government must itself create the conditions in which such people have confidence in themselves and government. Until such conditions are created, effective propaganda may produce good results under the surface, but they will remain submerged.[70]

The pervasive sense of inevitability and perhaps failure engulfing him regarding the imminent propaganda venture did not stop Reddaway coming up with a 'General Directive for the Propaganda Services' in October 1955, after consulting with the British Middle East Office's J. H. Peck.[71] In this directive he set out the principles, the political basis, the aims and targets of propaganda, the objects of the attack, the media, the issue of political guidance and ideas regarding the 'alternative to the appeal of *enosis*'.[72] Much of this was inspired by Glass's advice given at the meeting at the BMEO.

According to this directive, propaganda services in Cyprus would need to have a clear-cut and continuous policy that would agree with policies in other fields, namely the political, economic and social. There had to be discipline in the execution of this policy as all propaganda organs should work in concert to achieve a common objective. The political basis for propaganda policy was the proposals put forward by the British government at the London Conference for 'the political development of Cyprus'.[73] The main aim of propaganda was to encourage Cypriots 'to look inwards to Cyprus as the stage for their own political development and outwards to the Commonwealth as the setting in which their country would play its part in the world'.[74] Therefore, there had to be a persistent effort to spread understanding among the Cypriot people on the potential of the Commonwealth, on their expectations from it and on their benefits.

In order to ensure and encourage this special connection between Britain and Cyprus, the colonial government's propaganda would focus on 'broadening the horizon of the Cypriot people so that they cease to look on their political aspirations in isolation and acquire a proper realisation of the international complications which are involved'.[75] The greatest 'complication' was perceived to be 'the threat of Communist expansion in the Middle East' both by military aggression and by subversion. At the same time, the disadvantages of Cyprus's potential union with Greece had to be highlighted, and work had to be performed towards regaining the confidence of the Cypriot people in the British authorities. As Governor Armitage had emphasized in his letter to the Secretary of State, this confidence had ceased due to 'venomous' Greek propaganda of the previous decade. As a consequence 'the advantages of democratic processes' were to be displayed and put in contrast to 'the disadvantages of sterile extremism', meaning such as that of EOKA. Last but not least, an alternative to *enosis* had to be established and 'sold' to the Cypriots.

As far as 'targets', as they were called, were concerned, there was a general one: the Greek Cypriot people as a whole. There was also scope for 'specially angled propaganda', targeting different sections of the Greek Cypriot population, for example those who were perceived to be 'most vulnerable to arguments of self-interest' against change in sovereignty, such as the farmers earning a living from the export of agricultural products; the mercantile class trading externally with the Sterling Area; the urban middle-class that included government employees and whose standard of living had significantly increased while being on the colonial government's payroll. However, during this research no other evidence was identified regarding this 'specially angled propaganda', instead as will be analysed further on, only general propaganda targeting all Greek Cypriots.

Government propaganda was to focus on attacking, discrediting and undermining EOKA, discrediting and refuting Athens Radio, and arousing doubt among the majority of the Greek Cypriots regarding 'the wisdom of their present political leadership' and the extent to which their leader Archbishop Makarios was 'serving the true interests of Cyprus'. At this point, material for a personal attack on the Archbishop, as well as on other 'nationalist leaders', was to be accumulated and held in reserve. This material was indeed used at later points in the emergency campaign.

The media available in late 1955 for immediate use for propaganda purposes were first and foremost the Cyprus Broadcasting Service. In the government's effort for expansion, a political editor and a news editor were to be added to its staff. The rest of the available media were regular government publications such as *Radio Cyprus*, *Cyprus Review* and *Countryman*; two mobile cinema units; press communiques, handouts; official government pamphlets; and leaflets covertly produced and distributed.[76] Some other media missing at the time – however it was envisaged that they were to be developed in the near future – were a television service (this was to become a priority of Harding's government and it was finally inaugurated in October 1957 when Harding was leaving the island), locally produced news films, word-of-mouth propaganda, a nominally independent Greek newspaper subsidised and controlled by government, a government produced newspaper, a pro-constitution 'Third Party' fostered and backed by government, and a clandestine radio station.

Only selected media were to be used for 'psychological support'. Sometimes in the official correspondence 'psychological warfare' was euphemistically referred to as 'psychological support'. An example of 'psychological support' was the distribution of leaflets by the security forces in conjunction with house and road searches. It was estimated that leaflets handed out upon personal contact were more effective than airdrops, because readers were more likely to be detected using the latter method. Furthermore, there was some use of pre-recorded tapes in loudspeaker trucks in operations, and pre-recorded statements were being played aloud during roadblocks, searches and cordons. There was also some limited use of voice aircraft.[77] The above media are going to be examined in detail in the chapter 'The Propaganda Offensive in Sound, Print and Vision'.

Having planned how propaganda was to be disseminated and what its broader themes would be, what remained obscure was its specific content. The governor was to decide on this in light of the London conference on the future of Cyprus. At this point, one thing that was clear was the government's approach towards the issue of *enosis*. It was agreed that it was futile to try to develop 'an alternative emotional appeal' to that of *enosis*. Therefore, on the emotional plane propaganda had to circumvent *enosis*, not to challenge it. It had to bypass it by highlighting the said material appeal of prosperity under continued British rule. Even though this was the preferred course of action, it was not without some risk. Government propaganda had to be very careful not to provoke antagonism by denying the natural affinities of the Greek Cypriots with the people of Greece and at the same time not to exaggerate or encourage those affinities to the point of provoking nationalism. The government's long-term propaganda goals for Cyprus were to influence the Cypriots against the 'narrow nationalism of their present outlook by engaging their loyalty and self-interest on a wider and more international plane'.[78] In other words, it was a delicate situation that required delicate handling. John Reddaway could not do it alone. Leslie Glass and the other experts at the British Middle East Office were not enough either. They needed to branch out, and so they did.

Requesting information on 'counter-propaganda and/or psychological warfare or call it what you will'

The analysis of a series of secret and confidential letters between John Reddaway, officials of the Far Eastern Department and the Information Department of the Colonial Office on the issue of propaganda/psychological warfare has proved most interesting because it provides evidence of the significance that was assigned to propaganda, as a definite and powerful instrument of policy, during colonial insurgencies. At the same time, a certain amount of scepticism emerges regarding the use of psychological warfare during colonial emergencies. This scepticism also existed within official circles of the empire's departments. As will become evident below, doubt and disbelief, and very often cynicism, came hand in hand with confusion. These were also accompanied by a lack of effective communication and consequently a lack of effective coordination between the various responsible departments of the British government, regarding the dissemination of useful information on the designing and application of efficient propaganda and/or psychological warfare in colonial hotspots.

The correspondence shows varied attitudes among the empire's officials regarding propaganda, psychological warfare, information and publicity. Many times this attitude depended on whether these men were 'on the spot' or in the metropole and whether their role required the use of psychological warfare. For example, some officials of the Foreign Office tended to completely disregard and ridicule 'the art of psywar'. On the other hand, colonial administrators in rebellious territories craved for glimpses of useful information and propaganda material as a means of containing an insurgency and furthering the British government's interests.

This material also suggests that the process of decolonization was less 'connected' than some of the recent historiography might lead us to believe. Although there was certainly an intention on the part of British colonial administrators to 'connect' counter-insurgency experiences, at least in the case of Cyprus, this largely failed in execution. There were clear limits to attempts at borrowing and to the flow of ideas between different colonial settings, for example the borrowing of psychological warfare techniques from Malaya and Kenya in order to implement them in Cyprus, as well as limits to their effectiveness. As it was admitted in one of the notes on propaganda about Cyprus: 'There can be no guarantee that what has been tried with success in one part of the world will succeed in another. The psychological warfare methods evolved in Malaya and Kenya have been of little effect in Cyprus.'[79]

Taking the above into consideration leads to another argument: that the British propaganda machine was less formidable than the Anglophone historiography on colonial insurgencies up until the early 2000s has led us to believe. In the following chapters, this argument is examined and supported by recently released archival evidence. British experts on propaganda were severely lacking and those who did exist could not simply parachute into diverse colonial fields of conflict, for example from Malaya to Cyprus, in order to help the colonial government take back control. In the case of Cyprus, colonial officials, who were assigned the role of propaganda officers, such as John Reddaway, had limited or no experience in this sector.

Therefore, many times they depended on the information they would receive from outside sources, such as the British Middle East Office and other colonial outposts experiencing 'emergencies'. In particular, Leslie Glass's advice was almost desperately sought even before the official start of the revolt and as late as January 1959, shortly before its end. Another significant factor hampering investment in a well-designed, well-equipped propaganda machine, as Glass had warned, was limited financial resources. Even so, the colonial government could not just simply 'leave it alone', even though they knew that they would need to convince the sceptical Foreign Office and the busy Colonial Office 'to spend liberally on it' in order for their effort to be 'continuous and effective'.[80]

The analysis of the archival material also shows that British officials of the Foreign and Colonial Offices, who were remote from the field of action but nevertheless involved in the decision-making process about the colonial government's course of action in Cyprus, were out of touch and consequently misguided about the situation on the ground. Therefore, advice or orders coming from these sources in London, and often from other British representatives in Athens, Ankara and Washington, were often unhelpful and/or ignorant to the colonial government's effort to contain the insurgency and win over local and international public opinion. In other words, the Colonial and Foreign Offices' ambitions for the Eastern Mediterranean region and the Middle East did not necessarily mean having the necessary knowledge, much less the experience, required to translate these ambitions into achievements or being able to plan successfully and act accordingly in order to secure them.

However, it was not only a matter of internal coordination and cooperation within the various and diverse departments of the imperial government that were dealing with the future of Cyprus. One cannot underestimate the external, international developments affecting British ambitions during this period, such as the Suez debacle in November 1956 which radically changed London's attitude towards Cyprus. Furthermore, the deadlock between the interested parties, Britain, Greece, Turkey and the considerations coming from the United States and Russia, effectively shaped all aspects of British policy on Cyprus. These external influences will be explored in more detail in the following chapter.

In September 1955, six months after EOKA began its armed liberation struggle against the British colonial government, John Reddaway, unofficially head of propaganda and officially Administrative Secretary in the Cyprus government, wrote a personal and confidential letter to J. A. C. Cruickshank of the Far Eastern Department of the Colonial Office, requesting information about psychological warfare in Malaya during the British counter-insurgency campaign (1948–1960). Reddaway had been put in charge 'of counter-propaganda and/or psychological warfare or call it what you will' in Cyprus, 'rather late in the day' as he ironically commented.[81] Reddaway's confusion, and even perceivable annoyance with this vague and tiresome task, was eagerly picked up by his correspondent whose confidential reply echoed Reddaway's tone. Cruickshank wrote:

> I find there are some 'phoney' people in the Services Departments in Whitehall who, in an effort to build themselves an empire, are endeavouring to get it recognised that Psychological Warfare is an important though esoteric branch of the military art. They have written several papers, which seem to me to be rubbish. The result is that everyone here now eschews to use the phrase 'psychological warfare' and, even more, the use of the special abbreviation for it which has been adopted by these charlatans – 'psywar'. What I take it you

are really after is useful information from Malaya, not about psychological warfare, but about the Information and Propaganda services there.[82]

Cruickshank was deeply doubtful about the merits of psychological warfare in rebellious colonial settings. He was also unable to provide useful information, because the Far Eastern Department had 'little or nothing' on it.[83] He therefore forwarded Reddaway's request to S. Harold Evans, Head of the Information Department of the Colonial Office, even though he considered it doubtful whether Evans would possess useful information either. Indeed, Evans in his reply to Reddaway reinforced Cruickshank's view, adding that there was in Whitehall 'a certain amount of scepticism' regarding the popular catch-phrase '"psychological warfare"'.[84] As he explained, this was chiefly because some of its exponents had attempted to give it 'an almost mystical significance', by implying that it is 'a science apart which provides the key to all things but can be understood only by a chosen priesthood'.[85] Similarly to Cruickshank, Evans defined psychological warfare as little more than the intelligent and imaginative use of propaganda to assist in achieving a military objective. In the Cold War era, he attested, the term had also acquired the connotation of 'propaganda without inhibitions'.[86] This evidence arguably implies a certain disdain for the idea of 'psywar', but as it already shows this is not the case for the idea of 'intelligent and imaginative' propaganda. During the Cyprus revolt a lot of faith was invested in the potential of propaganda for all actors involved, the British colonial government, Archbishop Makarios and the EOKA movement.

With Reddaway's request for primary information on the use of counter-propaganda during the Malaya Emergency still pending, Evans finally recommended Alec Peterson's report 'Info Services in Malaya 1952–54'. Evans thought that this would probably provide a useful angle on the necessary reorganization, direction and coordination of information services in Cyprus now that EOKA, with the support of the *Ethnarchy* and the majority of the Greek Cypriot people, had embarked on their own national liberation struggle. Evans estimated that even though Peterson was, possibly, faced with the problems that Reddaway was now facing, nevertheless he also considered that the Malaya example 'is perhaps not very close' to the Cyprus one.[87] Reddaway rather defensively assured Evans that he had not fallen for 'the mystique of "psychological warfare"' and shared both the Information Department's and the Eastern Department's scepticism on the issue. However, most importantly he admitted that this was 'the one side of our propaganda activities here [in Cyprus] where we cannot at present see the way very clearly ahead, owing to our lack of specialist experience and advice'.[88]

Reddaway hoped that if Cyprus's colonial government acquired more detailed knowledge of previous 'psywar' operations in other colonial outposts such as Malaya, Kenya and Palestine, it would be able to decide how fruitful a similar approach might be in the present circumstances in Cyprus.[89] Nevertheless, having spent years in the island in official posts, Reddaway was in a position to discern some 'fundamental differences', as he called them, between Malaya and Cyprus. These differences generated valid doubts as to whether a cross-examination of colonial emergencies would help the Cyprus government see clearly ahead. In the course of the Cyprus Emergency, these considerations became severe limitations on the British attempt to create and disseminate efficient, meaningful propaganda about the future of Cyprus to its people and to a diverse international audience.

An example was the different level of media literacy between the indigenous populations in Malaya and in Cyprus. Reddaway wrote that one great difference between conditions in the two countries was that

> [in Cyprus] the 'man in the street', or better, 'the man in the field' is literate and takes a very active interest in political affairs. He already reads one or more daily newspaper (inevitably hostile) and listens assiduously to Athens Radio. He is already fairly blasé about the cinema. Our problem is thus to break down a long-established fixation in the Cypriot people's mind [union with Greece] and, in doing this, we do not have the advantage of novelty in the use of media, which was so obviously one of the strong points in favour of the work in Malaya. Once again, television seems to be the answer.[90]

This observation was confirmed when Reddaway finally got hold of the information requested on counter-propaganda operations during the Malayan Emergency. He concluded that Cypriots were 'far more sophisticated' than 'the people whom the psychological warfare division was trying to reach in Malaya', in the sense that in Cyprus the British had to deal with 'a literate European population who have already acquired a fixation on the subject of their political future and who are inured to most forms of publicity'.[91]

Importantly, drawing to any considerable extent upon the British experience in Malaya was a questionable venture because, whereas in Malaya the insurgents were physically separate from the mass of population and therefore propaganda could be directed specifically to them in their hideouts in the jungle, in Cyprus the insurgents were inextricably mingled with the public.[92] Therefore, it did not take Reddaway long to realize that the material provided on psychological warfare was limited, unhelpful and, to a large degree, irrelevant to Cyprus's context. In fact, he believed that propaganda directed specifically towards individual insurgents could do 'more harm than good' if it was distributed among the island's general population. He also foresaw that the propaganda line used at that point in late 1955 in Cyprus, aimed at causing disaffection among the insurgents, would prove to be ineffectual.

Instead, Reddaway proposed that the application of psychological warfare should wait until 'we begin to get them [EOKA] on the run'.[93] Serious, coordinated efforts in achieving this had to take place only after Governor Harding was sent to the rebellious colony. Until then, attention should be given to another important figure in the history of propaganda during the revolt: Lawrence Durrell, the well-known cosmopolitan novelist and poet, also Foreign Office employee and colonial government propagandist during his three-year spell in Cyprus, between 1953 and 1956. In the following section, it is argued that Lawrence Durrell was of significant importance in the initial steps of designing, applying and disseminating propaganda, as well as in information collection at the beginning of the Cyprus revolt.

Lawrence Durrell and 'Cypriotism': 'I became something like the head of propaganda'

While Reddaway was requesting useful information on propaganda from experts and non-experts in London and other territories, he was also coordinating propaganda in Cyprus. During this transitional period until the beginning of the emergency, he was in close collaboration with Lawrence Durrell, who at that time was residing in Cyprus. The British expatriate arrived in Cyprus in 1953 and stayed until August 1956, before the Greeks 'push us [the British] into the sea', as he wrote in one of his many letters to his friends.[94] Durrell served as the Director of Public Relations in Cyprus, but his services terminated in August 1956 when, afraid for his life, he fled. Durrell left Cyprus, persuaded that persuasion could no longer be effective for the Greek Cypriot audience and remarking that the island had become 'a sort of Kenya now and rather a nightmare for me'.[95]

Up until recently, information about Durrell's relationship with Cyprus was drawn largely from his autobiographical novel *Bitter Lemons*, published in 1957, amidst the Cyprus revolt. Although Durrell has certainly been given more attention in the secondary literature than other less well-known cosmopolitan personalities who also visited or stayed in Cyprus during the revolt, such as Freya Stark and Patrick (Paddy) Leigh Fermor, Durrell's role as an employee of the Cyprus colonial government remains largely unexplored.

Bitter Lemons sheds some light on his activities as the island's Public Relations Director and Information Officer. Fascinating archival material on Durrell's professional endeavours in Cyprus during the revolt has emerged during this research. This material, primarily coming from the Migrated Archives but also from other published, primary sources such as Durrell's correspondence, expands our understanding of the use of propaganda for Cyprus shortly before and during the early years of the revolt. Furthermore, it reveals another, largely unknown, aspect of Durrell's personality that does not relate to his famous literary persona but instead shows a much more prosaic persona, one that follows orders and whose otherwise artistic temperament is restrained by day-to-day cumbersome office tasks. This is Durrell the public servant, Durrell the propagandist.

Below there is a short excerpt from an interview he gave in 1959, in which he briefly referred to his activities in Cyprus:

Durrell: I had a little money. I bought, for 200,000 francs, a dilapidated
            Turkish house. [...] I went to Cyprus only because it was in the
            sterling zone and I could get my money there.
Juin: Then came the events of the Greek revolution?
Durrell: And at the same time as those, the Foreign Office. I became
            something like the head of propaganda. I quickly saw that all the
            issues had been decided: the Turks, the Greeks, the English were like
            rocks, unshakable. I resigned.
Juin: And you took refuge where this time?
Durrell: To England.[96]

Durrell first came to Cyprus to write his novel *Justine* (1957). He was in need of money and his friend Maurice Cardiff, Director of the British Council in Cyprus, introduced him to Constantinos Spyridakis, the headmaster of the Pan-Cyprian Gymnasium in Nicosia, 'a known hotbed of anti-British propaganda', as Cardiff called it.[97] Through Cardiff, Durrell secured a job as a teacher of English at the Pan-Cyprian Gymnasium. In 1955, and again via Cardiff's intercession, Durrell became Information Officer at the Cyprus Public Information Office, later to be renamed 'Press and Information Office'. Durrell's frustration regarding the state of the island's Information Services could be summarized in a sentence, found in one of his letters to his friend Freya Stark in 1954: 'I have been working like a black – they have made me a pasha and I am grappling with the moribund Information Services of the island, trying to make our case against the united howls of Enotists, British Pressmen and fact-finding MPs'.[98]

Durrell's new position disappointed his Greek Cypriot friends and bred considerable suspicion, as he was immediately branded a government mouthpiece promoting its illiberal views on prolonging colonial rule or 'slavery' as it was called in the Greek and Greek Cypriot media (through the press, Athens Radio and literature). Some Greek Cypriot and Greek intellectuals were quick to notice Durrell's false tone. The Greek poet and diplomat George Seferis, the Greek Cypriot novelist Costas Montis, and the Greek author and diplomat Rodis Roufos were a few who sought to refute his propaganda through their writings.

Durrell was a well-known figure in Greece, where he had lived from 1935 until 1941, first on the island of Corfu with his family, then in 1939 in Athens at the British Embassy Information Services as a press attaché due to his fluency in Greek, and then, at the British Council teaching English. Due to his knowledge of the Greek language he was able to develop a personal relationship with the people both in Greece and in Cyprus.[99] During the Second World War, between 1941 and 1944, he served as a press attaché to the British embassies in Cairo and Alexandria, but unconfirmed sources say that he was also recruited by the Special Operations Executive. After the war he held various diplomatic and teaching jobs. He worked on the Greek island of Rhodes and in Belgrade in the diplomatic service.[100]

In Cyprus, Durrell described his new role as 'telling the people of Cyprus what the government is doing for them'.[101] The colonial government's Information Department opened in July 1954 and two months later Durrell became its director. As previously mentioned, Governor Armitage had decided to restructure and upgrade the colonial government's media and public relations facilities. Jonathan Stubbs argues that the revamping of the department was decided on two reasons: first because the new headquarters for Britain's Middle East Land and Air Forces were to move to Cyprus, making it Britain's largest overseas airbase.[102] Thousands of military personnel and support staff were to be relocated to the island, and it was expected that the number of visiting foreign press correspondents would dramatically increase. The second reason was because in the summer of 1954, the Greek government appealed to the UN to apply the principle of self-determination in Cyprus, a strategic move that, ideally, would have led to *enosis*. Therefore, the island's Information Services had to build a counter-propaganda mechanism that would push forward Britain's position in Cyprus, threatened to be out-voiced by Greek and, increasingly, Greek Cypriot media campaigns.

Durrell wrote of his first impression of the Information Department in his novel *Bitter Lemons*:

The Information Office had a beguiling air of good-natured shabbiness [...] I had been led to believe that much needed to be done, but I was unprepared to find so few of the means for doing it. My inheritance seemed in pitiable shape; a cellar full of discarded blocks and photographic equipment so shabby and mouldering as to be a disgrace; an aged film van or two; a moribund house-magazine; and various other odds and ends of little practical use.[103]

On receiving an early note on 'Publicity and Propaganda on the Cyprus Problem', Durrell had wittingly replied to the Colonial Secretary that he was 'familiar with the facts of life [...] here, as its pattern is standard Foreign Service. Almost all these requirements are being met despite stock shortages and administrative delays'.[104] Even with shortages and delays, under his new but arguably familiar role, Durrell created and disseminated propaganda in various media and methods, primarily through the government's primary propaganda medium at this point, the Cyprus Broadcasting Service. Durrell significantly facilitated the process of propaganda by monitoring the broadcasts of Athens Radio, translating large parts of them into English and passing them on to his superiors, such as John Reddaway. Moreover, between 1954 and 1956 he was the director and editor of the *Cyprus Review* magazine, a local British illustrated monthly (the 'moribund house-magazine') that ran from 1946 until Durrell left the island in 1956.[105]

It could be argued that the *Cyprus Review* followed the government's policy of 'Cypriotism'. It did so by publishing articles and visual material produced by Greek Cypriot, Turkish Cypriot and British artists and writers, promoting in a mix-and-match way a hybrid Cypriot identity[106] (Figures 2 and 3). Durrell's task was to revive the magazine in order to use it as a medium to attract the Cypriots' support. In a letter to his friend and contributor to the magazine, Freya Stark, Durrell suggested that the changes he was about to effect in the magazine were intended to make it an instrument of more effective propaganda for the government. In another letter to Stark, he mentioned that the *Cyprus Review* 'will be something to stand the government in good stead – something worth owning. The Governor is very pleased with it but the Administration tends to grumble and regard it as frivolous. But the troops are buying it out and incoming tourists like it'.[107]

An identity for Cyprus was to be produced and marketed not only in the island for the Cypriot local and foreign population to consume, but also outside, disseminated by tourists visiting Cyprus, in this way formulating a favourable international public opinion. These attempts were to be reinforced under Governor Harding, as public opinion was vital to the success of his plan.[108] It is worth mentioning here that Durrell also disseminated the government's viewpoint through his published articles in the foreign and local press and arguably, first and foremost in terms of long-term impact, through his book *Bitter Lemons.*

Although Durrell was a declared philhellene, he considered the Greek Cypriots as having nothing to do with the 'Hellenes'. There are several instances in the archival material where he lapses into racial stereotyping about the Greek Cypriots. For example, 'Cypriots are afflicted by a "native torpor", which makes them unable to comprehend the British attitude to work, they are "almost oriental"' and they 'betray most of the character defects of Mediterranean Irishmen'.[109] It still remains obscure whether he expressed his thoughts out

Figure 1 (sitting, from left) Greek poet and diplomat George Seferis; Ministry of Information director and writer Lawrence Durrell; Antoinette Diamanti; British Council Director Maurice Cardiff; (standing, from right) Greek Cypriot painter and teacher Adamantios Diamantis and his son (1953).

IPLIK PAZZARI MOSQUE

JANUARY

SIX PIASTRES

Figure 2 *Cyprus Review* magazine, Cover page, Press and Information Office publ., ed. by Lawrence Durrell, January 1955.

loud when in company with Greek Cypriot and Greek influential personalities such as George Seferis, Evangelos Louizos and Adamantios Diamantis. His personal relationship with them served a purpose: through cultural diplomacy he attempted to collect information, passing it on to the island's Intelligence Services. Lawrence Durrell was acting as a 'middleman' between the British and the Greek sides (Figure 1).

CYPRUS REVIEW

Figure 3 *Cyprus Review* magazine, Cover page, Press and Information Office publ., ed. by Lawrence Durrell, July 1955.

We find an interesting insight into Durrell's stay in Cyprus in Maurice Cardiff's little-known but revealing memoirs *Friends Abroad* (1997). According to Cardiff, whom Durrell regularly visited at his house in Nicosia, 'two or three times a week for lunch or dinner', they discussed the political situation in the island and their love of books. During the revolt, Cardiff mentioned, Durrell 'was a fair game for the assassin's bullet', that is why whenever there was a knock on his door he opened 'armed with a 12-bore double barrelled shotgun pointed at close range at one's chest'.[110] During daytime, Durrell also carried 'a minute pearl-handled pistol stuffed into his breast pocket'.[111] Shortly after EOKA began its liberation campaign (Durrell had not predicted this, as he believed that Greek Cypriots would not support an armed struggle), and after Governor Harding took over the reins, Durrell expressed his displeasure with the government's hard line. By August 1956 Durrell had already left as his life was in danger. In a letter to his friend Alan G. Thomas, in August 1956, just before he fled Cyprus, Durrell wrote that 'after this long spell of Balkan service – nearly seven years flat I feel I need Debarbarising [sic] and re-gilding', not much of a 'philhelleno-cypriot' here.[112]

Lawrence Durrell and John Reddaway provide only two examples of the innate prejudices that existed among colonial officials and their collaborators regarding indigenous populations, in this case the Greek people of Cyprus.[113] The following excerpt from a long note on propaganda, information and publicity, is of particular interest as it focuses on the perceived issues surrounding the use of propaganda on the specific cultural terrain of Cyprus, but also in the Eastern Mediterranean region.

> Propaganda is a word which has acquired an ugly meaning. Often publicity material which a reader finds unpalatable, however true it may be, is dismissed as 'sheer propaganda'. Similarly publicity material which a reader wants to see or hear, however untrue it may be, is accepted as 'here are the facts'. This is especially true of the highly emotional people inhabiting the Levant area. Reason, logic, thought, common-sense, analysis, all the processes which are usual in the Western mind are absent. Once the Greek Cypriot has taken a side in an issue, he will tenaciously cling to a belief in that side, not yielding an inch in even the smallest detail. His capacity for self-deception and self-hypnosis is a factor which is hard to believe until experienced in dealings and conversation with him. To him 'truth' is what he chooses to believe whether or not it bears any relation to the facts.[114]

Through an assemblage of impressions a Greek Cypriot 'type' is identified, if not constructed. The Greek Cypriot was perceived as a 'far more sophisticated' (than the Malayan) 'literate European population'. Yet he was politically 'fixated' since it was lacking a traditional Western mind by reason of geography, as he was 'inhabiting the Levant area'. Therefore, he was 'highly emotional', stubborn, self-deceptive and delusional. Furthermore, this otherwise 'charming in so many ways and invariably hospitable and kind' people was 'intimidate[d]' and kept 'cowed' by EOKA because it was 'not endowed with much courage'.[115] In an attempt to follow a similar train of thought, it becomes only logical to assume that the British colonial Administration in general, being Western-minded by nature, was also culturally incompetent at fathoming the depth (or surface) of 'the people inhabiting the Levant area', and vice versa.

It was upon these fixed ideas that the concept of 'Cypriotism' was built. The concept of 'Cypriotism', in a rather vague manner, rested upon persuading the Greek Cypriots that they were 'an independent manifestation of Greek culture, rather older than and superior to that of modern Greece'.[116] Without denying that they were Greeks, the important thing was 'to free them from the idea that they are an inferior, colonial people', while encouraging associations between Britain and Cyprus.[117] Here a fascinating manipulation of the idea of national self-determination is found based on flattery and persuasion and targeting the political ambitions of the Greek Cypriots or, rather, their representatives.

It is only logical to argue that British assumptions about Greek Cypriots influenced and eventually shaped policy-making for Cyprus. The archival material accessed during this investigation supports the argument that racial stereotyping had an effect on colonial governance, especially on propaganda issues that targeted the Cypriot psychology. At the other end of the scale, as will be discussed in more detail in the following chapters, General Grivas, EOKA's leader, had attributed EOKA's success 'not to experience, but to my deep understanding of Cypriot psychology and my "sense of war" – the quality of judgment that brings correct decisions in moments of crisis'.[118] In his memoirs, Grivas discredited Harding's and his team's attempts 'to understand the people' they were ruling.[119] Durrell, therefore, was no different from other administrators, as his personal understanding of the Greek Cypriots also shaped his work as a propaganda officer.

Conclusion

In this chapter, an international debate on the issue of propaganda for Cyprus, discovered in unpublished secret and confidential official correspondences, was pieced together for the first time. This material dates back before the start of EOKA's campaign in April 1955 and reveals that since the early 1950s the Cyprus colonial government was in desperate need of propaganda in order to influence the Greek Cypriots, who were rapidly becoming nationalized by organs of Greek Cypriot and Greek propaganda, first and foremost by their Archbishop

Makarios III. At the same time the archival material has shown a deep-rooted scepticism within official ranks surrounding the idea of 'psychological warfare'. Nevertheless, no matter how doubtful the British propaganda venture for Cyprus may have been, the colonial government needed to reshape Cypriot consciousness turning them from Greeks into Cypriots, as the discussion on 'Cypriotism' has shown. This was in order to safeguard Britain's interest in Cyprus and in the region. Even though 'local men', such as John Reddaway, saw no great potential in the British propaganda effort in Cyprus, men in Whitehall believed otherwise. Therefore, it was decided that propaganda was to be used as a decisive instrument of policy and as a weapon during the British counter-insurgency. British attempts to counter Greek and Greek Cypriot propaganda, and to influence local and international audiences, are going to be studied in the following chapters, along with Britain's vision for Cyprus.

'Stepping up our propaganda on Cyprus', October 1955–October 1957

Introduction

The problem was phrased vividly in a stray note on propaganda in Cyprus: 'Long before a State of Emergency was declared H.M.G. and the Cyprus government were a dozen laps behind in the propaganda race.'[1] Propaganda was a crucial factor affecting the development of the revolt in Cyprus. How the propaganda game was to be developed would serve as an indicator of the spoils that each side, British and Greek Cypriot/Greek, was getting from Cyprus. As seen in the previous chapter, during the early discussions among colonial officials in Cyprus, propaganda experts at the British Middle East Office and the Colonial Office on the issue of propaganda and psychological warfare, there was a pervasive sense that during the revolt the Greeks had the upper hand. This understanding did not change under Governor John Harding who, in succeeding Robert Armitage in the governorship of the island some months into his rule, wrote to Allen Lennox-Boyd, the Secretary of State for the Colonies, that 'so far, the Greek Government and the *Ethnarchy* seem to me to have made a good deal of the running in this contest'.[2]

Justifiably Harding was agitated regarding the past inadequacy and present inefficiency of British propaganda about Cyprus, locally and internationally. Solely responsible for the containment of the insurgency as he now was, he had good reasons to be disturbed by the energetic propaganda campaign vigorously mounted by Greek and Greek Cypriot propaganda agencies active in Cyprus and abroad. The governor was convinced that the British and colonial governments' 'failure', as he called it, to make progress 'against the flood of misrepresentations from Greece', was due in large part to 'our having been too much on the defensive in the past'.[3] 'Misrepresentations' were coming from various sources, primarily Athens Radio and the Greek press, from Greek government representatives in international bodies such as NATO and the UN, as well as from within Britain such as members and supporters of the opposition and press editors, not to mention propaganda agencies in Cyprus such as EOKA's subsidiary bodies and the *Ethnarchy*'s affiliated organizations.

Under these circumstances, Charles Peake the British Ambassador in Athens rather defensively wrote that 'as long as they [the Greeks] do propaganda for their point of view they cannot expect us not to do likewise'.[4] Governor Harding had to catch up. What he did was to set as one of his priorities the reorganization of the island's Information Services in order to tackle the insurgency efficiently, both militarily and politically, and in order to put over the British case to the people of Cyprus, as well as to numerous overseas press correspondents who covered the emergency and therefore shaped international public opinion.[5] However, as will be presented below, his use of coercive measures to contain the revolt and to re-impose law and order and his undiplomatic handling of the situation, for example his exiling of Archbishop Makarios to the Seychelles in March 1956, were to bring about a total 'splitting of sympathy' between the British colonial government and the Greek Cypriot population. His strong-arm tactics and mishandling of propaganda would also alienate large sections of international public opinion.

Governor Harding, Greek propaganda agencies and the Cyprus Information Services

Governor Harding was 'parachuted' into Cyprus in October 1955, as he was making plans for his retirement. Prime Minister Anthony Eden proposed his assignment. Harding's previous experience in tackling Emergencies in Malaya and Kenya and his prestigious position as Chief of the Imperial General Staff (1952–1955) seemed to be the ideal prerequisites for yet another challenging task. Nevertheless, David Hunt, Harding's biographer, wrote that 'Harding accepted reluctantly, from a sense of duty'.[6] In November 1955 Harding declared Cyprus in a state of emergency. He left the island two years later, on 22 October 1957, without having succeeded in getting EOKA 'on the run' and thus having failed to bring the revolt to a halt. He was replaced by Sir Hugh Foot, a diplomat, not a military man.

Existing historical analyses of Harding's role in the Cyprus Emergency have emphasized the failure of his negotiations with Archbishop Makarios, the coercive measures he used against the people of Cyprus in his attempts to capture the insurgents, and his general inefficiency as the island's hardliner governor in leading a counter-insurgency campaign against the guerrilla organization EOKA and those who supported it. 'Harding enacted seventy-six new laws that permitted security forces – term that British officials used in reference to both police and military units – to wield significant coercive powers.'[7] Declassified archival material used for the current analysis shows Harding's dependency on propaganda, information and psychological warfare in colonial governance. Harding's anxious longing to utilize efficiently Cyprus's Information Services and other emergency propaganda means, such as clandestine propaganda exerted by unofficial sources, becomes evident through the study of his private and confidential correspondence with other empire officials. Propaganda was supposed to facilitate Britain's ambitions to secure its position in the Middle East and the Eastern Mediterranean region by gaining the acceptance of its policies by the local Cypriot population and international public opinion. Winning 'hearts and minds', therefore, would contribute towards Britain's objective not to lose its 'world power' status after the end of the Second World War and into the Cold War era.

During his two-year stay in Cyprus, Governor Harding and his team on the ground, which included the Cyprus 'veteran' John Reddaway, invested in restructuring the island's Information Services and in 'put[ting] out overtly and covertly', internationally and locally, 'a very heavy stream of propaganda' on behalf of the colonial and London governments.[8] Harding requested from Allen Lennox-Boyd, the Secretary of State for the Colonies, additional staff for the local information and broadcasting services for research and writing of publicity material, both for Cyprus and overseas. Specifically, he asked for a full-time Information Officer who would be devoted to presenting 'the British case on Cyprus'.[9] He asked for an expert.

This expert was to be none other than Leslie Glass, who in November 1955 moved to Cyprus and became the new Director General of Information Services responsible for the coordination of all forms of publicity and propaganda, succeeding John Reddaway in this role.[10] It is highly possible that he was recommended to Harding by Reddaway, as Glass and his team at the British Middle East Office had provided the colonial government with advice on propaganda and psychological warfare issues before Harding's arrival.

Glass stayed in Cyprus for a year or so before joining the Foreign Office and becoming the British Ambassador to the United States. Like Durrell before him, Glass remained unimpressed by the state of the local Information Services. In a letter to the Colonial Office he expressed the view that 'a "peacetime" Press Organisation with inadequate staff has been trying to keep up with "wartime" conditions'.[11] During the first eight months of the EOKA campaign, Lawrence Durrell at the Cyprus Public Information Office had been issuing information from the British point of view about day-to-day events in rebellious Cyprus. However, as an anonymous note on propaganda observed: 'It [the Public Information Office] was not geared to do this effectively'.[12]

The Greek and Greek Cypriot agencies that Governor Harding considered responsible for inflating and exploiting the emotions of the Greek Cypriots to the point of violence were 'the *enosis* leadership' and especially that 'ruthless priesthood', Athens Radio and the 'Greek press' (i.e. press from Greece).[13] Harding believed that the only way to tackle effectively, in other words 'to crush', the guerrillas and their collaborators was by attacking and limiting the reach and power of the above agencies. As Aaron Edwards writes, it didn't take long before Harding 'began to bear the brunt of Greek propaganda. Athens Radio, the main organ by which the Greek government "provided moral support to the insurgents", was remarkably anti-British, leading Harding to request that the Foreign Office "should seriously consider taking more forcible steps by diplomatic or other means to put an end to the lying abuse" being transmitted from Greece'.[14] Only a month into his governorship and his prediction was grim: the British government could not 'expect in any short time to induce the Greek Cypriots to see their basic Hellenism in perspective'.[15] Harding's estimation corresponds with Reddaway's considerations sent previously to Governor Armitage when he was first assigned the role of head of propaganda. Reddaway was one of the closest, if not the closest, advisor to the new governor as well. It is therefore highly possible that Harding was influenced by Reddaway's views.

Throughout the Cyprus Emergency Harding was more often than not expressing the views of John Reddaway and Leslie Glass on propaganda issues. This partly diffuses responsibility from a single individual, in this case the governor, and shows that emergency policy was designed by a group of people. In this way it becomes logical to argue that in order to better understand how colonial policy was formed, the 'supporting actors' need to be identified and studied.

As with mid-1954, in mid-1955 the colonial government was once again identifying a need for a well-staffed Information Service, which would counter hostile propaganda, prepare background briefing papers and propagate the government's point of view. As seen in a note on propaganda for Cyprus, although it was acknowledged that 'the British have an inherent dislike of anything that smacks of propaganda or publicity [...] in the modern era of mass communications through the press, radio and television this self-effacement can do untold harm. Certainly the opponents of Britain have no inhibitions about making the fullest use of these methods'.[16]

With this in mind, at the end of 1955, after Harding declared a state of emergency in Cyprus, 'a Civil – Security Forces – Police information organisation was established', headed by Glass.[17] During the 'saturation period of press visits', as it was called, between November 1955 and February 1957, Leslie Glass had direct access to Government House and was in charge of all information services. He spent most of his time briefing individual pressmen, thus shaping international public opinion from the British point of view.[18]

Archival evidence suggests that Glass left Cyprus in early 1957 and the post of Director General of Information Services was abolished.[19] As will be examined later on, Glass was to return to the island at the end of the revolt to provide some final advice on the 'Practicabilities for Psychological Warfare in Cyprus' in January 1959.[20] In this fascinating report, discovered during this research, Glass recalls the structure of Information Services in Cyprus during the emergency. This is important as no other account, primary or secondary, is currently known setting down the structure of Information Services in Cyprus during the revolt. Consequently, most of the information in this report is still absent from the historiography and is therefore reproduced and analysed here for the first time.

When Glass became Director General of Information Services, he assigned the role of operational propaganda officer to an Edward Wynne. 'For reasons of security', Glass recalled, Wynne 'remained in his old room marked with his old title, "Community Development Officer"'.[21] Here an important point emerges, namely that secrecy regarding the government's propaganda machinery was common practice. Similarly, Reddaway had kept his previous title as Deputy Colonial Secretary when he became head of propaganda in August 1955. The Greek Cypriots and the press had to remain in the dark regarding the government's organized efforts in propaganda. This was because 'knowing' would provide them ample material for counter-propaganda and/or violence.

Edward Wynne, after Glass left Cyprus in 1957, became assistant commissioner at Troodos but later resumed his past activities at the Information Research Unit. He was responsible for writing propaganda material. During 1956, Wynne was assisted by a Richard Wayne 'studying interrogation reports and keeping in touch with feelings in the countryside'.[22] Both Wynne and Wayne were Greek-speaking.[23] There was no full-time liaison officer with the operations staff. In hindsight Glass estimated that this was a mistake as a liaison officer was needed to 'go round in the field' and also to do appraisals for the operational requirements of the Information Research Unit.

Although it was intended for a Greek Cypriot to take a post within the unit, this proved impossible to achieve, because it was believed that 'anti-EOKA work of this nature was too dangerous'.[24] Glass, in his 1959 report, mentioned, but did not name, two Greek Cypriot collaborators, carefully classified by Glass as 'advisers' on propaganda matters. According to EOKA and Athens Radio these were 'traitors'. General Grivas had warned of 'severe punishments' for those who did not follow EOKA's orders and who did not comply with its rules.[25] However, even before EOKA's campaign, Athens Radio broadcasting from Greece was naming and shaming those Greek Cypriots who, in their understanding, were not acting in a patriotic manner and who were, in their words, 'traitors'. For example, under Governor Armitage and during the discussions for a new colonial constitution:

> The Governor [...], having failed to effect a conference of local representatives of the Cypriot people and notables of the island for the examination of the [...] constitution is now indulging in secret contacts with certain persons who he is trying to influence in return for well-known exchanges to make them renounce their homeland and agree to the enlisting of their names as traitors to their country by those of John Klirides and Paul Pavlidis and two or three others who will remain stigmatised in the pages of Greek history.[26]

Furthermore,

> You [Armitage] know quite well that with the exception of the notorious traitors Klyridis and Pavlidis and five or six others who have sold their souls and their glorious country to the devil you will find no other true Cypriot – that is true Greek – who would dishonour his name and that of his family before history. And when the gallant people of Cyprus celebrate their freedom the renegades will be compelled to take refuge in Britain where they will find only the contempt of the proud British people because no one has ever cared for traitors.[27]

In the case of Glass's 'two Greek Cypriot collaborators', he mentioned that the first had twice narrowly escaped assassination and the second's father was, after several attempts, killed by EOKA members. Therefore, Greek Cypriot 'individuals' were commissioned to prepare drafts, translate and type in Greek, in complete secrecy, usually in their own homes.

In this way, although Glass estimated that sufficient Greek Cypriot help was provided to produce some limited amount of propaganda material in Greek, this was not enough to maintain an intensive campaign.[28] In fact, up until the end of the emergency, there was an absence of full-time Greek Cypriot staff for the reasons mentioned above. This was a significant limitation for British propaganda activities. Glass, an expert in psychological warfare, was resolute: 'It is one of the axioms of propaganda that it can only be effectively done through nationals of the country addressed. [...] Only Greek Cypriots or Greeks, capable of thinking themselves into the skins of the target groups they are addressing, can produce really effective propaganda.'[29]

Therefore, as becomes evident through study of the archival material, another reason significantly affecting the quality and effect of British propaganda targeting Greek Cypriots was the lack of sufficient Greek Cypriot sympathizers to assist the colonial government in its propaganda campaign. Examples of British propaganda copying Greek propaganda in order to reach, trick and finally influence the Greek Cypriot audience, for instance through the use of forged leaflets, will be examined in the following chapter.

However, a well-staffed and well-organized Information Service to counter 'top level *enosis* leadership' would not suffice. In a top-secret telegram to the Secretary of State for the Colonies, Harding proposed legislative and administrative actions to be taken to diminish the political power of the Church and to confine the clergy to their sacerdotal duties.[30] Harding was convinced that the Church was exploiting its position for seditious ends, actively engaging 'in a conspiracy to overthrow the Government by force'.[31] It was Harding's firm position that 'as long as the top level Enosis leadership remains untouched, the inflammation will continue to be very severe and the conduct of the security campaign will suffer accordingly'.[32] In a 1984 interview for the Imperial War Museum's archive, Harding admitted that during his time in Cyprus, he found it 'difficult to understand' the Greek Cypriots. Specifically, he found it difficult to

> understand the willingness of the Greeks in Cyprus to hand over themselves, body, soul and spirit, to their so-called spiritual leader [Archbishop Makarios]. [...] also difficult to understand how the spiritual leader of the community could adopt and support and carry on with the use of violence for political ends. That is part of the tradition behind the leaders of the Greek Orthodox Church. And Makarios was a brilliant advocate of that general philosophy.[33]

Harding's correspondence reveals how overwhelmed he was by his political opponent, who he perceived as competent, but also ruthless, a wolf in priest's clothing. Harding often appeared exasperated in his correspondence: 'Practically the whole leadership of the Church has been deeply and directly implicated in launching the campaign of violence on Cyprus.'[34] The governor needed to 'render it [the Church] less of a danger to peace and order'.[35] His plan for delivering a blow against the Church's political power, while safeguarding the colonial government's policy in front of public opinion, included excluding members of clergy from the legislature, annual audit of church accounts, prohibition of the use of church funds for any purpose other than a religious, charitable, philanthropic or educational scheme, and proscription of the organization OHEN (Orthodox Christian Union of Youth) because of its 'subversive activities' such as inciting nationalistic feelings through word of mouth. Harding had even proposed more invasive methods to curb the Church's power, such as making it illegal for it to use the power of excommunication, marriage and divorce for political purposes such as sanction against disloyalty to EOKA and the Cypriot cause.[36]

The argument on the importance of secrecy is also applicable here. An interesting and telling element of Harding's correspondence was his wish not to make any public announcement on the colonial government's new policy against the Church. He feared that this 'might have the effect of marshalling public opinion' against the government and, at that point, this would make Greek Cypriots accepting Lord Radcliffe's proposals for a constitution even more difficult.[37]

Secrecy, therefore, was a component of British policy-making, and only research into the available archival material (much of which was inaccessible up until recently and some of which still is) will allow historians today to re-evaluate the history of British policy-making during decolonization. It will also inform the history of those territories experiencing revolts during their formal disengagement from foreign rule and towards independence. Here, this issue is brought to the foreground in relation to the specific aspect of propaganda during the Cyprus Emergency. It is however highly possible that, since secrecy was a common practice within the British and colonial governments, these did not only use it for one aspect of the counter-insurgency campaigns such as propaganda but instead applied it to other aspects of colonial governance. One infamous and known example is the extreme violence used during the British counter-insurgency in Kenya and the painstaking lengths the British and colonial governments went to in order to hide it, resulting in 2012 in 'the Mau Mau torture case' where the Kenyans won a ruling against the UK.[38]

The importance of 'public opinion' and inflammation of Turkish Cypriot feeling

Governor Harding often stated in his private correspondence that he had to improve Cyprus's Information Services in order to catch up with the 'propaganda race' to win over 'public opinion'. During the 1950s, the Committee on the British Oversea Information Services, based in London, defined the real genesis of the services' work as lying in the increased influence exerted at that point in time by 'public opinion' upon the policies of governments and in the development of modern techniques for the mass dissemination of news and views. As Simon J. Potter writes, 'Patterns of long-distance mass communication in the nineteenth- and twentieth-century British Empire were influenced by particular institutions' such as the British Oversea Information Services one could argue 'and marked by an unevenness and a tendency toward systematization that shaped the nature and the extent of connections between different parts of the world'.[39]

By 'public opinion' or 'world opinion' as it was alternatively called, the British government largely meant the United States, the UN, NATO and Soviet public opinion, as well as the opinion of former colonies rapidly changing into 'emerging states'. The committee defined two important objectives to be met by the services active around the world. The first objective was 'to strengthen the bonds of sentiment and enlightened self-interest between the colonies, Britain and the rest of the Commonwealth', as it was envisaged that political control coming from London was to be progressively loosened for many imperial territories during the 1950s. The second objective was to counter communism by direct counter-propaganda and through an emphasis on Britain's 'democratic alternative'.[40] As Rory Cormac writes:

> Policymakers and intelligence analysts alike feared nationalist unrest would be exploited by Moscow and these fears grew as more colonies neared independence, creating a potential power vacuum. This was the era of competitive coexistence and an enticing opportunity for Khrushchev to intervene in parts of the world previously out of reach. Whitehall braced itself for a subterranean battle for influence, although much Soviet activity targeted American ascendency rather than the old colonial powers, for Moscow was already confident of British decline.[41]

Public opinion was believed to be a significant determinant of public policy 'in a world plagued by profound ideological differences'.[42] Revealingly, 'governments must not only carry their own public opinion with them but use public opinion overseas to influence other foreign Governments. In seeking to make use of public opinion overseas competition is encountered from yet other Governments who are also seeking to influence this public opinion'.[43] With regard to the colonies, of which Cyprus was one, they were thought to be affected by 'what the world thinks and says of them'.[44] At the same time, public opinion was formed and influenced by indigenous perceptions of the failure or success of British policy in colonial territories.[45] As a consequence 'no policy would be likely to-day to obtain international acceptance, unless it was understood and accepted by peoples as well as by Governments'.[46]

In regard to the future of Cyprus, the study of confidential correspondence has revealed that public opinion was an issue of utmost importance to the colonial governor but also to Greek Cypriot leaders, Archbishop Makarios and General Grivas. Public opinion shaped the decision-making process and eventually colonial policies themselves. It is here argued that, in turn, public opinion was shaped by propaganda. This consideration has not been given emphasis in the relevant historiography; it is however highlighted here. Governor Harding felt that the British side had to deal with the revolt and 'win the battle for the support of public opinion' locally and abroad, by using 'far more imagination and vigour', and by adopting 'a much more robust and offensive policy', to speed up the 'propaganda race'.[47] This would have entailed the use of various and diverse media and methods to be identified and analysed in the following chapter.

The issue of 'public opinion' was a constant worry for the British and colonial governments. Governor Harding's official correspondence proves that he was very much aware that in conjunction with a military counter-insurgency targeting EOKA, he had to apply a propaganda policy that would safeguard the Greek Cypriots' sympathy towards the colonial government and British rule. In one of his early reviews of the security situation in the island, Harding identified two aspects of the counter-insurgency campaign that had to be successfully approached in order to deal with the political requests of Makarios and to restore 'law and order' in a place where both 'had ceased to function'.[48] The first aspect was the active operations against the insurgents. This was largely a matter of intelligence, organization, methods and resources, on which he managed to secure absolute authority as Governor and Director of Operations shortly after he arrived in Cyprus.[49]

The second aspect was the measures directed 'at the root causes of the trouble', meaning 'the unscrupulous inflammation and exploitation of Hellenic nationalism amongst the Greek Cypriots amounting in many instances and cases to fanaticism'.[50] This second aspect, which can be arguably summed up as Greek and Greek Cypriot propaganda, has been traditionally neglected in academic research. This neglect may lie in the fact that Greek Cypriot and Greek popular historians have taken for granted that the Greek Cypriot people innately supported EOKA's struggle and Makarios's demand for *enosis*. An enquiry into the methods of Greek Cypriot and Greek propaganda would possibly imply that the Greek Cypriots' support was not instinctual or unquestionable. It would potentially undermine the power of the *enosis* demand, as it would suggest that the people were influenced and persuaded into supporting the struggle and that they did not do so spontaneously.

On the other hand, the fact that the study of Greek and Greek Cypriot propaganda by foreign researchers is very limited is also due to language limitations. Most Greek and Greek Cypriot propaganda was published in Greek, needing translation into English before analysis. Currently most of the original material remains in Greek, and research into it is available only to Greek-speaking researchers. Even though this book does not go as far as to argue that the Greek Cypriot desire for *enosis* was 'artificial' (although this was claimed by officials in the Colonial and Foreign Offices in the early phases of the revolt) it does argue that powerful Greek and Greek Cypriot propaganda organs were definitely at play during the period of the Cyprus revolt. These unquestionably inflated, but did not create, the Greek Cypriots' national feeling.

As will be examined in detail in the following chapter on propaganda media, even though Harding's government acknowledged the centrality of public opinion, the decisions it took were not the right ones for winning it over, either in Cyprus or abroad. On the other hand, for the Greek Cypriot audience Archbishop Makarios's propaganda had an emotional appeal due to its message: liberation from foreign rule and political union with motherland Greece. This message also resonated with international developments. British colonies were becoming independent one by one; why would Cyprus stay behind? Furthermore, and rightly so, Harding was worried about Makarios's appeal and outreach to the international community and particularly his reach in Britain. It was believed that Makarios was successfully evoking sympathy for the Greek Cypriot cause and exerting pressure on the British government to re-adjust its position by making 'further concessions', leaving open the possibility for *enosis*.[51]

Leslie Glass considered Makarios 'the most powerful of nationalist leaders'.[52] He 'and his henchmen' ruled political life on the island.[53] The Greek Cypriots, being a religious and pious people, were afraid of the threat of religious sanctions for failing to follow the Church's word, and this, the British colonial government thought, was enough to keep them in line with it. Furthermore, Makarios's 'enlightenment' world tour, for example in the United States, where he lobbied for the Greek Cypriot cause, gained international support and secured funding from foreign governments, the Greek diaspora and former colonies ('emerging states') which were 'anti-colonial' and more sensitive to the requests of a people under foreign rule. Makarios's vigorous policy, and his skills in diplomacy, his role as the representative of a religious institution vexed the colonial and British governments and their counterparts in Athens and Ankara, just as his persona and activities harmed Britain's public image and prestige.

Charles Peake, the Athens Ambassador who was also included in Harding's close circle of correspondents, had written to J. C. Ward of the Foreign Office about the situation in Cyprus, complaining that 'the Greeks' had 'been allowed to make the running'.[54] He was 'much concerned here to see how ignorant, and in some cases unconcerned' public opinion in Greece and abroad such as in the NATO countries was.[55] However, it was not only Makarios and Greek propaganda that were harming British prestige. While Harding was governor, his strong-arm tactics significantly contributed to 'the splitting of sympathy' between the people and the administration. Before moving on to the issue of the 'splitting of sympathy', another more controversial aspect of British emergency propaganda for the sake of public opinion needs to be brought into the foreground.

The incitement of Turkish Cypriot public opinion and feeling, and by extension the inflammation, prompting and urging of the Turkish government to step up its propaganda campaign on the legitimacy of the Turkish case over Cyprus's future, was a significant aspect of the British propaganda effort. This emerges during the study of confidential correspondence for this book, between officials of the Colonial Office and the Foreign Office during the period of the revolt but it has also been debated in the historiography on other aspects of the revolt.[56]

There was an urgent need to boost the promotion of the British case over Cyprus by 'stimulat[ing] the Turks into greater activity in putting over their case on Cyprus in other foreign capitals', W. Hilary Young of the Foreign Office admitted in a confidential letter titled 'Turkish Publicity on Cyprus' on 6 June 1956.[57] In mid-1956, a few months after Makarios's deportation, Turkish publicity was perceived by the British government as 'certainly [...] very disappointing so far', partly putting the blame on Turkish political leaders, such as Prime Minister Adnan Menderes and his Minister Fatin Rüştü Zorlu who were perceived as 'rather old-fashioned believers in blood and iron' and fell behind the more experienced Greek in the propaganda race.[58]

As far as Turkish lobbying of foreign governments was concerned, specifically NATO governments, the Foreign Office thought that the Turkish way was 'apt to be heavy handed'.[59] Therefore, the Foreign Office suggested persuading the Turks to replace their representative to the NATO Council with 'a more effective [... and] impressive' one.[60] The British government was anxious to ensure that the Greek government, whose representatives were perceived as more able than their Turkish counterparts, 'should not have the NATO floor to themselves for propaganda purposes'.[61] They recommended that the calibre of the Turkish representation at NATO be raised. Furthermore, they urged that the Turks make sure that they would take advantage of every opportunity given 'to ensure discreetly that their views are understood in NATO capitals'.[62]

Although the British government considered Turkish claims to be an essential part of the British case on Cyprus, nevertheless, it believed that the British case would not make an impact on world public opinion unless it was articulated effectively by the Turks themselves. Simultaneously, the British government was to do everything it could, primarily through a policy of general publicity, and by lobbying foreign governments, to ensure that the Turks made their case known internationally.[63] Regarding the issue of general publicity, the Foreign Office supported the view that although there were sufficient statements by Turkish spokesmen concerning Cyprus, including the 'rather old-fashioned' Turkish prime minister, the problem was that these had received insufficient attention from the international press and this somehow had to be reversed.

On the other hand, the British government was satisfied that through the manufacturing of 'sensation stories' (or a 'smear campaign' as it was called) EOKA was creating communal disturbances and giving prominence to the Turkish attitude. Nevertheless, it could be argued that communal disturbances were not only created due to EOKA's 'sensation stories', which anyway had little to do with the Turkish Cypriots, but in fact were concerned with the behaviour of the Security Services on the island. Disturbances were not only created because of the Greek Cypriot demand for *enosis*, a demand that was indeed contrary to the Turkish government's ambitions over Cyprus. Disturbances also took place because the colonial government was employing Turkish Cypriots in the Police Force, ordering them to hunt down EOKA and its sympathizers. EOKA's sympathizers, however, could be anyone. As a consequence all Greek Cypriots were suspects. More importantly, this research has also revealed that the Police Force was in search of Turkish Cypriots who knew the Greek language to serve as interrogators of Greek Cypriot prisoners. This no doubt was a significant factor contributing towards the 'splitting of sympathy', to use Leslie Glass's pertinent phrase, between Greek Cypriots and Turkish Cypriots.

Director General of Information Services: Predicting 'the future of Cyprus'

There is not much information on Leslie Glass's time as Director General of Information Services in Cyprus. However, one important archival finding of this research was his six-page secret note on 'The Future of Cyprus', a recurring title in official documents for Cyprus during the revolt. It is worth examining this document in some detail as it is particularly relevant to the use and role of propaganda in Cyprus during the revolt. Not only this, the document was produced by an expert in propaganda and psychological warfare who personally experienced the situation in Cyprus. His take is therefore much more relevant to the specific conditions of the emergency than any other estimation coming from British officials in Britain and abroad. The note, dated 1 April 1956, conspicuously aligned with the beginning of the liberation struggle on 1 April 1955, submitted to Governor Harding as well as to the Southern Department of the Foreign Office.[64] Glass produced it informally, since he was neither an official representative of the Foreign Office yet nor an accepted political adviser. However, due to his previous experience in the Middle East, and his foreseeable future career in the Foreign Service, his views were welcome.

Tackling the revolt efficiently depended on comprehending the situation in Cyprus. From what we have seen so far, it could be argued that officials in London and elsewhere, with no direct experience of the revolt in Cyprus, could not do that. Harding, a field marshal himself with experience in emergency situations, was aware of this fact. Among his suggestions to the Secretary of State for the Colonies was for a member of the Foreign Office Information Department to come to Cyprus and see at first-hand what the colonial government was doing, what they sought to achieve 'and how the lives of the Cypriot people are being affected'.[65] This was in order for the government in London to be supplied 'with first-hand up-to-date knowledge' of the propaganda and information material the colonial government was supplying, for example, to press correspondents on the island.[66]

Glass's note may be characterized as a pragmatic, unambiguous, frank, personal estimation of the situation in Cyprus. It summarizes the British policy on Cyprus based on four postulates: (a) Britain had to have a strong point in the Middle East, (b) Cyprus was the only place available, (c) Greece wanted sovereignty over Cyprus but might not agree with Middle East policy, (d) therefore Britain had to hold on to the sovereignty and control of Cyprus for several years ahead. Glass asked the simply phrased yet essential question: Could Britain do this?

It is important to emphasize here the fact that this note, like many other documents accessed during this research, was secret. Therefore, although Britain's policy on Cyprus at that time may seem straightforward, certainly it did not seem so to either the Greek Cypriot representatives pushing for their case, or to the Greek Cypriot audience, or to the international audience. More often than not, and perhaps more importantly, it was not straightforward to British colonial officials on the ground either. This was because they were not informed of the discussions taking place in parliament or in the Foreign Office.

The pre-1957 British government knew very well that it wanted to stay in Cyprus and the reasons behind this desire. However, it also acknowledged that it could not use its strategic reasoning overtly and directly in order to provide an explanation for its position. There were concerns that this reasoning was to be used for propaganda purposes by its enemies, such as Greek and Greek Cypriot propaganda, as well as Soviet propaganda, both active in the colony and abroad. As a result, many vital interested parties were insufficiently informed and fragmentarily updated. These interested parties were, for example, the colonial government, the Greek Cypriot representatives, the Greek government and also Turkey after Britain 'introduced [it] as an interested party, a role she undertook with increasing zeal, and the first criterion for a settlement became agreement between Greece and Turkey' as Diana Markides argues.[67]

What was central to Glass's discussion was the significance of public opinion in relation to Britain's handling of the Cyprus issue. Glass's considerations came just before the Suez Crisis, when public opinion in Britain, the United States and the UN played a major role in discussions about Britain's imperial future and policy options and decisions in a Cold War context. Glass estimated that for political expediency, the British government needed to reconcile its policy with British public opinion, with world public opinion and with Cypriot public opinion. In his understanding the first two depended on the latter. Perhaps in a lapse of judgement, or more probably unaware of the Foreign Office's priorities and/or machinations, Glass expressed the view that the power to decide whether the Greek Cypriots would achieve *enosis* would not remain in British hands for much longer. Neither could the British stay on the island by force, because they would not be able to sustain this in the face of British and international public opinion.

Therefore, in acknowledging the centrality of the role of public opinion in general, and on the guiding role that Cypriot opinion had, he foresaw three possible outcomes depending on the British treatment of the latter. If it was to defy Cypriot public opinion this 'may well mean that Cyprus will end up like Palestine and Ireland'.[68] It is safe to assume here that what he meant by this was partition. If British treatment wished to change Cypriot public opinion this would require several years. In fact, if a substantial change was envisaged meaning to deflect Cypriot public opinion 'away from Greek nationalism and the emotional urge to *enosis*', Glass considered this impossible. In his opinion, the only viable solution regarding Greek Cypriot public opinion was to come to terms with it. He believed that British post-deportation policy (i.e. Makarios) would stand or fall by the colonial government's ability to deal effectively with EOKA to 'get EOKA on the run' as Reddaway and Harding had stated earlier.[69] In fact, he warned that 'it will be a close race whether we can penetrate the hard core of EOKA and capture its leaders before the measures we take drive the population into open and general sympathy with EOKA. If the latter comes about first, we have lost the battle'.[70]

Glass believed that most Greek Cypriots were 'shocked by certain EOKA methods' and that they were all 'terrified by the threat of EOKA vengeance'.[71] Nevertheless, he also estimated that 'almost all have at least a sneaking admiration and sympathy for them as darling patriots who are fighting for noble nationalist ends'.[72] This is a significant point made by an expert on civilian psychology under conflict conditions, which was not raised by any of the advisors in the field or in the Colonial or Foreign Office up until that point. Harding, in his 1984 interview, reiterated this. He acknowledged that during the counter-insurgency in Cyprus, he was not up against a small group of 'terrorists', as EOKA fighters were named by the British colonial government. It is worth mentioning here that the term 'terrorist' was not applied without some consideration. 'Outlaws' was the second best choice but due to its romantic connotations, its Robin Hood-like aura, it was rejected.[73] Harding, instead, had 'to convince EOKA, and the people who supported EOKA, which meant 90 per cent of the Greek population, that they couldn't achieve their political objective that is self-determination leading to *enosis* by violence'.[74]

The above admission is significant because it provides information on the scale of support that EOKA had within the island. This information comes, not from self-validating archival sources of the Greek Cypriot side such as General Grivas's memoirs, but from EOKA's opponent, the protagonist of the British counter-insurgency campaign in Cyprus. This statement also explains and justifies, to some extent, Harding's difficulty in winning over Greek Cypriot public opinion.

The Greek Cypriots' support of EOKA's efforts was not always acknowledged by the British colonial government. On the contrary, in the official correspondence between British officials in Cyprus, London and elsewhere, regarding the various aspects of the counter-insurgency, it was often stated that Greek Cypriots were neither for nor against EOKA, their overpowering feeling being primarily fear. This fear was also projected in the colonial government's propaganda themes, which claimed that the Greek Cypriots were terrified of the armed guerrilla organization and the reprisals they would suffer in case they did not follow its orders or if they dared to help the British Security Services in their attempt to break EOKA's back. Although this arguably bore some truth, archival research conducted for this project showed that it was also an exaggeration, a hyperbolic claim constructed to serve British propaganda efforts against EOKA, as it focused on disengaging the Greek Cypriot public from the armed guerrillas in the eyes of international opinion. If British propaganda succeeded in doing this, the message saying that EOKA was isolated and alienated from the Greek Cypriot masses would empower the colonial government's position by justifying the counter-insurgents actions in the eyes of the international community.

At the same time, using this propaganda line within Cyprus would ideally enable pro-British influential 'moderate' Greek Cypriots to come forward and provide the Greek Cypriot public with an alternative to EOKA and Archbishop Makarios. This alternative for the future of the island was to be approved by the London and colonial governments. It was also to be in agreement with Britain's political, economic and strategic interests. These 'moderates' belonged to a school of Cypriot 'level-heads' as they were described and were the colonial government's emergency solution, quite literally in the midst of the emergency.[75]

Official correspondence reveals that there were desperate searches for these 'moderates', to be pushed forward onto Cyprus's political arena and take the reins from the Archbishop. However, they were quite hard to find and much less to secure. John Reddaway wrote about this in his book *Burdened with Cyprus: The British Connection* (1986).[76] In his experience there always existed a substantial minority of Greek Cypriots who favoured the connection with Britain, although not in the form of maintaining indefinitely Cyprus's colonial status. He admitted that the British did not succeed in fully and thoroughly 'mobilising and bringing out in the open this element'.[77] However, he attested that this was probably impossible because of the pervasive influence of the Church, the nationalist press and politicians.

With the effort to find moderates failing, and with Harding turning towards coercive measures to contain the revolt, Leslie Glass in his 1956 report firmly advised against the latter. He believed that the British counter-insurgency campaign neither should nor could attempt to frighten the population into cooperating with the British by using more brutal methods than EOKA did, nor could the British make Cypriots lose sympathy for the organization by stressing the brutality of EOKA's methods. Instead, British propaganda had to convince the Greek Cypriots that EOKA had outlived its usefulness and that the British were prepared to grant political terms that the majority of the Greek

Cypriot population would be willing to accept. By distancing the people from the organization, and by satisfying their pride with 'a reasonable political offer', it was estimated that the Greek Cypriots would gladly 'return to peace, normality and business as usual'.[78]

Glass's use of language is telling: the British, he thought, 'stood a good chance of being able to sell' to the Greek Cypriots a 're-fashioned political programme' for Cyprus. In summary, this policy proposed that the British were in Cyprus to stay and that they were to rule for an unspecified but long period of time. They would also, sooner or later, defeat EOKA whose brutal methods corrupted Cypriot society. Furthermore, the British accepted that the principle of self-determination was applicable to Cyprus and that they would draft a constitution for the Cypriots. In case the Greek Cypriots were not willing to participate in this process, the British would be willing to proceed with the 18 per cent minority of the Turkish Cypriots. This last point would arguably resonate as a threat in the ears of the Greek Cypriot representatives and push them to negotiate more leniently.

Furthermore, the constitution would be introduced as soon as 'terrorism and disorder have been put down'.[79] After this the British had to reassure the Greek Cypriots that they respected their Hellenic tradition and that they intended to foster it in the island, as they would also promote its economic prosperity. Glass also proposed that Harding should set up a committee to 'go into the whole question of what we can do to flatter and conciliate the Hellenism of the Greek Cypriots'.[80] Harding mentioned in his 1984 interview that the Greek Cypriots 'were schizophrenic to some extent [...]. Emotionally and psychologically they wished to be Greek, commercially and financially they were anxious to retain their British connection'.[81] Here again the early plans of the British committees for the Oversea Information Services to focus on the material benefits of the British connection come into the foreground. The emotional appeal of *enosis* could only be downplayed by emphasizing the material aspect of British rule – or so it was believed.

Glass predicted that if this was not to be, the Greek Cypriots would get embittered with the colonial government's tough, coercive measures, and more and more of them would pledge their allegiance to EOKA, considering the organization their voice, helping and protecting the guerrillas, and providing them with recruits. He was right in his prediction. Glass had warned that if the colonial government's 'policy of repression' continued to be accompanied by 'inadequate political offers', this would likely lead to *enosis* in two to three years.[82] Eventually, Glass's plan was largely rejected for downplaying, even dismissing, Turkey's demands and position vis-à-vis Cyprus. Neither the Colonial Office nor colonial administrators in Cyprus were in a position to know the discussions taking place within the Foreign Office and its plans for Cyprus, which soon were going to change with the Suez Crisis of late 1956 and as soon as Harold Macmillan's government came to office in early 1957. Estimations coming from all sources, in the field of action, the Colonial or Foreign Office, were bound to change with these developments.

The 'splitting of sympathy': An Archbishop in exile and coercion

Leslie Glass had emphasized the danger of the 'splitting of sympathy' between the Greek Cypriots and the British in Cyprus. For Glass, this issue stood very high on the colonial government's priority list, 'even higher than the security consideration'.[83] Harding's government could not ignore anymore the political implication of its actions. However, Glass's admonitions were brushed aside in favour of, or overshadowed by, Harding's coercive methods, used previously in Kenya and Malaya. This book agrees with Glass's warning and further argues that a crucial reason why British propaganda in Cyprus failed was because of the 'splitting of sympathy'.

When Harding declared Cyprus in a state of emergency, he also declared martial law through the imposition of strict and very often collective measures against the Greek Cypriots. Since the British colonial governments in Cyprus did not invest in the education of the Cypriots during the British occupation, propaganda could not have immediate results. Thus, the weapons used to fight EOKA and its supporters had to be immediately and blatantly invasive. Governor Harding introduced several coercive measures in his attempt to contain the rebellion, reinstate law and order, and safeguard Britain's political, economic and strategic aspirations, while concurrently doing propaganda for local and international audiences.

Carrying arms was punished by death: 18-year old Evagoras Pallikarides was hanged for this. Sabotage meant life imprisonment. Strikes were declared illegal. The police were given powers to arrest, incarcerate and interrogate without warrant. The government could expel anyone from the island, ban public meetings, close down places of public resort and entertainment, and seize newspapers or private property. There were curfews, evictions and 'village bashing' as Harding called it in his 1984 interview. There were collective fines and searches. Harding had ordered the reorganization of the government's counter-insurgency equipment, including improving intelligence and developing communications. Last but not least, he requested soldiers to be brought to Cyprus in order to restore peace through violence. Security Services patrolled the island. Cypriots were prisoners in their own homes.

Brian Drohan writes that as the war raged in Cyprus, in early 1957, 'the Labour Party peer Lord Strabolgi rose during a heated debate in the House of Lords. Criticizing Britain's colonial government in Cyprus, Strabolgi demanded, "What sort of State is this? Is it a police State? Is it a State like that set up by Nazi Germany, or a State which is trying to copy the methods of Soviet Russia?"[84] The most evident example on the use of colonial violence during the Cyprus Emergency is the hanging of nine insurgents. As Martin Thomas writes, 'The violence of colonial security forces in Cyprus, though, was a prelude, not the main event. With the worst of the Algerian War and revelations about the killing of Mau Mau detainees in Kenya still to come, external condemnation of colonial dirty war methods was set to increase.'[85]

As Robert Holland argued in his book *Britain and the Revolt in Cyprus, 1954–1959* (1998), after Governor Harding exiled Archbishop Makarios to the Seychelles on 9 March 1956 'a trial of force [was] inaugurated in which there could only be one winner.'[86] This book argues that physical force was not the only form of power mutually deployed by the enemy sides. In fact, the British colonial government's attempts in the sphere of propaganda were used very much as a weaponized policy and an instrument towards handling the population in Cyprus, and international public opinion in the United States, the UN, Greece and Turkey. Before embarking on a more detailed study of the specific propaganda methods and media used during the Cyprus revolt, the coercive aspect of the counter-insurgency should be briefly sketched. In this way the study of propaganda media will be presented in a more informed context.

Harding arguably acted more as field marshal and less as governor in spite of the fact that he very well understood, and was also advised by his administrators, that 'it is possible that a continuing deadlock on the political front would result in an increase in support for EOKA from the Greek Cypriot community as a whole. It is therefore of the greatest importance to keep the political ball in play until we have defeated the terrorists.'[87] He could not adhere to this. After the first rebellion of October 1931 and the results it brought, a feeling of distrust and suspicion developed between the British administration and the people and especially the people's representatives. This fact is also documented in the secret correspondence of the time. The British administrators did not trust the Cypriots.[88] During the EOKA campaign this was reflected, for example, in the police force which was successfully infiltrated by EOKA, where the majority of Greek Cypriot police officers were under EOKA's command.

Furthermore, a secret note for 'UK eyes only' contains information on 'a reluctance by Greek Cypriot Policemen to serve in ranks of Special Branch and so "stick out their necks"', for fear of EOKA's retaliation.[89] The police force was soon manned with Turkish Cypriots. As James S. Corum aptly perceived: 'If Harding carefully had planned to alienate the entire Greek population of the island and push the moderate Greeks into full support of EOKA, he could not have done better than by his policy of unleashing a horde of untrained, poorly-led Turkish police on the population.'[90] In the secret note, a more sinister way of giving an active role to the Turkish Cypriots during the emergency is revealed. Namely, the colonial government's intention to hire Turkish Cypriot government servants who spoke Greek and were willing to act as interrogators in order to assist 'the interrogation of terrorists and terrorist suspects'.[91] The colonial government's role in developing inter-communal bitterness is evident here. This bitterness was soon to become open hostility and conflict in the decade following the island's independence.

A pervasive distrust between the British, Greek Cypriot, Greek and Turkish representatives was being firmly established and consequently affecting negotiations on the island's future. For example, Francis Noel-Baker, a Labour MP's comments upon his visit to Cyprus in February 1956 are revealing. In his understanding, 'Reddaway was so suspicious of the Archbishop's motives that the Archbishop regarded anything which might derive from Reddaway with equal suspicion.'[92] This analogy may also be projected onto the people of Cyprus, British and Cypriot alike. The Greek Cypriots lost trust in the British and vice versa. It was a 'splitting of sympathy' as Leslie Glass had warned. In his memoirs, General Grivas quite accurately wrote that Harding's '"security forces" set about their work in a manner which might have been deliberately designed to drive the population into our arms. [...] the population were merely bound more closely to the organisation and the young scorned the threat of the gallows.'[93] He claimed that the British colonial government, and specifically Harding, not only lacked the means (expert staff, financial sources, equipment) to win the Greek Cypriots' hearts and minds, but in fact, they lacked understanding of their target audience; thus their attempts were futile:

> The British, in misunderstanding the Cypriots so completely, contributed generously to their own defeat. I laughed aloud when I heard that General A or Brigadier B had come to Cyprus to put into operation the methods which had won him fame elsewhere. They could not understand that the Cyprus struggle

was unique in motive, psychology, and circumstance, and involved not a handful of insurrectionists but the whole people.[94]

Harding, in spite of his attempts during his two years in the island, did not succeed in containing or destroying EOKA. Furthermore, after a series of negotiations he also failed to reach a political agreement with Archbishop Makarios. What is interesting, paradoxical and important to stress here is that while Harding was designing an elaborate scheme against the Cypriot Church as seen earlier, in order to curb its power, and while legitimizing this move in the eyes of public opinion, at the same time he acknowledged that no action taken could 'be more than partially effective' and that eventually the clergy could not be prevented from intruding political matter into their sermons.[95]

After Makarios's exile in March 1956, and in light of the Radcliffe Constitution which was to be introduced to the people of Cyprus, Harding decided to relax a number of emergency regulations. In this way he hoped to convince the Greek Cypriots to trust the colonial government. At that point in time, Harding perceived that the Greek Cypriots were 'in a state of confusion to put it mildly. Past history, present fears and emotions, lack of sufficient time as yet to understand and weigh the Radcliffe proposals, their impetuous rejection by the Greek government and certain vocal Greek Cypriot personalities and the local press have all contributed to this'.[96] Under the pretext of making a fresh start by 'refashioning a political programme' as Leslie Glass had called it, and as Athens and London advised him to do, in order to achieve rapid progress towards peace and harmony in the island, Harding revoked the regulation under which males under the age of 18 could be sentenced to be whipped for certain offences.[97] He also revoked the regulation under which fines could be levied collectively on the inhabitants of particular areas, shops and dwelling houses (Collective Punishment). He allowed places of public resort to open, except if they were to close temporarily as part of a particular 'anti-terrorist' operation. He also relaxed the regulations requiring persons to obtain exit permits whenever they left the colony. Harding would also review cases of persons detained under the Detention of Persons Law.[98]

Nevertheless, as Glass had warned, Makarios's exile was one serious slip leading to the people's 'splitting of sympathy', a glaring example of bad decision-making, a radical, undiplomatic move that was deeply criticized outside and inside Cyprus and caused outrage and deep disappointment among the Greek Cypriot public.[99] For example, a few days after Makarios was ousted, EOKA managed to place a bomb under Harding's bed in the Government House, which failed to detonate. When asked about his night's sleep Harding replied that he had slept better than usual that night. Harding thought that by exiling the 'archterrorist', as Makarios was often called within administrative circles, he had created the perfect opportunity to reveal the Church's 'complicity in terrorism', with the least offence to religious opinion throughout the world. When documents were captured at the Archbishopric in Nicosia, after being translated into English they were to be published for propaganda purposes.[100] Harding was to 'take every opportunity of exposing publicity cases of religious blackmail and other cases of ecclesiastical abuse of office or injustice'.[101] Another example of the Church's complicity was when several caches of arms and ammunition were found on the grounds and buildings of a church.[102] Harding thought that based on this kind of evidence, the colonial government could support its decision to exile Makarios and take legislative and administrative action to diminish the political power of the Church.

The governor thought that the Greek Cypriot acceptance of the proposed constitution depended on the defeat of EOKA by the British Security Services and on inducing Makarios 'to start the ball rolling towards co-operation', as Harding put it.[103] Harding considered Makarios to be the only one who could give 'a lead away from terrorism', but up until that point the Archbishop remained 'intransigent and unreasonable'.[104] Makarios had rejected the constitution and refused to get into discussions as long as he was in exile.[105] He felt that 'no helpful consultations or exchange of views could be made in an atmosphere of detention'.[106] Due to this, Harding estimated that he should not be returned to Cyprus, considering in fact to release him 'on parole', to Malta or to London, until he was brought to his senses, at least not until self-government was tried out successfully and other Cypriots, more moderate in nature, had a taste of political power, with the British government's blessings.[107]

Harding thought that although the average Greek Cypriot unquestionably repeated Greek propaganda, claiming, for example, that the Radcliffe constitution was a trap, at the same time there was evidence of many 'thoughtful Cypriots', as he called them, who were attracted by the Radcliffe constitutional proposals. However, all other potential moderate political leaders were too afraid of EOKA to speak, indeed afraid for their lives.[108] When Makarios was finally released from exile on 28 March 1957, a little more than a year after his incarceration, the Intelligence Committee prepared a secret report for his homecoming. The excerpt that follows is an example of how the Greek Cypriot people reacted to this event and, significantly, how propaganda heightened their reaction.

The scenes of wild enthusiasm which hailed the news of the Archbishop's release on the 28 March, could be taken as an expression of the intense relief that, at long last, there was some positive sign that the end of the emergency had arrived. The crowds, for the most part were friendly disposed, and, turning like the sunflower, were prepared to cheer anything and anybody, without thinking about what it all meant, or what the next step would be. However, there was something more sinister behind this purely emotional demonstration. As soon as it was seen that they would be allowed to blow off steam, the priests and youngsters (fans and erstwhile recruits of EOKA plus the ladies of OXEN [Christian Orthodox Youth Association]) did their best to get the thing turned into an EOKA victory, and make people believe that the road to ENOSIS was finally open. This was further emphasised in the Archbishop's statement to the Press. It is believed it needs strong counter propaganda.[109]

When Harding was asked during his 1984 interview about the public's reaction in Cyprus when Makarios was deported, he quite cynically replied: 'Well it was a lot of shouting and screaming ... but it did die down of course ... As far as I was concerned it was a necessary thing to do.'[110] When he was asked whether, looking back now, he thought that it was the right decision to make (perhaps the interviewer implying that it was not), he said: 'Oh yes, most certainly, oh yes, I'm sure of it.'[111]

Nevertheless, archival sources show otherwise. Harding's move was criticized not only in Cyprus and Greece, but also in the wider international community, and from within Britain's press and the opposition, as will be studied later on. Regarding Makarios's exile Grivas wrote later in his memoir: 'I believed Harding had made the greatest mistake of his career and I took full advantage of it.'[112] Even though denying it in 1984, Harding indirectly admitted failure at the end of 1956. Months into Makarios's exile and in a telegram to the Secretary of State for the Colonies, Harding wrote that 'for the time being at any rate, Makarios remains in an unassailable position, exercising a power of veto over Greek Cypriot opinion' even from the Seychelles.[113]

Lawrence Durrell's perceptive and, arguably, cunning criticism of Harding's propaganda methods should be emphasized here:

Clumsy propaganda tends to widen the gap between government and the people – and create the impression that we are at war, not with Athens, but with the people of Cyprus. This is really playing EOKA's game: they want us to be as harsh, repressive and irritating etc. as possible in order to increase the peasantry's annoyance with us and recruit sympathy for themselves. I feel we should take every opportunity of accusing peasants of being too honourable and sensible to feel opposed to law and order – even though it may not be true.[114]

The following important admission, found in the above extract, should be emphasized: the colonial government should 'accuse peasants of being too honourable' to rebel against it 'even though it may not be true'. This will be considered in conjunction with Harding's admission, that 90 per cent of the Greek population in Cyprus supported EOKA, and other colonial officers' estimations regarding the honesty or dishonesty of *enosis*.[115] The conclusion arising from instances of 'secret and confidential' honesty in the private correspondence of British officials is that British propaganda consciously misrepresented, suppressed (e.g. through jamming Athens Radio) and even fabricated the truth at the time of the Cyprus revolt (e.g. forging EOKA's leaflets).

It is worth clarifying here that although the Greek Cypriot people were enraged over Harding and the Security Services, at the same time several Greek Cypriot and British primary sources, such as memoirs, show that quite often the local people were sympathetic towards British soldiers on the ground, who were brought in overnight to fight for the British flag in this unknown, remote, dry and hot island, so different from home, the 'Red Planet' as it was half-jokingly referred to by Martin Bell, who served as a soldier in the Suffolk Regiment during the revolt between 1957 and 1959.[116] The soldiers' disorientation created by the bombs, the panic, the fear, the absurdity of it all, the island's emergency status, the faceless enemy of bomb-throwing mountain guerrillas and their branding as 'terrorists', could be sensed by the local people. Whereas EOKA was taking advantage of it to attack and retaliate, others were reluctant to put Harding and his team in the same boat with the average British soldier-in-the-street who had no other choice but to follow orders blindly. This goes both ways. Paradoxically enough, although the Greek Cypriots were perceived by the British as pretty much all EOKA, the British insisted in stressing how much the average Greek Cypriot differed in temperament from the guerrilla fighter. This however remains complicated as EOKA fighters came from every class and every rank in Cyprus, secrecy in the organization was essential and therefore no one knew (at least no British were supposed to know) who was EOKA.

EOKA's 'propaganda of the deed': Breaking British morale

EOKA's 'propaganda of the deed' or 'war of nerves' as General Grivas called it should be given some attention here, as its eventual goal was to be used for propaganda purposes. Propaganda of the deed was a strategic move used by EOKA since the beginning of the revolt. Its purpose was to break the morale of the British security forces on the ground. This would then instigate the forces' reaction against the Greek Cypriot population. In turn, this would be used by EOKA for propaganda purposes in Cyprus and abroad in order to win the attention of international public opinion and gain support for the Greek Cypriot struggle.

As seen here, international public opinion was not an issue preoccupying exclusively Cyprus's political leaders, Governor Harding and Archbishop Makarios, but at the other end of the scale, the military leader of the revolt, General Grivas. It is argued here that EOKA's 'deeds of heroism and self-sacrifices' were not an end in themselves. This realization is neglected in the relevant historiography, where the Greek Cypriot popular historian has focused on these 'deeds of heroism and self-sacrifices' as a means towards romanticizing the struggle in the Greek Cypriot public memory.[117] On the other hand, 'imperialist' historians have translated these 'deeds' as 'terrorist actions', again providing a limited interpretation. On the whole, the interest of historians of the empire and its colonies (Anglophone and Grecophone) has focused on other aspects of the emergency/revolt. Therefore, 'propaganda of the deed' in the literal sense of the phrase, as a means towards influencing public opinion, remains under-researched. This section will attempt to offer a different view on it, using material from archival sources.[118]

During the Greek Cypriot insurgency and the British counter-insurgency campaigns, there were many instances when the patience of both sides was wearing thin, ultimately leading to a 'crisis of trust', as Robert Holland called it, between the Greek Cypriots and the British in Cyprus. Below is an extract of a message written on 18 November 1956, to be read on parade to all ranks of the security forces of Cyprus. A fuming Governor Harding, using highly emotive, dramatic language and in an enraged tone, writes:

> The savage brutality of terrorist outrages, and the many biased and unfounded allegations of misconduct by the Security Forces that have recently appeared in the press, have added to the provocation to which the Security Forces are exposed. The high standard of patience and restraint maintained in the face of this almost unparalleled provocation reflects great credit on all ranks of the Security Forces. It is essential for the good name of the Security Forces, whether they belong to the Armed Forces or to the Police Force, that this high standard should be maintained no matter how great the provocation. [...] Searches of individuals and premises will always be carried out with scrupulous thoroughness, but there will be no rough handling of persons, or avoidable damage to property. [...] We will maintain our own high standard of behaviour no matter to what depths of degradation our enemies may sink.[119]

What had instigated Harding's public message was several disturbing incidents that took place across the island; for example, on 23 October 1956, two teams of British soldiers played a football match on a ground on the outskirts of the village Lefkoniko, while they were off duty. This was not an unusual event. The match was being watched, as many times before, by Cypriot villagers. However, what was unusual this time was that the villagers had left the grounds before the end of the game. When it ended, the players gathered round a drinking water fountain. Then came a severe explosion at the base of the fountain, caused by an electrically detonated charge. One soldier was killed on the spot and five others were injured. While the soldiers were fleeing in a military vehicle to obtain medical help, it was believed that a bomb was thrown at them but at the time did not return to investigate. After the event, troops of soldiers returned to the village embarking on a search. However, in a spirit of vengeance, they indiscriminately attacked the villagers, physically wounding them, damaging private and public property, and stealing. Harding wrote that 'the troops may have jostled and hurried the villagers in the course of their investigation but the Government rejects any allegations of serious physical violence because there is no supporting evidence'.[120] He also accused the Greek Cypriot witnesses of 'greatly inflating and dramatizing' their 'allegations'. Nevertheless, he announced that compensation would be given in cases where the government confirmed that damage was inflicted.[121]

The colonial government seldom admitted that physical and material harm was being inflicted on the Greek Cypriot public, collateral damage during the hostilities between Greek Cypriot guerrillas and British soldiers. Although accusations coming from both sides and allegations of mistreatment of people and property are a common finding in the archival material, what is not so common to discover is validation that confirms or discredits them. In this way, there are times when research is inconclusive. Nevertheless, for the above example, it was possible to find archival corroboration. In another telegram discovered, created two days after Harding's message, written by Larnaca's commissioner and endorsed by most commissioners on the island, we find information on the issue of the 'hardening of the feeling of Security Forces against the civil population'.[122]

> This is perfectly understandable in view of the number of brutal and treacherous attacks on troops. The question of reprisals based on this feeling is a difficult one and there is some risk that more harm than good will come of a 'tough' policy. The view is held among the few Greek-Cypriots who dare to discuss such

things than no one will mind if an EOKA man is beaten to death, but what good does it do to Government to make more enemies by needlessly inflicting hardship on ordinary villagers? No one who gives information to Government is safe thereafter, and why should Government hold it against villagers who do not give information in these circumstances. This is a matter of long term view; if we wish to remain in Cyprus, we must do so on good terms with the inhabitants. Every village subjected to avoidable hardship or distress is a village gained by EOKA. In the long run this cannot pay.[123]

A vital aspect of the EOKA campaign was maintaining secrecy throughout. Secrecy, therefore, was not only the British and colonial governments 'accepted and promoted policy, but it was also the guerrillas'. However, EOKA ordered that secrecy was to be followed not only by the fighters, but by all Greek Cypriots. 'Traitors', informers and the faint-hearted were to be punished accordingly by the organization, very often by execution in the name of the cause. As Charlie Standley writes, 'The usual methods employed by the police – paid informers – elicited no information on EOKA, as so thoroughly had the insurgency infiltrated Greek Cypriot communities that only a tiny minority were prepared to run the risk of providing information, even for money. Therefore the security forces relied almost wholly upon the fruits of interrogation.'[124] In his memoirs Grivas was very clear about it. An example that displays how the Greek Cypriots obeyed EOKA's orders, even if they knew that they were going to be punished by British security forces and the police about it, is the following.

EOKA was planning to execute a difficult and dangerous assignment: to dynamite British army trucks outside Yiallousa's police station. The mission was undertaken by a 15-year-old boy. The trucks packed with soldiers stopped close to the police station. As the men were jumping out, the mines detonated. There were about twenty casualties. As Grivas recalled in his memoirs, the unusual aspect of the operation was that almost the whole village knew about it. Several villagers saw the young boy, and everyone was warned to avoid the road area close to the police station when the trucks were to arrive. The secret was kept until the assignment was completed, with success. Grivas explained that public executions of British soldiers were meant to severely damage police and army morale.

From the discussion above certain conclusions can be drawn. Firstly, EOKA's attacks had a psychological objective; the logic behind them was to break British morale. Calling its members bloodthirsty, fanatic 'terrorists', was arguably a publicity trick meant to discredit the organization in the eyes of the local and international public opinion. Grivas wrote about the effects of

EOKA's propaganda of the deed which arguably once performed resulted in what British experts called 'psychological warfare'. Grivas confirmed this using another example: 'The mine was detonated, blowing the truck apart and killing three soldiers. Pieces of mangled metal and flesh were found 200 metres from the spot. It was an appalling sight, and the moral effect on the troops who witnessed this, and dozens of similar incidents, was tremendous – much more important to me than the casualties themselves.'[125]

Secondly, as with the example of the incident of the exploding fountain at Lefkoniko village, Greek Cypriot fighters and British soldiers were not the only targets during the conflict. The Greek Cypriot public was very often the victim of violent actions, as reprisals were targeted against them in the absence of the culprits. A third conclusion is the realization that even under the threat of imminent reprisals by the security forces, the Greek Cypriot public did not dare give information on EOKA. This may be attributed to the fact that they may had been supporting EOKA or were afraid of EOKA: most probably, a combination of both. Last but not least, colonial administrators at the end of 1956, such as Larnaca's commissioner, still held the idea that Britain was to stay in Cyprus 'forever', which in turn shows the tenacity characterizing the enemy sides, as neither of the two retreated in its ambitions regarding the future of Cyprus.

Susan Carruthers argues that the 'terrorization' of Greek Cypriots by EOKA was a dimension of the activities of the armed movement that was emphasized by British propaganda, because it suggested that a reluctant local population had to be frightened into support for 'the terrorist organisation'.[126] Nevertheless, Sylvia Foot, the wife of Governor Hugh Foot who was to succeed Harding as Cyprus's last governor, provided an alternative view in her autobiographical book on her stay in Cyprus, *Emergency Exit* (1960):

> It seemed to me that EOKA was composed to a greater or lesser extent of every Greek in Cyprus. It seemed to our weary hearts that we were once more up against the disastrous and childish and utterly hopeless theory that Force could overcome Ideas.[127]

Foot's approach corresponds to Greek Cypriot primary accounts and arguably captures a truer sense of the psychology of the Greek Cypriot. This realization, that more or less all the Greek Cypriots were EOKA, also reappears in many accounts of the time, from people who passed through and stayed in Cyprus during those tumultuous years. One example given earlier is Harding's own admission, in his 1984 interview, that 90 per cent of the Greek population supported EOKA.[128]

In April 1957, in a confidential letter to A. Morris of the Mediterranean Department of the Colonial Office, the Cyprus Administrative Secretary warned that after Archbishop Makarios's return to Cyprus, they were moving into 'a very tricky phase which will call for determination and fixity of purpose here and in London if the Greek Cypriot public is to be discouraged from assuming that the Enotist extremists have got the British on the run again, with all the damage that that could do to any hope of a settlement'.[129] Nevertheless, the damage had already been done. The 'splitting of sympathy', as Leslie Glass had warned, was unfixable. Speaking out of experience from his service in South-East Asia and the Middle East, Leslie Glass wrote that it was 'not possible to reason with emotional nationalism, particularly when it has got a hold on the younger generation'.[130] Even though artificially inflated, it was not artificially created. He believed that 'the Hellenic patriotism of the Greek Cypriot is genuine and deep-seated'.[131]

Despite this, the British and colonial governments went on with their only clear policy, that of procrastination and coercion, thus steadily losing the Greek Cypriot public's sympathy, as Glass had predicted. Glass, interestingly, also made a general comment on 'the forces of nationalism' that aptly describes the case of Cyprus. He had a 'profound doubt as to the practicability of any policy except that of coming to terms with nationalist feeling once it is really aflame. [...] I realise too that the situation in Cyprus is not necessarily the same as anywhere else in the world but [...] the pattern seems strangely familiar'.[132]

Glass, an expert in psychological warfare, could capture the psychology of the Greek Cypriot. Officials in London, many of whom had not visited Cyprus, but who were still given a key role shaping colonial policies, could not do this. It was, therefore, not so much the incapacity of Glass to design and implement an effective propaganda strategy, but rather the multiplicity of voices taking part in the decision-making process and different priorities and considerations they had by nature of their profession and expertise that hindered the British propaganda offensive in Cyprus.

Conclusion

In this chapter the propaganda issue in Cyprus, as perceived and experienced by Governor Harding and his close team of collaborators, such as Leslie Glass, Director General of Information Services, has been explored. This investigation has shown that Harding was convinced that a weak propaganda policy on the part of the colonial and British governments had allowed Greek and Greek Cypriot propaganda agencies (the *enosis* leadership, Athens Radio and the Greek press) to unleash a ruthless propaganda war against them. For this reason, there was a strong need to develop the island's Information Services to perform counter-propaganda. Glass became the head of this organization. The organization's action was, however, limited in reach. Therefore, Harding employed coercive and illiberal measures against enemy propaganda organs and, unavoidably, the Greek Cypriot population at large, which in turn alienated and hardened local and international public opinion (e.g. the Archbishop's exile). The result of 'the splitting of sympathy' had been predicted by Leslie Glass in his secret note on 'The future of Cyprus'. As an answer to the colonial government's miscalculated propaganda policies and coercive measures, EOKA embarked on its own 'propaganda of the deed'. EOKA intended to break the morale of the British security forces in order to instigate the forces' reaction against the Greek Cypriot population. This reaction would then be used by EOKA for propaganda purposes in Cyprus and abroad to attract international attention, sympathy and support. By this time the propaganda war for Cyprus was at full blast. In the following chapter, a comparative study on the propaganda instruments used by the opposing sides is going to be examined in detail.

4

The propaganda offensive in sound, print and vision

Introduction

This chapter is made up of three case studies on the use of propaganda media during the revolt in Cyprus. 'Sound' explores the history of radio broadcasting and radio jamming in Cyprus during the 1950s and how Athens Radio and the Cyprus Broadcasting Service (CBS) competed for the Greek Cypriots' attention and loyalty. Drawing information from unpublished archival material, this case study also reveals the use of other sound media by the British colonial government in order to divert the attention of the Greek Cypriots from EOKA, such as voice aircraft and public address vans. The way these two media were used in Cyprus was 'borrowed' from other 'Emergencies' such as Malaya and Kenya.

The second case study entitled 'Print' consists of two sections: the first looks at newspapers and publications, and the second at leaflets. The study explores how print media were given primary importance by the opposing sides during their campaigns, with the aim of winning over local and international public opinion. In this section EOKA leaflets are translated for the first time into English by the author of this monograph, providing a window into the language, tone, themes and intentions of Greek Cypriot propaganda. The rebellious colonized voice is given a platform to speak directly to the reader. By contrast, in most academic studies of the Cyprus revolt the Greek Cypriot perspective is drawn from colonial archival material; thus it is inevitably interpreted from the British point of view.

The third case study reconstructs the unknown but fascinating history of television in Cyprus, based exclusively on unpublished material from the Migrated Archives. The establishment of a television station in Cyprus by the colonial government was intended to take the lead in British efforts in propaganda; however when it was finally inaugurated in the island, in late 1957, it was arguably too late for it to influence the Cypriots into believing in the (material) benefits of British rule.

In this chapter, observations by Governor Harding and other protagonists of the emergency period, regarding the issue of the colonial government's defensive position towards enemy propaganda, continue to take a leading role in the discussion. In previous chapters the colonial government's bafflement and even annoyance regarding its ineffective approach to propaganda, information, psychological warfare and publicity was exposed through the study of private and secret correspondence, for example John Reddaway's private discussions with experts at the British Middle East Office, officials in the Colonial Office and the Foreign Office and British Ambassadors in Greece, Turkey and the United States. As seen earlier, information on other Emergencies, such as Malaya (1948–1960) and Kenya (1952–1960) which were unfolding concurrently with Cyprus, was eventually and reluctantly shared with Reddaway. However, this only left him feeling unsatisfied and deeply doubtful as to the efficiency of the proposed, borrowed methods.[1]

In the following case studies the application of these borrowed techniques from South East Asia, but also from other settings such as the Anglo-Irish War (1919–1921) and the Arab revolt in Mandatory Palestine (1936–1939) will be examined. It will be argued that borrowed propaganda techniques had limited effect in the Cypriot setting, where Cypriots had little in common with the populations of other territories under British rule. This is a conclusion drawn early on in the discussions on the use of propaganda media in Cyprus and recurs through this book. Up until this point it has been largely absent from the academic literature on the subject.

The discussion below will go a step further arguing that although British officials gradually became aware of the inefficiency of British propaganda media in Cyprus, this did not mean that they turned to other more effective means. As will be shown, these other means were not readily available and/or the colonial government could not come up with other innovative media or methods to reply to Greek Cypriot and Greek propaganda.

Instead, an argument that gains validity below is the mimetic tendencies of British propaganda. In the context of the Cyprus Emergency some of EOKA's propaganda methods were imitated by British propagandists. For example, EOKA's leaflets were mimeographed in order to confuse the Greek Cypriot public who read them avidly and turn it against the guerrilla organization. However, these methods did not have positive results as EOKA was quick to discredit the pseudo-leaflets; not only this, EOKA was quick in ridiculing the government's inefficient, unimaginative and arguably desperate, attempts at counter-propaganda.

Sound

Radio: Athens Radio vs Cyprus Broadcasting Service

During the period of the Cyprus revolt, an adversarial relationship developed between Athens Radio and the Cyprus Broadcasting Service. Investigation in the archival material has showed that these two instruments of Greek/Greek Cypriot and British aural propaganda were extensively used in Cyprus, with the former arguably winning the fight for local Greek Cypriot public support. Although the colonial government hoped and tried through the Cyprus Broadcasting Service's broadcasts to divert Greek Cypriot feeling and opinion from Athens Radio's patriotic rhetoric, which demanded a change in the island's sovereign status and union with another 'foreign' state, the service's effect on the Greek Cypriot public was weak. Very little research has been done on the use of radio during the Cyprus revolt. Nevertheless, unpublished archival material has revealed that the use of radio was a significant component of both the Greek/Greek Cypriot and British propaganda mechanisms from the early 1950s to the island's independence. Importantly, whereas broadcasting was used by both adversaries, the method of jamming radio signals as a countermeasure for the inflammatory broadcasts of Athens Radio was employed only by the colonial government.

'The cry to Greek Cypriots to man the ramparts' came from Athens Radio and the Greek press. These two were arguably fighting an anti-colonial struggle against British rule in Cyprus months before EOKA officially began its campaign in April 1955. For example, an Athens Radio broadcast from 20 August 1954 contained the following message:

> My enslaved Brothers, the battle has started. Today all the newspapers are faithful to the struggle and you can see whole pages depicting the Greek flag with Cyprus enfolded in it. ... the general slogan is: 'Cyprus is ours!' At the present moment we Greeks have all achieved the feelings of a soldier in the hour of battle, but this time the battle is being waged for union with our beloved island.[2]

The colonial government was informed about this through the monitoring of Athens Radio. A letter from the Administrative Secretary's Office to the Colonial Office 'in the three months or so preceding the outbreak of violence' claimed how Athens Radio broadcasts to Cyprus showed 'how consciously the Greeks were creating the atmosphere for their later activities and accusations'.[3] The colonial government soon came to the conclusion that the radio station based in Athens was an instrument of 'malicious propaganda' by a foreign power, preaching hatred and sedition, as well as incitement to violence, by rousing the peasantry to support EOKA and urging them to 'drive out the British invaders'.[4]

In mid-1955, during the early discussions on the design for propaganda for Cyprus, John Reddaway considered the Cyprus Broadcasting Service 'our greatest propaganda means'.[5] Government propagandists believed that Athens Radio had to be paid back in its own coin; in other words, it had to be countered via radio propaganda, through the broadcasts of the Cyprus Broadcasting Service. A competition between two radio stations was to begin, rivalling for 'political purposes' in front of a Cypriot audience.[6] At this point, although television was considered a stronger propaganda medium which could 'do more than the CBS can achieve to occupy the attention of the people and divert them from Athens Radio', it would take a few more years before a television service was established in the island.[7]

As Chrysanthos Chrysanthou wrote, the Cyprus Broadcasting Service had 'emerged during the crisis of the world colonial system and when the demand for self-determination arose in Cyprus'.[8] The service was established with the Programme for the Development and Prosperity of the Colonies. This aimed in inculcating obedience to the Crown, a sense of belonging to the British Empire and the feeling that British culture was superior. 'Thus, at first, radio and TV broadcasting in Cyprus were unpopular among Cypriots as they were regarded as colonial propaganda.'[9] Chrysanthou's assessment will be confirmed and expanded later in this book, when Greek Cypriot primary sources on the reception of the Cyprus Broadcasting Service will be examined.

The service first started broadcasting in Nicosia, the capital and hub of the colonial administration. In 1952 transmissions began on an interim basis and in three different languages, Greek, Turkish and English. The official launch took place a year later on 4 October 1953 with forty-three hours of broadcasting per week. There were approximately 14,000 radio sets on the island and 'the Greek-Cypriots listened to programmes from Athens and the Turkish-Cypriots from Ankara'.[10] Governor Andrew Wright (who preceded Governor Armitage) during his inauguration speech denied that the service was a tool of British propaganda and that instead it was an established British tradition to ensure that broadcasting was not intended to mould, or even to guide public opinion, but simply to inform.[11] However, Wright's argument did not convince the Greek Cypriots. In fact, as we have seen so far, 'moulding' and 'guiding public opinion' was exactly the intention of the British and colonial governments.

There were certain propaganda themes that were to be disseminated via the broadcasts of the Cyprus Broadcasting Service. These were summarized as follows: the catastrophic results of EOKA's terrorism and the danger the guerrilla organization was putting the Greek Cypriot public into, for example by bringing into the foreground the island's partition into Greek Cypriot and Turkish Cypriot parts as a last resort solution, a solution supported as the conflict progressed by the Turkish Cypriot community of the island; the international consequences of *enosis*, largely meaning Turkey's reaction; the disruption of NATO and the Baghdad pacts; victory for international communism; and finally and importantly, Britain's position and prerogative in being the only one who could help the Greek Cypriots get themselves out of the mess they had gotten themselves into.[12]

In July 1955, shortly before Harding took the reins as Cyprus's governor, Governor Armitage, who had already survived an assassination attempt, decided that

> the CBS should go out of its way to brand EOKA as a collection of murderers and gangsters, and should repeatedly use these terms in describing their activities. The aim should be to make the public realise that the people who carried out EOKA orders were the lowest type of criminal, and that 'terrorist' was too good a word for them to use.[13]

He was evidently angry, upset and anxious to discredit EOKA in the radio audience's ears.

During the early discussion on propaganda for Cyprus, taking place in mid-1955, it was decided that the service would start daily broadcasts in Greek. In this way 'the opportunity [...] arises slowly to introduce counter propaganda to Athens Radio and what one might call "offensive propaganda" to the Cypriots explaining the benefits they get from their existing circumstances'.[14] At that point, Commander John C. R. Proud, the radio service's controller, who was also involved in the early discussions with John Reddaway on propaganda for Cyprus, was building up a series of radio features. However, in discussions between the head of propaganda, the director of Intelligence Services and the controller of CBS 'the need to get an officer who would be fully occupied in seeing that a specific propaganda thread is woven into all the appropriate material that goes out on CBS' was highlighted.[15]

It is worth noting here that it was hoped that the Cyprus Broadcasting Service would be 'the first to have a "black" propagandist on its staff'.[16] This officer had to study the broadcasts of Athens Radio and work out the means required to counter it. In conjunction with this, he would also have to study the daily Greek press in Cyprus, again see what should be countered, develop a propaganda theme and put it in train. Although the Cyprus Broadcasting Service had intermittently broadcasted extracts from Greek newspapers, showing the financial and economic plight that Greece was in, and hoping that this would act as a deterrent to the Greek Cypriots' desire for *enosis*, up until that point it was considered useless as this was done in an irregular fashion. Therefore, it was envisaged that this officer would work out a recurring theme 'so that the pattern is presented week after week'.[17]

The intention was clear. 'Entwined throughout the CBS programmes there must run this thread, never ending, ever spinning, refuting Athens, carefully, moderately boosting Cyprus equally'.[18] For example, where Athens Radio called the EOKA guerrillas 'militant patriots' for killing a Police Sargent, the CBS was describing the event as a 'ruthless cold-blood of a murder by a bunch of gangsters'.[19] This brings to mind the discussion about Greek Cypriot individuals who were collaborating with the colonial government. These were called 'advisors' by the government, but Greek Cypriot propaganda media such as EOKA leaflets and Athens Radio broadcasts called them 'traitors'.

The selected officer for radio propaganda had to direct the radio propaganda effort, and in order to do this he had to read and speak Greek. However, most colonial officials did not have the language skills. They were therefore often oblivious to the content of Greek propaganda, especially because translating parts of this was time-consuming. There is an admission for this in the above example on 'militant patriots'/'bunch of gangsters' and the necessity of calling them 'gangsters' in the CBS broadcasts: 'They may be doing it [British counter-propaganda], but as I don't understand Greek, I can't tell'.[20] It could therefore be argued that the inability of most of the colonial government's staff to understand Greek worked as an advantage for EOKA and its sympathizers, who could act unobtrusively at least until their propaganda was translated into English. Although it was acknowledged that 'a stupid mistake made may set things back by months or years', nevertheless these issues of basic communication skills persisted until the end of the Cyprus revolt.[21]

The individual who became responsible for the CBS, although this was not his sole responsibility as hoped, was Lawrence Durrell. During his two-year stay in the island, he was particularly proud of the way he had made the service work, unlike the previous state of the local Information Services. In his understanding the CBS under his directorship had become 'better by far than Athens [Radio]'. Durrell gave great importance to the radio as a mass communication medium, the 'new metal God of the times' as he had called it.[22]

Nevertheless, CBS methods seemed to be failing. For example, the transmission of the 'Cyprus News' in Greek at the same time as the 'Athens News' did not appear to be having the desired effect. The listener tuned to the CBS for the headlines and then to Athens for the details. The CBS was therefore going to change its times so as not to coincide with the Athens broadcasts. Soon after Harding took over, Durrell started complaining that the service's news reporting had 'gravely compromised public belief in the objectivity of CBS'.[23] In one of his letters to John Reddaway he wrote: 'Every time I go to my village I have a tedious wrangle about the station, and am reminded by the village wiseacres that the Cypriot taxpayer is paying for it.'[24] A similar argument on the financial sorrows of the Cypriot taxpayer was given about the television station Harding managed to set up before finally leaving the island. When Durrell left Cyprus, John Proud, the service's controller, who was as Leslie Glass wrote 'an Australian who escaped to join the Psychological Warfare team in the Pacific as a Commander in the Australian Navy', succeeded Durrell in the role of the director of the Cyprus Broadcasting Service.[25]

Before jamming Athens Radio in February 1956, three months after Makarios's deportation, it was estimated that the station had a 'terrible effect' and did 'incalculable damage to Anglo-Cypriot relations'.[26] Jamming, 'however repugnant it may sound, should have been introduced much earlier', instead of resorting to diplomatic protests to the Greek government which did not produce the desired results (on the contrary, they merely confirmed Athens Radio's effect and British annoyance).[27] In the following pages, attitudes towards radio propaganda during the Cyprus revolt will be examined, in an attempt to understand how and why the British colonial government took the decision to jam Athens Radio and how this move was perceived by the local Greek Cypriot population and other audiences, such as the British press.

Jamming: 'An admission of defeat'?

Athens Radio 'inflammatory broadcasts' were monitored by the colonial government before Governor Harding arrived in Cyprus and before 'the law had ceased to function'.[28] In April 1955 the broadcasts had allowed Governor

Armitage to 'certainly welcome' the jamming of the station.[29] This happened right after Charles Peake, the British Ambassador to Greece, asked the Greek government to tone down Athens Radio broadcasts, but without effect. The Greek newspaper *Kathimerini* commented on Peake's request as follows:

> The British government's request about Athens Radio broadcasts to Cyprus has neither moral nor substantial justification. At this point Greece has chosen the line that decided as necessary to follow, the issue of the *enlightenment* [of the people] is considered a priority. The broadcasts of Athens Radio simply interpret the feelings and thoughts of the Greek people over the Cypriot Struggle. The Greek government cannot stand in the way of the people from evaluating British policy using its 'gut feeling' beyond the frame of strict diplomacy. It is strange that our English friends, instead of trying to get at the root of the problem and think, that it is high time that they put an end to the excuses that create Greco-British tension, they are preoccupied with details, which are unimportant compared to the extent of the issue.[30]

Governor Armitage, backed up by other colonial government officials, was gradually becoming eager, restless and desperate to utilize the method of jamming in order to suppress the growing Greek nationalism on the island. The tone in his telegrams sent to the Secretary of State for the Colonies shifted from proposing, to asking, to pleading: 'Is there nothing HMG can do to put an end to these broadcasts?' and 'I see little value in further complaints about Athens Radio. Let me try a little intermittent, selective jamming. Advice to do this would be unanimous here.'[31] However, two weeks into the EOKA campaign in April 1955, London was still reluctant to engage in any full-scale jamming operation against Athens Radio, unless the situation was perceived to be extremely urgent. The Secretary of State justified this position: Britain was a party to an international convention directed against jamming. If used there might have been repercussions on the BBC's Greek service.

More so, jamming was regarded 'as an admission of defeat'.[32] In October 1955, in his 'UK Eyes only' memorandum to the Secretary of State, the Chairman of British Joint Communications wrote that this special technique should be reserved only in very singular conditions and only where this was considered to be essential for security reasons. He also wrote that the jamming of broadcast transmissions was considered to be a negative form of psychological warfare, since it created a mass impression to the audience that the truth was being suppressed.

At this point, being only at the very beginning of the counter-insurgency campaign, proposals about negative forms of psychological warfare to be applied in Cyprus were still to be accepted by London. However, as the revolt progressed, positive as well as negative forms of psychological warfare were to be used. One example, as will be studied later on, was the colonial government's production of pseudo-EOKA leaflets, coming after the organization's successful method of leaflet dissemination which effectively guided the Greek Cypriots' attitudes and 'won their hearts and minds', in a complimentary manner to Athens Radio.

Nevertheless in April 1955, before Harding's arrival and before he declared Cyprus in a state of emergency, hostile broadcast propaganda had to be countered in a positive manner by a quick and effective counter-propaganda broadcast service. This being the proposed policy, it should be noted that experimental jamming lasting 'a minute or two' had been granted permission and was successfully effected before Harding's arrival.[33] It was suggested therefore that the Cyprus Broadcasting Service should be reorganized to provide throughout the island 'continuous, enlightened and incessant broadcast propaganda in Greek', designed specifically to support the policy of Britain and that of the colonial government of Cyprus.[34]

Even when Harding first arrived in Cyprus, although he certainly considered Athens Radio a powerful instrument used by the Greek government to intervene in the internal situation in Cyprus in favour of *enosis*, he also thought that political and psychological reasons made the possibility of jamming impossible. Thus, initially Harding was in accordance with London's stance. He believed that Greece station's 'unscrupulous stirring up of violence in the territory [Cyprus] of a friendly member state [Britain]' and its 'evil effects' could be partly 'counteracted by counter propaganda from here [Cyprus] and from London'.[35] He therefore agreed to and intended on using alternative measures, including setting up an island-wide television service. He finally did set this up in October 1957, merely two months before his departure from Cyprus.

Instead of jamming Harding asked urgently for personnel to be seconded in Cyprus, such as broadcast editors and technical personnel. Before creating for Leslie Glass the role of the Director General of Information, Harding assigned a handful of tasks to the then Director of Information Services in Cyprus, Lawrence Durrell. Durrell was asked to produce studies on alternative measures of positive psychological warfare/propaganda. The results of these studies would then be passed on to the Financial Secretary for approval. The first study was on the costs and requirements in staff and equipment for the refurbishment of CBS. The other studies included researching the costs of issuing a Turkish version of the *Cyprus Review*, which Durrell was already responsible for, and investigating the possibilities, both in Cyprus and abroad, of engaging a skilled cartoonist/illustrator to work on a *Radio Cyprus* publication as well as other printed material.[36] The issue of publications is to be studied separately in the following case study on print propaganda media.

In one of his pre-Harding confidential letters to the Colonial Secretary, Durrell gave his perspective on Athens Radio broadcasts to Cyprus, on the position of CBS in relation to the former, and his suggested course of action.[37] Drawing upon an analysis of reports, he concluded that even though Athens Radio had been enjoying great success among Greek Cypriots, and that it was perceived locally as 'a heart-warming performance, an earnest blood-brothership', it could not be considered 'as a purveyor of straight anti-British information'.[38] In fact, Durrell argued that the station's heated statements, which he called 'immoderate and foolish' as well as 'blood-thirsty' and 'rhetorical' (e.g. 'Cyprus the great concentration camp'), were putting a smile on the face of some level-headed Cypriots.[39]

Still, the animated rhetoric used by the station could easily excite young Cypriots. Durrell's appreciation of the effect of Athens Radio broadcasts on young Cypriots is validated in Greek Cypriot accounts about Athens Radio's reception discovered during this research and to be studied in the following pages. This point strongly resonates with Leslie Glass's analysis of 'emotional nationalism' and 'the Hellenic patriotism of the Greek Cypriots'. Glass argued that this 'has got a hold on the younger generation' and that there was no way to reason with it as it was 'genuine and deep-seated'.[40]

Among Durrell's responsibilities as Director of Information Services was to pass on to the governor the latest updates on Athens Radio broadcasts, providing him also with translations of broadcasts and of important Greek newspaper extracts relevant to the situation on the island. Durrell's role, therefore, was crucial to the government's effort in staying up to date with the content of Greek and Greek Cypriot propaganda. Durrell's knowledge of Greek was a great advantage that, as seen earlier, not many colonial officials shared, making his services valuable.

In August 1955 he was asked to produce a compilation of Athens Radio broadcasts, to exemplify the 'virulent and inflammatory material' directed at Cyprus.[41] Durrell chose only a few of the many objectionable passages, as he called them, chosen mostly for their 'open or ill-veiled incitement to violence'.[42] A copy of this broadcast potpourri was sent to the Secretary of State, but also to the British Embassies in Athens and Ankara, keeping them all in the loop and giving them access and space to voice their position, in the debate on the internal situation of the island. Extracts of this were to be used in the London

Talks regarding the future of Cyprus and for other official purposes such as the UN debate, the agenda of which included the Cyprus issue.

Even though Durrell emphasized the fact that the translated quotations inevitably lost some of their significance and punchiness if the reader was not able to listen to 'the vehemence and unrestrained frenzy with which some of the speakers deliver their piece', the two extracts are reproduced below, which translated by Durrell convey some of the tone of these broadcasts.[43]

> The authorities in London regard Athens radio's short-wave transmissions as one of the chief obstacles to the success of these efforts. They ignore the fact that for 3,000 years, during which no pressure, no force, succeeded in weakening the proud Cypriot people, there was no 'Voice of the Homeland' [programme] to incite in them the passion for freedom. There was no 'Voice of the Homeland' on the air when Bishop Kyprianos and his followers were hanged during the Greek revolution for refusing to betray their faith and their Hellenism. There were no microphones at that time. But the voice of the homeland reverberated in their souls. 12 February 1955

> If the young student of Nicosia is imprisoned, his place will be taken by another ten, twenty, or fifty, or by as many as are needed. The story of the monster Hydra is purely Greek. We say this beforehand, so that when it happens they will not inform us that this is again the fault of our radio. 15 May 1955

Durrell echoing London held the opinion that if CBS made the 'tactical error', as he called it, of attacking Athens Radio, this would alienate sympathy and would risk branding CBS a propaganda station, losing thus valuable collaborators, public confidence and listeners. In his understanding as the Director of the Information Services and Public Relations, he believed that the key to increasing a hold on public opinion in Cyprus was for CBS to act moderately in spite of boycotts and attacks coming from Greece and the *Ethnarchy* in Cyprus.[44] Three months prior to the commencement of the EOKA campaign, and in spite of the frequency, tone and content of the broadcasts, Durrell was reassuring London that at that point in Cyprus there was no direct anti-British feeling, open hostility or lawlessness, as yet. Therefore, the empire should not strike back, because there was a distinct possibility of instigating an unpleasant reaction among Cypriots.[45] This last point brings to mind Leslie Glass's futile warning more than a year later about 'the splitting of sympathy'.

By the end of 1955, Durrell as well as other colonial administrators in the island reconsidered and gradually became more apprehensive about the effects of Athens Radio. For example, a change in the attitude of Durrell is detected when he was asked to comment on a monitored extract from a broadcast sent to Harding in December 1955. The extract was talking about the EOKA fighter Charalambos Mouskos, who was killed by a 'gallant British officer'. The broadcast had called the officer 'a murderer' and the deceased 'a hero'. Durrell replied that in the absence of a policy directive, he proposed to take no action. Nevertheless:

> Athens Radio broadcasts to Cyprus are, as is well known, a continual stream of lies, abuse and misrepresentation, repeated day after day. I see no virtue in an occasional refutation of a particularly malicious and slanderous attack: the matter must be tackled as a whole.[46]

In a similar tone, Major General Ricketts wrote that in the span of a year (1954–1955) 'Athens Radio has contributed more to destroying the Greek Cypriot public's confidence in the British government and good-will and respect towards the British authorities than the Archbishop himself'.[47] Therefore, this is another piece of evidence proving that the 'splitting of sympathy' arguably started even before coercive measures were imposed as part of Harding's repressive emergency regime.

Coercive measures did intensify Greek Cypriot dissatisfaction with the British colonial government; however it was Athens Radio and the *Ethnarchy*'s persuasive rhetoric that triggered the people's reaction. In order to expand the calibre of the Cyprus Broadcasting Service, it was proposed that the service should improve and expand its programme quality, as well as increase the number of its broadcasting hours and its personnel.[48] Even though radio scripts were made available to local press, they were very rarely reproduced. Other, more imaginative scenarios regarding jamming were also being put on the table. For example, an ingenious method would be for the Cyprus Broadcasting Service and the British Middle East Office to put out a programme on the same wavelength as Athens Radio's, such as continuous gramophone records. This would not be 'jamming' per se, but merely 'unfortunate interference'.[49]

Finally, in early 1956 London and Nicosia were heading to the same direction regarding Athens Radio broadcasts. Harding decided that there was no point in broadcasting gramophone records, as this in effect would be jamming. Therefore, if the decision was taken to jam 'we may as well do it without disguise'.[50] In enquiries coming from the opposition about jamming, the Secretary of State would reply that the British government reserved the right to take jamming, or any such other countermeasures, as it may consider necessary and justified 'to preserve Cypriot and British lives from outrages directly provoked by these broadcasts which contain incitements for which it would be difficult to find a parallel in the history of broadcasting.[51] Another important reason that it was eventually decided to jam Athens Radio was because, based on Harding's information, the station was also being used by EOKA as a medium for passing operational messages in code. This proved to be true as it was admitted in the memoirs of Greek Cypriot EOKA members and collaborators.

Jamming eventually started in Cyprus in early February 1956, originating from the Cyprus Broadcasting Service in Nicosia. As Asa Briggs writes, 'The British Government, in reversal of all its wartime policies, had itself jammed Athens broadcasts to Cyprus.'[52] Interference began gradually until Athens's short wave broadcasts were made inaudible throughout Cyprus. However, in mid-February London denied responsibility when asked by the Associated Press and Reuter in Athens if the Cyprus government had jammed Athens Radio. Instead, they issued a brief and direct lie: 'Athens Radio transmissions to Cyprus have not been jammed.'[53] This relates to the issue of secrecy and further reconfirms the argument that secrecy was an accepted and widely used policy of the British government. Where this example differs from previous examples is that here the government went one step further by lying to keep a secret.

The British and colonial governments were never quite truthful with the press, and by extension, with the public, on how much jamming they were actually applying to the signal of Athens Radio broadcast in Cyprus. The unwillingness to admit this is reinforced further by a reprimanding telegram sent from the Cyprus government to the Colonial Office, after a BBC overseas service report in 1958, two years later after jamming operations began. The report said:

> The authorities have suspended since Saturday, the jamming of Athens Radio broadcasts to the island. A Colonial Office spokesman in London said that jamming had been wholly selective. The tone of Athens Radio broadcasts to Cyprus had improved at the time of Mr. Macmillan's visit [in Athens] and therefore jamming was no longer necessary.[54]

The colonial government complained to the Colonial Office that the above statement 'went a little too far' and that, although confirming the report's content, the only statement that should have instead been made publically was that 'jamming had always been selective'.[55] The British government must not have been particularly proud of succumbing to the 'defeatist' method of jamming to fight their enemy, but the situation in Cyprus was considered urgent, and desperate times called for desperate measures.[56]

Susan Carruthers called Athens Radio 'perhaps the most vexatious aspect of Greek propaganda, a source of irritation to the British government'.[57] Harding took a rare step when he was given permission by the cabinet to jam if he saw fit, if and when talks with Makarios broke down.[58] Given the 'unorthodox nature of the move', as Carruthers put it, the jamming of Athens Radio had to be accompanied by extensive and very persuasive propaganda, using British propaganda themes such as the station's 'incitement to murder', 'incitement to violence', 'incitement to terrorism', in order to convince local and international audiences about the validity of drastic measures used by the colonial government.

However, not everyone agreed with the practice of jamming. A large part of the British press opinion was critical of jamming in Cyprus. Newspapers such as the liberal, socialist *New Statesman and Nation*, unconvinced of the usefulness and the moral justification assigned to this method, wrote:

> To try to stop the Greeks from presenting their case must suggest to the outside world that our own is hopelessly weak. The Greeks can rightly retort that they do not jam our broadcasts. They can also point out that despite the animosities of recent months Athens radio continues to relay a daily bulletin broadcast by the BBC. By making a British monopoly of the Cyprus air we are suggesting that the Greeks have a monopoly of the arguments.[59]

Reception: 'Father, I heard Athens!'

Jamming Athens Radio in February 1956 occurred in close proximity to Archbishop Makarios's banishment to the Seychelles the following month. This was another one of Harding's controversial to some, reprehensible to others, moves that backfired. The Greek Cypriot public was outraged and, to use a familiar word, 'incited' amply and immediately. It was this type of spasmodic reactions, combined with coercive measures, that led to the Greek Cypriots' complete distrust of and antipathy towards Governor Harding and his close team of collaborators such as John Reddaway, and the Security Services.

Despite Durrell's vain hopes for the Cyprus Broadcasting Service to remain untainted by British propaganda in the eyes of Greek Cypriots, the station was perceived since its inception, both by EOKA and the *Ethnarchy*, as an instrument and mouthpiece of British policy. After all, it was no accidental move for EOKA to commence its campaign on 1 April 1955 by bombing the service's establishments in Nicosia. This could be interpreted as a symbolic gesture to silence the enemy who, after that first attack, trumpeted 'pathetic bleats of broadcast, of protest and condemnation', as General Grivas wrote in his memoirs.[60] At least a second time is recorded when EOKA bombed the service's establishments. On 11 October 1957 CBS and RAF radio stations in Nicosia were sabotaged by time bombs, putting the service off the air and causing damage amounting to £9000 to the RAF camp, cutting off its electricity.[61]

Nevertheless, one should ask what did CBS's programmes broadcast that was immediately branded as propaganda by the Greek Cypriot leadership. For example, a programme called 'After the News' included commentaries by a George Wilkinson, with titles such as 'Greco-Turkish alliances' (7 September 1955), 'The MacMillan proposals' (8 September 1955), on Grivas 'Patriot to Outlaw' (25 May 1956) and 'Portrait of a Failure' (1 June 1956).[62] In these commentaries what the commentator essentially attempted to do, according to the British point of view, was to talk some sense into the Greek Cypriot audience and to anyone else who was tuned in such as British and Greek audiences. This however was immediately branded as propaganda by the Greek and Greek Cypriot sides. Two extracts follow:

> 'Patriot to Outlaw' – It's extraordinary even in these days of fast and thorough communications how distance can still distort values and make nonsense of the truth. It's extraordinary to read that there are still people in England who are prepared to give the terrorists the benefit of doubt and try to believe that they see themselves as patriots. It's extraordinary even to think that there are people in Greece who are so committed to the theory of the objects of the terrorists that they find themselves more and more forced to ignore what the theory has become in practice. [...] fellow-country men [Greek Cypriots] were carelessly slaughtered in the name of patriotism.

> 'Portrait of Failure' – It's often been said that the story of a failure is more interesting than the story of a success. Although we read the lives of the Great and follow their well-documented course through to their honoured ends, there's no doubt that there is a fascination in the pathos or the tragedy of a life that goes wrong. [...] It's easy enough to see roughly when the soldier turned into the political plotter. It's easy enough to imagine thwarted ambition going bad and surrendering increasingly to bitterness. It's easy enough to watch the habit of murder taking hold and the disappointed careerist, frustrated of legitimate command, tasting power by ordering secret killings.

Both the Greek and the British press and radio, when speaking about a nation's activities and efforts, were aiming at reconfirming the national community; therefore, their published and broadcasted material was part of a 'nationalisation project'.[63] For example, a memorable incident used for CBS's propaganda campaign, exploiting EOKA's use of violence, was the murder of Sergeant Hammond by EOKA on 2 August 1958.[64] The 23-year-old was taking his 2-year-old son to buy an ice cream when he was shot down; his wife was expecting another baby. The troops were subjected to an emotional broadcast by CBS radio describing 'this most brutal and cowardly murder' – as if many, from both sides, had not already died in every horrible way. The radio announcer told, in quivering tones, of the ice cream and added that an officer who went to Hammond's aid asked Greek Cypriot bystanders for a handkerchief to staunch the blood and they refused. By now everyone in Cyprus knew there could be no bystanders at a shooting, but the story was too good for any enterprising London newspaper to reject; one correspondent even had Cypriots standing 'grinning and smirking' by Hammond's corpse.[65] What was customarily described by CBS as 'the hysterical malevolence of EOKA' produced a feeling among the British that they were all in this together.

Athens Radio broadcast a heavily nationalist programme aiming at stirring the sentiments of the Greek Cypriots by advertising EOKA's beliefs.[66] Its broadcast programme to Cyprus was made of diplomatic commentaries by Greek and Cypriot contributors, news bulletins including headlines from Athens newspapers, reading of EOKA leaflets, the Greek military march, and music such as folk-song interludes, recitation of Cypriot poetry and patriotic slogans. Three of the most popular programmes broadcast from Greece to Cyprus were the 'Voice of the Fatherland', 'Our Cyprus' and 'Our Blue Cyprus', with the first allegedly inspired by Archbishop Makarios. The programmes openly denounced the British presence in Cyprus, castigating its activities, accusing it of various atrocities and of 'Fascism' and even 'Genocide'.

In fact, Athens Radio broadcasts complemented EOKA's activities which ran an effective campaign accusing British security forces of brutality and of running 'concentration camps' in which torture was routinely used to extract information, a 'smear campaign' as it was branded by the British. Athens station's voice boomed out from the coffee shop radios every evening: 'Become a tornado, O youth of Cyprus. Sweep away any who may block your path. Rout the imperial dynasts. Take the holy road to freedom. Struggle calls for sacrifice. Freedom is won only with blood!'[67] As Lawrence Durrell wrote in his *Bitter Lemons* (1957), 'Disorders increased under the stimulus of rhetoric and the envenomed insinuations of Athens radio', which 'blared and rasped out its parrot-like imprecations' exercising moral pressure on its listeners.[68]

Behind closed doors Greek Cypriots listened to Athens Radio insatiably. The programme's content was about the British stance in relation to Cyprus, namely that the British government avoided reaching a settlement and was deliberately stalling and putting obstacles in the way of any agreement discussed with the people's representative Archbishop Makarios. Also, that the British government was using its infamous 'divide and rule' policy, doing everything in its power to set Greek against Greek and Greek against Turk, that it was provoking Turkish intransigence, that there was no British plan, and that even if there was it would have been full of traps. From the evidence we have examined so far these accusations don't seem to be far from the truth.

From February and until the end of May 1956, the colonial government had no precise information on the effect of jamming on local reception. There were, however, indications which showed that the listening habits of the Cypriots had somewhat changed after jamming began. Instead of trying to receive Athens, the Greek Cypriots tuned to other channels which had made up for the loss of Athens Radio, for example Cairo news broadcast in Greek and also other regional transmitters of Greece's Home Services and Greek Armed Forces such as in Thessaloniki, Komotini, Jannina and other towns.[69] When a channel's wavelength was jammed, usually additional channels were provided which would repeat complete or abbreviated forms of programmes. This method was largely used as a countermeasure to jamming.[70] By September 1956, nearly sixty Greek broadcasting channels needed to be monitored regularly, of which only seventeen could be heard effectively in Cyprus.[71]

A significant source of information, largely absent so far in the Anglophone historiography of the Cyprus revolt, is Costas Montis's novella *Closed Door* (1964). This contains information on the Greek Cypriot reception of the radio during the revolt. Montis, who is considered today as Cyprus's national poet and novelist, who lived through the Cypriot struggle for independence, wrote about it from a Greek Cypriot perspective. *Closed Doors* was in fact explicitly written as a reply to Lawrence Durrell's book *Bitter Lemons* (1957). Montis in his introductory 'explanation', as he called it, wrote: 'Suddenly came the Revolution to penetrate my whole being, to patch together (carelessly? Okay, carelessly) the fracture. [I] could not take it anymore, someone had to speak. Someone who had lived those extraordinary four years.'[72]

In his novella Montis gave special importance to the radio and its vital role during EOKA's campaign. His anonymous, teenage male narrator, a symbol for all the young Cypriots fighting with EOKA, explained: 'We besieged it [the radio] in the mornings, during the noon and evenings to listen to the latest news from Cyprus's and foreign stations, from Athens, London, Cairo, Moscow.'[73] The radio took on mythical proportions, its voice becoming for Cypriots the long-awaited rain, their greatest century-old worry. 'Will it rain this year?' the narrator wondered. Cypriots woke and slept with this agony. So much was this question embedded in their psyche that it became a psychosis, an unchanged pattern of repetition living through generations. During the struggle, this angst expressed through a compact verbal utterance was pushed into the background, as if it was not that important anymore. The narrator wrote: 'Our morning worry did not look at the sky anymore, but nailed the ear to the radio. ... What did London say? We had caught the words "Cyprus", "Famagusta", "Limassol" [on the English broadcasts]'. The radio was personified and it invited diverse reactions by its listeners. During the CBS's and London's broadcasts, the Cypriot gamut of responses ranged from irony, to mockery, to annoyance, to fury, 'I feel like punching it [the radio] smashing it into a million pieces'. This anger corresponded to the angry tone of many of EOKA and PEKA leaflets. For example:

> The Nazi government of our island is fuming as our people listen to the repulsive propaganda being poured out from the loudspeakers of its Radio station and [our people] laugh and pity its foolish inspirers. [...] The reason why the Radio station was established has failed miserably.[74]

But when Athens spoke:

> When that beloved voice was heard ('Cypriot brothers ... ') we held our breath .... The radio left its table, it was now somewhere above us, while clutching it in our arms we felt it speaking closely to us about everything that had taken place, its breath stroking us gently, and we, listening to its heart (for the heart listened to its heart).[75]

Amidst curfews imposed by Harding's Security Services, the radio was the medium to Athens and a 'conduit for EOKA broadcasts' as Carruthers called it.[76]

> And how differently it resounded within the isolation of the curfew – that voice (had a timbre as from another world), how it dissolved it [the curfew]. But soon the English jammed the show and we were left alone. ... We stacked our ear on the loudspeaker ... one word was enough, two syllables were enough. ... – Father, I heard Athens![77]

Montis used his narrator to tell his reader that Greek Cypriots were critical of what they were listening to.

> Of course, we heard one thing from London's and Nicosia's station and we understood, comprehended another. This was not difficult since we had learned (and we learned fast) how English propaganda thought, what it attempted to hide, what it tried to suggest. And the truth is that so much it had not changed its method (Its method, only? It didn't even change phraseology) that it

became naïve (Come on, tell us something different for a change! we exclaimed ironically) and childish.[78]

Interestingly, the narrator remembered a leaflet (most probably of EOKA or PEKA) which placed side by side extracts of announcements of English propaganda in Ireland in 1921 and in Cyprus thirty-four years later. They were very similar.[79] Grivas in his memoirs went a step further accusing CBS of 'poisonous rubbish and lying' and of 'a never ending stream of propaganda' presenting EOKA 'as riddled with doubt and dissension' after Makarios was exiled.[80] Grivas also reported how during Harding's rule, the people '[were] fed with a great deal of false news … though the Cypriots knew the truth well enough'.[81] This is evident in many EOKA announcements made, by leaflet or reported on the radio, seeking to refute many of CBS's news items. For example:

> The Gauleiter of Cyprus announced via the radio station [CBS] that he has discovered large amounts of weaponry belonging to the Organisation [EOKA] in Varosha [in Famagusta]. We declare that Absolutely Nothing belonging to the Organisation has been found by the Nazi troops of the Gauleiter. Let the Cypriot people judge on its own the reason why he disseminates this kind of information the Panicky Field-Marshall of Kenya.[82]

Grivas had made a distinction between radio audiences. He thought that contrary to Greek Cypriots, 'the gentlemen of the Press are easily deluded. […] And I made use of the fact myself when it became necessary. […] At once extraordinary rumours would begin. […] It was a trick that worked however many times it was used'.[83]

Some limited material could be found in the Greek Cypriot bibliography on the local population's reception of the radio, such as in Costas Montis's novella *Closed Doors*. Unfortunately, no reports or studies made by the colonial government could be found on the reception of jamming in Cyprus. For example, evidence shows that in late March 1957 the Secretary of State for the Colonies, having been informed that an analysis of the jamming operations against Athens Radio was being undertaken, asked for a report on the psychological effectiveness of the operation, in terms of 'keeping the Cypriot population well-disposed and halting the progress of the terrorists'.[84] However, this is currently missing.

Concluding interferences: 'Little room left for further incitement'

In April 1957, the Director of Public Relations in Cyprus P. J. P. Storrs (Lawrence Durrell and Leslie Glass had both left the island by this time) proposed that since the broadcasts of Athens Radio were 'less venomous', as a result of EOKA having declared a truce between March 1957 and March 1958, jamming could be discontinued.[85] This proposal was backed up by the new governor of Cyprus, Sir Hugh Foot. Athens Radio had toned down its broadcasts and Cairo Radio Greek had been confined to world news of which reception in Cyprus was very poor.[86] Eventually, from June 1957 jamming was reduced to a minimum. Broadcasts continued being continuously monitored so that more intensive jammers could and would be used 'within seconds' if needed.[87] Broadcasts from Radio Athens to Cyprus were still being jammed as a matter of Her Majesty's Government's policy, 'although the occasions on which it is necessary have diminished since the operation began'.[88] For a short period of time in late 1958, Foot had considered re-imposing radio interference because of Athens Radio's renewed 'incitement to violence', believing that if he did not 'interfere' he would risk mass disorders within the local population.[89]

When Foot asked the town commissioners' opinion as to what course he should take on the matter, their replies were as multiple as their number. For example, from Nicosia's commissioner: 'Athens Radio broadcasts are widely listened to and undoubtedly, by dint of constant repetition affect public opinion and keep nationalist fervour at a high pitch [...] I do not see how we can avoid resumption of jamming.' Lefka: 'Only slight attention is paid to Athens Radio broadcasts these days [...] they are not likely to increase materially the risk of mass disorders. To jam Athens Radio at this stage would tend to give it greater publicity. Cairo radio is as bad, if not worse [...].' Famagusta: 'The effect of these objectionable broadcasts is no longer such as to justify jamming [...] people are already so incensed against the British Government, the Security Forces and even the local administration that there is little room left for further incitement.' Kerynia:

> Very little interest is being shown in these broadcasts in public places. [...] coffee-shops tune in to CBS for news and music [...] rarely in Athens radio [...] although there is no doubt that privately many people do so. [...] whipping up the feelings of the youth [...] causing an increase in violence [...] I am in favour of re-imposing jamming.[90]

By the end of February 1959 Governor Foot had decided to close down and dismantle the jamming organization 'as soon as possible', by mid-March the month that the emergency came to an end. This was after vaguely noting that jamming had proved 'a most resourceful efficient and effective unit'.[91] A full report on jamming including problems, lessons learnt and technical details was to be produced but, again, could not be found in the archival sources.

Metaphorically speaking, jamming, disrupted communication, interference, was also very much in use within the colonial machinery. This multi-frequency signalling within the Cyprus colonial ranks, and between Nicosia and London, created such an erratic combination of tones and timbres between officials that a cacophony of personal temperaments, understandings and misunderstandings, expertise and inadequacy, made it almost impossible for the colonial government to devise an effective line of action, a stratagem against the propaganda campaign mounted by EOKA, the *Ethnarchy* and Greece. On a more general plane, Aaron Edwards's conclusion on 'the nub of the problem' is valid: 'There was a lack of synchronization in policy between Nicosia and London, which invited a military stop-gap and ultimately left EOKA decisively undefeated.'[92]

Voice aircraft and public address vans

More elaborate methods of sound propaganda and psychological warfare were borrowed from other colonial Emergencies such as Kenya and Malaya and applied in Cyprus. For example, voice aircraft was tried out, but largely without effect.[93] These aircrafts, Susan Carruthers explained in her chapter on the Malaya Emergency in her book *Winning Hearts and Minds: British Governments, the Media and Colonial Counter-insurgency 1944–1960* (1995), were fitted with loudspeakers that either announced propaganda messages or played music or other distracting noises to intimidate local populations.[94] Andrew Mumford in his book *The Counter-insurgency Myth: The British Experience of Irregular Warfare* (2012) also mentioned this method in relation to the Malaya Emergency. Voice aircraft would fly over the jungle broadcasting messages to the insurgents, urging them to surrender. As the war began to turn against the MRLA (Malayan Races Liberation Army) after 1952 and morale severely plunged, the effectiveness of this method became more obvious. In 1955 interrogations revealed that 100 per cent of surrendered enemy personnel said that they had heard propaganda being broadcast from voice aircraft. Many of these agreed that what they heard played a large role in their decision to surrender and offer intelligence.[95]

Kumar Ramakrishna, in his book *Emergency Propaganda: The Winning of Malayan Hearts and Minds 1948–1958* (2013 edition), explained how voice aircraft was introduced during Alec Peterson's tenure in Malaya. Peterson was responsible for the organization of the Information Services there. This medium 'was able to reach terrorists with news if important developments very quickly, and hence joined the leaflet as a key tactical propaganda instrument'.[96] The voice aircraft would fly over a designated area, broadcasting General Templer's congratulations and 'exhorting the people to keep the terrorists out'.[97]

The available archival information on the use of voice aircraft in Cyprus is scant. During this research it was discovered that the possibility of using this method during the emergency was John Reddaway's idea after getting hold of Peterson's 'Report on the Information and Development of the Information Services 1952–1954' in Malaya.[98] Reddaway had asked for this as a possible manual for his handling of propaganda and psychological warfare in Cyprus, and voice aircraft was finally one of the methods borrowed. Four years later, in Leslie Glass's 1959 report on the 'Practicabilities for Psychological Warfare in Cyprus', the expert tellingly wrote that there were very few times that voice aircraft in Cyprus was 'other than useless. It is of more value to illiterate and remote targets', bringing to mind earlier discussions about the Cypriots' media literacy.[99]

Similarly, 'public address vans with recorded tapes' were of occasional value during the British counter-insurgency campaign in Cyprus and were only good for admonishing the villagers during the searches, cordons and curfews. They were of some importance when they were used by individual Security Committees when they were publically addressing the civil populations.[100] In 1959, as stated by Leslie Glass after re-evaluating the issues of finance, equipment, establishment and personnel for the resumption of psychological warfare in Cyprus, there were six loudspeaker trucks with equipment both for direct addresses and repetition of pre-recorded tapes. Tape-recording facilities were available at the Forces Broadcasting Service.[101] However, these were not to be used as political agreement was reached before applying Glass's renewed plan for psychological warfare.

As seen earlier, the complaint and worry of many colonial officials in Cyprus was that they were 'always on the defensive' regarding propaganda issues. Their confusion was felt and perceived by EOKA and by the Greek Cypriot people, and it was only natural during a war for liberation and in light of Governor Harding's harsh methods, to take advantage of it. Their campaign was many times assisted by articles in the foreign press, such as Irish contributions of solidarity supporting the Cypriot cause, commentaries by the British opposition opposing the London and colonial governments' actions, even letters by prominent intellectuals such as Albert Camus's 'L'enfant grec' in *L'Express* on 6 December 1955 on the imminent death of Michalis Karaolis, a 23-year-old EOKA member sentenced to death by hanging in May 1956. Press and publications during the period of the Cyprus revolt are therefore the next case study.

Print

Newspapers and publications: 'Turning off an important tap of hostile propaganda'?

News about Cyprus generated on the island and abroad, and disseminated in print among various audiences, influenced, if not shaped, public opinion(s). The issue of public opinion was of crucial importance to the British and colonial governments, as well as to their rivals, the Cyprus *Ethnarchy*, EOKA and their collaborators in Greece, Britain and abroad. This section focuses on print media and agencies, primarily in Cyprus and some abroad, producing news material (newspapers) but also stories (travel literature, magazines) and targeting diverse publics, such as the Greek Cypriot, the British and the international public.

This section investigates the print media used in the effort to present the British and Greek cases on Cyprus, by accessing primarily archival material such as official correspondence, reports, publications such as illustrated editions on the Greek 'character' of Cyprus commissioned by the Church of Cyprus and memoirs. Newspapers and publications were a popular, influential and effective means of communication between agents of propaganda and their respective audiences. Simon J. Potter writes that British policy-makers sought to counter-insurgent propaganda 'in part through censorship, but also by engaging in a wide and often covert propaganda operation to shape the news agenda. Terrorist actions and proclamations were placed in a wider context in official publications and press briefings, designed to show the illegitimacy of the insurgents' cause and the limited support they enjoyed among the wider public'.[102] These imperial policies of countering insurgent propaganda were also implemented during the Cyprus revolt and are to be examined in the following pages.

During the 1950s, the colonial government attempted to silence Greek and Greek Cypriot press outlets because these were considered producing hostile anti-colonial propaganda, thus influencing negatively public opinion. Greek newspapers coming from Athens were interpreted by the colonial government as inflammatory and inciting in a similar way that Radio Athens broadcasts were. For this reason, as a note on propaganda succinctly put it, 'Dangerous foreign propaganda interference in a British territory must be suppressed as quickly and effectively as possible. The lesson of Athens Radio must be remembered.'[103]

Before the beginning of the Cyprus Emergency, during 1954, the colonial government announced the strict enforcement of a 'Seditious Publications Law' which criminalized the publication of articles which were perceived to 'excite disaffection' against the government.[104] Newspapers from Greece which had been devoting large sections of their print material to Cyprus, successfully 'whip[ping] up public opinion' as Charles Peake, the Athens Ambassador, wrote in a confidential letter, were banned from entering the island in 1956.[105] Banning the Greek press was considered regrettable and a negative form of psychological warfare, as jamming Athens Radio was. In spite of this it was effected in a coordinated effort to re-impose 'law and order' in a place where both 'had ceased to function'.[106] Under Governor Harding's emergency regulations it was estimated that some twenty newspapers published outside Cyprus were excluded, including all Athens newspapers, thus 'turning off' 'an important tap of hostile propaganda'.[107]

Greek Cypriot/Greek press

Greek Cypriot newspapers were believed to be 'under EOKA's thumb', too scared to move in a different direction because of EOKA's threat of reprisals.[108] For this reason Greek Cypriot newspapers could not be an outlet for the British position, as the colonial government originally hoped. Towards the end of 1956, 'a spate of invariably anonymous complaints and allegations against the Security Forces began to be published in the Cyprus press'.[109] These 'complaints and allegations' were perceived by the colonial government as 'exaggerated and irresponsible reports', intended to cultivate a climate of prejudice within Greek Cypriot society regarding the nature of British emergency operations. This had the alarming result of straining relations between the civil population and security forces, a 'splitting of sympathy' as Leslie Glass called it.

As Simon J. Potter aptly writes, 'In the British Empire, as elsewhere, newspapers often courted the loyalty of readers, listeners, or viewers by playing consciously on ideas about community'.[110] In order for this to be stopped the colonial government introduced Control of Sale and Circulation of Publications regulations in November 1956.[111] These regulations allowed Governor Harding to prohibit by order the sale and circulation of newspapers 'which printed matter prejudicial to operations; contained incitement to violence; contained matter likely to promote violence, ill-will or hostility between different races or classes of the population or between the public and the Security Forces'.[112] Furthermore, the colonial government, having the power to prohibit or restrict publications, compiled a 'stop list', as it was called, of topics not to be mentioned in the press, for example names of security forces casualties until these were officially released. These regulations were to be revoked after Archbishop Makarios's release, and under Governor Foot's command, in April 1957.

Arguably it was not the effect of Greek Cypriot newspapers that 'strained relations' between the Greek Cypriots and the security forces but Harding's strong-arm techniques which targeted civilians in the hope they would confess anything they knew about EOKA. In addition to this, Harding's undiplomatic moves such as exiling Archbishop Makarios further 'strained relations'. Although Greek Cypriot newspapers certainly exacerbated this feeling of discontent, what is being argued here is that Harding's coercive measures and undiplomatic decisions were the primary means to bring about this 'splitting of sympathy'.

Prohibiting the sale and circulation of 'suspicious' newspapers was in essence censorship though it was not admitted as such. Nevertheless, it was interpreted as such by the Greek Cypriot intelligentsia who not only considered these regulations illiberal but also a flashback to the harsh rule of Governor Palmer during the 1930s. The above regulations were also perceived by the Greek Cypriot public as hypocritical. Prohibiting press material which 'contained matter likely to promote violence, ill-will or hostility between different races or classes of the population or between the public and the Security Forces' was deeply ironic as, for example, the colonial Police Force by this point was replete with Turkish Cypriots who were ordered to curb EOKA's power, thus inevitably affecting the Greek Cypriot population.

About a month after the implementation of regulations Harding wrote in his correspondence that comment in the Greek Cypriot newspapers was 'markedly reserved', focusing mainly on the position of Archbishop Makarios and the question of self-determination.[113] However, this was not entirely true as regulating the Greek Cypriot newspapers did not to go unchallenged. On the contrary, as will be studied in more detail below, it was used for propaganda purposes by EOKA and its political arm PEKA, who regularly criticized Harding's tactics through their leaflets. In this way, they further incited the Greek Cypriot people who, by this point, had every reason to be frustrated.

As Jonathan Stubbs writes, whereas Greek-language newspapers in Cyprus were 'reliably hostile towards British policy during this period, [...] the Turkish-language press was dominated by a nationalist discourse of its own'.[114] Regarding the Turkish Cypriot press on the island this was perceived to be fairly pro-British and not objectionable to any degree to British policy, though this did not mean that the colonial government could count on it to remain so, as the Turkish Cypriots 'take their cue from the Turkish Government'.[115] Tellingly, after the events of 27/28 January 1958, the Turkish Cypriot press became strongly anti-British.[116] In Jonathan Stubbs and Bahar Taşeli's article 'Newspapers, Nationalism and Empire' (2014), the authors examined the development of an indigenous

Turkish-language press in Cyprus during the British colonial period. They argued that Turkish Cypriot newspapers, shaped by the strict anti-nationalist censorship of the British colonial government and also by the intensification of the Greek Cypriot campaign for *enosis*, became highly influential in the propagation of ethno-nationalist ideology, finally endorsing separate Greek and Turkish communal identities on the island and promoting ethnic attachments to Turkey.[117]

Greece on the other hand was publishing printed propaganda for Cyprus and it was doing it successfully. There was, for example, an organization called the Pan-Hellenic Committee for Self-determination for Cyprus, chaired by the Archbishop of Athens, which according to the Cyprus colonial government had 'worked at full blast pouring out anti-British propaganda lies'.[118] Between May and December of 1956, it was believed that it had issued thirty-six publications in seven languages (3.5 million copies). It also had a card index of 3,500 names of prominent persons and organizations abroad and a nominal role of 60,000 persons abroad. Another example is the 1956 propaganda booklet published by the Greek government entitled *British Opinion on Cyprus* stating that 'the majority of the British people disagree with their Government's policy on Cyprus'.[119]

This kind of printed material was designated to achieve 'extensive enlightenment of world public opinion on the question of Cyprus'.[120] It is worth noting here that the Greek government brought the issue of mistreatment of Greek Cypriots held under interrogation by the British forces before the European Commission of Human Rights. In this way British security activities in Cyprus were brought under international scrutiny. The presentation to the UN of a note on 'British atrocities' in Cyprus was perceived by the British government as a severe breach of trust between the former wartime allies Greece and Britain. Governor Harding's anger found in a private and secret letter to Allen Lenox-Boyd, Secretary of State for the Colonies, in May 1956 is evident:

> I am convinced that our failure to make more headway against the flood of lies and misrepresentations from Greece is due in large part to our having been too much on the defensive in the past. We have, by and large, allowed the Greeks to make the running and have contented ourselves with refuting their most outrageous allegations and answering and manoeuvring them at the UN.[121]

In Cyprus, the *Ethnarchy* was responsible for the commission, funding, sometimes printing and dissemination of diverse printed material, for internal and external use. For example, local magazines such as *Elliniki*

Kypros (*Greek Cyprus*), the Greek Cypriot intelligentsia writing in the Greek press, such as Konstantinos Spyridakis in *Kypriaka Grammata* (*Cypriot Letters*), *Kypriakai Spoudai* (*Cypriot Studies*). The *Ethnarchy* was also funding publications for international circulation such as illustrated historical editions reconfirming Cyprus's long Greek tradition, such as *KYPROS* (*Cyprus*) in two volumes, illustrated by Greek illustrator and writer Athena Tarsouli. Some of these publications were rich in visual material; others were solely visual material and essentially a form of visual propaganda. For example, Fokion Demetriades, a Greek cartoonist, was promoting the Cypriot cause abroad through the publication of his caricatures. Artists were even brought from Greece, such as Greek Royal photographer, Apostolos Ververis who captured with his camera a Greek Cyprus, rich in Greek visual imagery and symbolism. This material was then exported abroad and was arguably a way to perform and establish in the minds of the international audiences the Greek character of Cyprus. In this way the Greek Cypriots' aspirations for *enosis* were to be validated.

English-language newspapers in Cyprus

The English-language press in Cyprus consisted of two newspapers, the *Cyprus Mail* and the *Times of Cyprus*. The *Cyprus Mail* was owned by the Greek-Cypriot businessman J. K. Jacovides and manned by a British editorial staff. Before the relocation of the headquarters of Britain's Middle East Land and Air Forces from Egypt to Cyprus in 1954, the newspaper had a small readership consisting mainly of British expatriates, government employees and military personnel. However, with the headquarters opening in Cyprus the island's English-language newspaper market was expected to expand considerably.[122] Lawrence Durrell, then Director of Information Services, had plans of launching another English newspaper on the island in the hope that Cyprus would produce 'a really good Middle Eastern paper' covering the whole region.[123]

Charles Foley's proposal was the only one to materialize. Launching in May 1955, the *Times of Cyprus* was run by the British journalist Charles Foley who had moved to Cyprus that year. He was a former *Daily Express* foreign editor (1940–1955). In 1962 he published his book *Island in Revolt* where he wrote about his experiences as a newspaper editor. His second book *Legacy of Strife: Cyprus from Rebellion to Civil War*, later on *The Struggle for Cyprus* (co-authored with W. I. Scobie), was published in 1975.[124] Foley also published, edited and translated *The Memoirs of General Grivas* (1964).

The *Times of Cyprus* slogan was 'a paper with ideas of its own'. From day one the newspaper was regarded with suspicion by the colonial government and it did not take long to brand it 'a most dangerous and damaging EOKA propaganda organ' in the English language.[125] In official correspondence, John Reddaway, Cyprus's Administrative Secretary, and James H. Henry, the Attorney General, referred to Foley's 'clear identification with the terrorist movement' and him being 'the mouthpiece of EOKA' respectively.[126] 'Its influence has been appalling, and not least on visiting journalists reporting and commenting for the overseas press.'[127] Jonathan Stubbs in his article 'Making Headlines in a State of Emergency: The Case of the Times of Cyprus, 1955–1960' (2017) examines the problematic relationship between Foley's newspaper and the colonial government against a backdrop of social instability and political violence during the last five years of British rule in Cyprus.[128] Stubbs emphasized that the newspaper 'which proved most troublesome for the Cyprus government was published neither in Greek nor in Turkish but in English', while across its five-year lifespan 'it played a prominent and provocative role in the political life of the island'.[129] Although the newspaper sold considerably fewer copies than the leading Greek Cypriot newspapers, the British administration considered it more dangerous because of its ability to influence the overseas press and therefore to shape British public opinion and the international debate about Cyprus.[130]

Stubbs argues for the role of the newspaper 'as a conduit of information between Cyprus and Britain', as it conveyed the experience of colonial rule to an influential readership in London and reported British support for self-determination.[131] Stubbs reveals that the newspaper was widely read among the Greek Cypriots. Charles Foley in the *Times of Cyprus* was publishing quotes from EOKA's propaganda leaflets, and whereas these were certainly newsworthy and while they received considerable informal distribution, as will be examined below, nevertheless the local media were expressly prohibited from making any reference to their content.[132] This ability to undermine official control over the flow of intelligence between the colonial periphery and its metropolitan centre unsettled the British administration. This anxiety was exemplified in repeated attempts to proscribe the newspaper; however, the administration's efforts proved unsuccessful.[133]

As with Susan Carruthers and David French, Jonathan Stubbs also supports the view that 'the colonial Government's ability to impose control over dissenting media outlets, particularly when their influence extended overseas, was [...] vital in their effort to maintain sovereignty'.[134] Stubbs in his article offers important and original insights into the broader relationship between colonial power and media communication during the revolt in Cyprus through the examination of the example of Charles Foley and his newspaper. In retracing the history of the newspaper before its closing in 1960, Stubbs argues for the 'significance of colonial media management and the perceived vulnerability of the British government to adverse public opinion, both home and abroad, as the state attempted to retain sovereignty in its imperial territories'.[135] He also relates the case of the *Times of Cyprus* to the role of newspapers in a broader process of communication between the metropolis and the colonial periphery, and the dangers that this communication posed. Out of the efforts to suppress the newspaper, he finally made an argument for 'a larger colonial double standard in which a free press was allowed to flourish in London while Britain's colonies were subjected to highly authoritarian rule'.[136]

Foley had the support of Labour MPs in the UK, such as Francis Noel-Baker, whose help was recruited when he and his newspaper were put on trial by the colonial government in December 1956 for publishing material which was felt to 'cause alarm or despondency' among the public.[137] Under Harding's governorship and shortly after Foley's prosecution, the colonial government further tightened press censorship by granting the governor new powers to immediately suppress any newspaper which was felt to 'prejudice the success of measures taken to bring about an end to the state of emergency'.[138] Crucially, these measures could be taken without prior warning and with no public hearing.[139] Charles Foley antagonized the administration during this period by republishing articles about Cyprus by influential international journalists who had arrived on the island to cover the Suez Crisis, such as James Cameron and Geoffrey Thursby of the *News Chronicle* and the American Serge Fliegers of the Hearst Corporation's International News Service.[140]

The British and colonial governments depended heavily on the press for the generation of positive international and local public opinion. One of Leslie Glass's main responsibilities in Cyprus was exactly this, to handle overseas press representatives visiting the island to cover the revolt. The Public Information Office, originally established as a 'peace time' organization, was responsible for publishing information about daily life in the colony. When EOKA embarked on an armed struggle, the office continued to act as the main generator of information and propaganda for the following eight months; however, it 'was not geared to do this effectively'.[141]

When Governor Harding arrived in Cyprus and declared it in a state of emergency, he reorganized the Office, establishing a 'Civil – Security

Forces – Police information organisation'. Whereas previously the press was said to be highly critical of the inadequate and delayed release of press material from the colonial government, this new organization was to cover that need. The organization of the Office was also Glass's responsibility as Director General of Information Services. The Public Relations Department (by this time Lawrence Durrell had left the island and no longer offered his help on propaganda) and the Cyprus Broadcasting Service, under the watchful eye of the director general, were feeding news to the Central News Room. The staff that manned these services were 'retired, persons who had settled the Island'.[142] It was believed that these expatriates knew Cyprus and its people, and this was considered to be an advantage that other territories of the empire did not have, making Cyprus 'more fortunate than many' others.[143]

Cyprus was easily accessible by air, as it was not too far away from the various European capitals. In 1956 it was estimated that 323 press representatives visited the island.[144] International journalists reporting from the Canal Zone used Cyprus as their communications base. Their reports were heavily vetted by a Joint Press Censorship Unit on the island.[145] The expanding media presence in Cyprus, largely due to the Suez Crisis but also due to the revolt developing in the island, concurrently exposed the British operations in Egypt and Cyprus to increased scrutiny.[146] Leslie Glass spent most of his time briefing individual journalists. Similarly, Governor Harding, and Governor Foot later on, spent a lot of their time meeting, liaising and building good public relations with the press, in another 'enlightenment campaign' one could say, similar to the one undertaken by Archbishop Makarios before his exile, even though Harding, a hard-line military man, was not that successful at it. Hugh Foot, a diplomat and therefore a persuader by profession, who had also presided over moves towards independence in other territories such as Jamaica and Nigeria, as governor and chief secretary respectively, was highly skilled and aptly trained and experienced.

The colonial government depended on journalists, even though it did not particularly appreciate their profession; nevertheless it had to keep them content. The following extract is revealing:

> There are always third-rate pressmen, as there are third-rate men in every walk of life. But however irritating they are, it is no good crossing them. Like the poor, the press are always with us and they back each other – dog does not eat dog.[147]

During the Cyprus revolt several local publications were in print such as *Radio Cyprus* a weekly Cyprus Broadcasting Service illustrated magazine capable of carrying a considerable volume of government propaganda in an attractive form.[148] Under Harding's rule, the governor proposed a daily commercial newspaper in Greek which would support moderate views, instigating in this way the founding of a 'middle-of-the-way' political party, which would stand between the 'extreme views of the right and left parties'.[149] Furthermore, Lawrence Durrell's *Cyprus Review* predated Harding's rule. The magazine intended to foster a new identity for the Cypriots, based on 'Cypriotism' and not directly affiliated with the 'mother nations' of Greece and Turkey.

Government publications for international use

During the Cyprus revolt the colonial government in collaboration with the Foreign and Colonial Offices was responsible for producing printed propaganda material for international dissemination in Britain, the United States, Greece and elsewhere. This aspect of British propaganda was given great importance. The Cyprus government considered external briefing to be of paramount importance at a time when international fora, such as the UN, were 'invariably resorted to for the ventilation of views', especially where colonialism was concerned.[150] 'Publicity material' as it was called, a reminder of the British distaste for (the word) 'propaganda', and briefing papers were compiled in order to expose and brand the aims of the Cyprus *Ethnarchy* as 'seditious', the role of the Greek government as 'subversive' and 'the whole history of a planned campaign of murder, threats and intimidation'.[151]

This material was being circulated among the Colonial Office, Foreign Office and Embassies (primarily Athens, Ankara, Washington) and other information posts overseas, keeping all interested parties on the same page. This material was also circulated among the Anglophone media in order to be used as reference point by newspaper editors, radio broadcasters and other media professionals. The aim was to encourage a sympathetic attitude towards British policies on the future of Cyprus and, at the same time, creating antipathy and horror against EOKA 'the terrorists', Makarios 'the archterrorist' and Greece the collaborator of 'terrorists'. This material, although primarily produced for international consumption, was also made available in Cyprus, although a large part of the Cypriot audience was immune to imperial propaganda due to EOKA's and the *Ethnarchy*'s counter-propaganda.

Indicative titles of government publications were *Terrorism in Cyprus (The Grivas Diaries)* and *The Church and Terrorism in Cyprus: A Record of the Complicity of the Greek-Orthodox Church of Cyprus in Political Violence* which contained chapters such as 'The Prostitution of Religion', 'The Preaching of Violence', 'The

Corruption of Youth', 'On the Record: Statements by Makarios', '*Enosis* and Only *Enosis*', 'The Cyprus Problem: Basic Facts and Background Notes', 'Cyprus: Peace or Violence'. *The Church and Terrorism in Cyprus*, for example, was a secret publication for official use only. It contained several extracts on the dubious activities of the Church of Cyprus during the revolt, such as accusations of the incitement of schoolchildren by priests and on the facilitation of EOKA's leaflet campaign by hiding, for example, duplication machines in monasteries. A most interesting excerpt, setting the tone and language used in this material, is the one below on the 'prostitution of religion':

> The church leaders sought to dragoon their flocks into unquestioning accord with their political adventure by a [...] process, more subtle than intimidation, more insidious, and with effects more difficult to eradicate. It is illustrated by the popular theme: 'To Greeks religion and motherland are one and the same thing'. By devoting sessions to politics rather than true religion a confusion is purposely brought about in the pious mind, a confusion between Christianity and Hellenism. 'Cypriots pray to the God of Hellenism for their liberty' says Athens Radio. And the words of Holy Writ are insinuated into the Church's political gospel.[152]

There was a difference of opinion between British officials regarding the issue of international propaganda for Cyprus. Some progressive officials, for example, lamented the prospect of all the diligently prepared press material getting 'pigeon-holed or inefficiently released in London' due to the British 'inate [*sic*] aversion to propaganda' and tendency to 'shrink from publicity'.[153] Others took a different stance, arguing that the inefficiency of British publicity about Cyprus was neither because of an insufficient supply of publicity material coming from London nor because of the lack of activity on the part of the Information Office in Cyprus. Instead, they identified three basic difficulties hindering British attempts: 'a) the fashion of anti-colonialism, which run strong not only in the US but also in many NATO countries; b) *schadenfreude*, for example of Germany and Italy; c) statements coming from Britain's opposition and other prominent "uncommitted" figures.'[154]

'Harding and his influential chief secretary, John Reddaway, both men identified as Tory placemen', as Martin Thomas calls them, were known advocates of propaganda's great potential for successful use and went to great lengths to secure agreement in London.[155] They wanted to create 'a special and effective organisation for dealing with the propaganda side of the Cyprus issue' in Britain.[156] Before Prime Minister Harold Macmillan's decision to 'retreat from

Empire', Harding put forward a more radical idea.[157] He proposed that the British government should produce a White Paper, as he said 'placing squarely' on the Greeks their responsibility for the troubles in Cyprus.[158]

It was a common belief in Cyprus government circles that Greece was largely responsible for the island's agitation, especially due to Athens Radio's broadcasts and the Greek press. Charles Peake, the Athens Ambassador, while agreeing with Harding's proposition for a White Paper, saw a disadvantage in its format.[159] White Papers, he wrote, 'all look alike. Whether it is a report by the Scientific Committee of the Privy Council recording their views about the growth of vegetable organisms in Stilton Cheese or whether it is a coruscating record of what is going on in Cyprus'.[160] Having previous experience in the Foreign Office News Department and in the Ministry of Information, Peake strongly supported the view that 'familiarity breeds contempt'.[161] This brings to mind Leslie Glass's ambition 'to sell' to the Greek Cypriots a re-fashioned 'political programme'.[162] Similarly, Peake believed that the British had to find a more imaginative way to present the British case to the wider public, be that British, international or Cypriot. He energetically proposed that the British side should 'enlist the arts of display' in order to achieve this as this was a commonplace of propaganda. However, he knew from experience 'that natural distaste which the Department [Foreign Office] has always had for descending, as it were, onto the very floor of the street. But it is an aspect of the situation that I am sure we must bear in mind'.[163] Peake was convinced that the British case on Cyprus had to be presented by experts 'who knew the tricks of the trade', not amateurs.[164]

For example, Roger Makins, the ambassador to Washington, who was also participating in this secret international debate on propaganda about Cyprus, in one of his responses to Harding's circulated letters, offered an insider's view of American public opinion regarding the situation in Cyprus. According to him, American public opinion is 'largely hostile or indifferent to, if not in ignorance of, our [British] case' on the Cyprus issue, partly because of the American attitude towards 'colonialism' which was acting as a barrier to the assimilation of the British case over Cyprus.[165] He also expressed the complaint, as many Cyprus government officials did (starting with Harding himself), that the British were on the defensive and they did not have the initiative in the propaganda battle for Cyprus. He seemed in fact offended by this apparent failure as 'this sort of line is not well suited to this country', and therefore 'anything that can be done to reduce the volume of British criticism', for example, in the British press, would be helpful.[166]

There are two important points to be made here. The first is to emphasize the fact that, like Leslie Glass, Roger Makins was writing a few months before the Suez Crisis. The second is Makins's disappointment and worry regarding the inefficiency of British propaganda in relation to the Cyprus issue. He was arguably concerned that negative comments in the British press would have a knock-on effect in the United States. Conclusions reached from consulting posts in other NATO capitals showed that in many countries, including the United States, 'we [the British] have not, in spite of very considerable efforts, made the impression which was hoped'.[167] However, the Foreign Office did not seem willing to admit this. As far as propaganda for Cyprus in the United States was concerned, the Foreign Office was in fact reassuring the worried Cyprus government that British Information Services in New York were conducting an all-out campaign on Cyprus from the speaker's platform, as well as from broadcasting and television studios. They were acting as such in their attempt to offset 'the bias of emotional anti-colonialism or plain Schadenfreude, which unfortunately affects the outlook of so many people in NATO and elsewhere'.[168] Perhaps this was done in order to avoid further disheartening the colonial government. Perhaps indeed they could not evaluate the situation from London as they were detached from the realities of the colony and from the roots, so to speak, of international public opinion such as the United States. The traditionally suspicious Foreign Office, although agreeing with Harding on a more aggressive line on propaganda in London and in Cyprus 'to put more punch into it', took a more conservative attitude to Peake's progressive suggestions on Harding's White Paper. The tone used in their letter is familiar: 'There are certain immemorial traditions about the form and content of White Papers and if we are going to embark on "advertising" techniques we shall have to choose some other medium'.[169] So they did.

However, there was another contributing significant factor hindering the efficient dissemination and reach of British propaganda, and at the same time, facilitating enemy propaganda. This was the division existing between the two main political parties in the British Parliament. Internal dissension regarding the future of Cyprus, as well as diversity of opinion regarding the efficiency of oversea propaganda, were said to serve the needs of the pro-*enosis* movement, and at the other end, to have inflated Turkish mistrust of British policy. In Conservative circles, this dissension was believed to be 'one of the most tragic features about the Cyprus problem'.[170] Parliament was seen as 'utterly divided' regarding this issue. During the revolt years, Cyprus 'continued to be a party political bone of contention'.[171] The debate did not stay within parliamentary circles. It was recorded, for example, that a Labour MP visiting Cyprus before the beginning of the insurgency urged the Greek Cypriots: "'Why don't you fight for what you want, like they did in Palestine, India, Ireland etc.? If you can't get what you want by constitutional means you have to fight.'"[172]

The Labour Opposition was therefore accused of being unhelpfully pro-Greek, while it ignored the Turkish attitude. In government circles in Cyprus and in London, it was estimated that this political rift between the Conservative government and the Labour Opposition had done 'untold harm, not only in Cyprus and Greece, but in Turkey, which has shown strong mistrust of British intentions'.[173] In July 1956 a Foreign Office minister declared: 'The attitude of the opposition constitutes the greatest weakness in the presentation of our Cyprus policy in the USA and abroad generally.' As Jonathan Stubbs rightly suggests, these criticisms resonated with the more serious allegations of abuse in Kenya, which Labour MPs such as Barbara Castle had publicized in the press and the House of Commons.[174]

As a result of this rift, the British and international press had also taken sides, condoning or criticizing British policy in Cyprus. Editorial criticism in London's newspaper 'giants' regarding British policy in Cyprus, specifically on Governor Harding's coercive regime and undiplomatic moves, such as Archbishop Makarios's exile, was putting the colonial government in a delicate position. For example, the British press systematically accommodated in the correspondence columns articles by Greek Cypriots based in London 'with their version of the Cyprus problem', as Harding tellingly wrote.[175] These were supposed to influence public opinion in Britain and in the Anglophone sphere.

Travel literature

Travel literature set in Cyprus, published by British publishing houses in the middle of the Cyprus revolt, such as Lawrence Durrell's *Bitter Lemons* (1957) and Penelope Tremayne's *Below the Tide* (1958), was arguably an opinion-former on its own right, being particularly popular with the British reading audience. In these two examples, although the authors' denied the 'political' nature of their works, their claim does not withstand scrutiny. The Greek and Cypriot audience were suspicious about the purpose and function of such literature since its publication. Durrell's book, for example, as soon as it was published, provoked a negative reaction among Greek Cypriot and Greek intellectuals. Costas Montis's *Closed*

Doors (1964), Rodis Roufos's *The Age of Bronze* (1960), as well as George Seferis's poems dedicated to Cyprus are only a few examples of this reaction in print.

Seferis in his 1955 poem 'Salamina of Cyprus', based on his experiences on the island during the autumn of 1953, talked about 'tools' the British were using 'to change them [the Cypriots]'. 'They gather tools to change them; / they won't succeed: they'll unmake them only / if souls can be unmade.'[176] Roufos who also spent time in Cyprus during the revolt, in his novel *The Age of Bronze* (1960) talked about the Cypriot struggle. The original language of his novel was English. It was published in London in 1960 'to present to the English audience the Greek point of view'.[177] However, his book 'was essentially ignored by this audience'.[178] It is worth mentioning that both Seferis and Roufos were working for the Greek government as diplomats. Their profession brought them to Cyprus. Both of them being writers transferred their experiences, views and concerns about the situation in Cyprus almost concurrently to their stay on the island. In the Cypriot literature, Costas Montis's *Closed Doors* was first published in Greek in 1964 as a reply to Durrell's *Bitter Lemons* (1957). It was only translated into English and published in 2004 by an American publishing house, owned by Montis's daughter. All the above are a sample of sources which were meant to reach a wider English-speaking audience to present the other point of view, the view of EOKA and the colonized.

Furthermore, foreign intellectuals moved by the situation in the island wrote about it in the press. One of these famous figures was Albert Camus. His open letter titled 'L'enfant grec' about Michalis Karaolis, a 23-year-old EOKA member sentenced to death by hanging in May 1956, was published in *L'Express* on 6 December 1955.[179] Irish statements of solidarity with the Cypriot cause appeared in the press, underlying their common experience.[180] Paddy Leigh Fermor ('Paddy') also visited Cyprus at least two times during the 1950s, in September 1953 and in May 1955, a month after the beginning of EOKA's campaign. During his second visit he stayed with Lawrence Durrell and joined him in Paphos where they 'witness[ed] the trial of a group of EOKA rebels who had been captured while waiting for a caique loaded with guns and ammunition'.[181] According to Fermor's biographer Artemis Cooper, he was frustrated with 'the Cyprus debacle' which 'left its bitter taste' on everything related to the Greece he so cherished.[182] Fermor published two articles in *The Spectator*, the first one titled 'Friends Apart' on 9 December 1955 and the second 'Friends Wide Apart' on 16 December 1955. Both commented on the situation in the island and on the effect this had on the relationship between Cyprus, Greece and Britain.

Leaflets: An island 'knee-deep in paper'

EOKA and PEKA leaflets

The role of EOKA's and PEKA's leaflets is largely absent from the Anglophone historiography of the Cyprus revolt. This may be partly because of the language barrier, as the leaflets were written in Greek and to this day they haven't been translated into another language. However, the leaflets also remain under-researched by Greek-reading researchers. It was not until 2013 that the Cyprus State Archive published a comprehensive catalogue in Greek, titled *Propaganda – Counterpropaganda: Liberation Struggle 1955-1959*.[183] In this edition 235 propaganda and counter-propaganda leaflets of the Cyprus revolt were reproduced, several for the first time, in this way giving the reader access to EOKA's '"public speaking"'.[184] Some of these leaflets have been translated into English here to facilitate the analysis.

In the foreword of *Propaganda – Counterpropaganda*, Petros Papapolyviou elaborates on the process of EOKA and PEKA's leaflet production and dissemination. The first leaflet of the Greek Cypriot struggle was issued in the early hours of 1 April 1955, the beginning of the armed revolt, and signed by 'Leader Dighenis', who was no one else but General Georgios Grivas, EOKA's leader. In this first leaflet Grivas took responsibility for the explosions taking place simultaneously in the island's largest towns, in this way introducing EOKA to the Cypriots and to the British colonial government. Papapolyviou writes that this leaflet was accepted by the Greek Cypriots with 'unique, unprecedented emotion'.[185] The final leaflets were disseminated in March 1959 at the end of the revolt.

Responsible for the leaflets' transfer, typing, reproduction and dissemination were hundreds of Greek Cypriots, the vast majority of youths and children.[186] Papapolyviou argues that EOKA caught the colonial government unprepared with the beginning of the war of leaflets and that it was only gradually that 'the British realised the importance of the leaflets in EOKA's struggle and their transport or simply their possession carried heavy penalties'.[187] New evidence brought to surface here shows that the colonial government was designing a propaganda war of its own, several months ahead of the official start of EOKA's campaign. Leaflet production and dissemination was an important aspect of the British propaganda offensive.

Charis Alexandrou, editor of the *Propaganda – Counterpropaganda* volume, argues that leaflets were EOKA's primary medium of communication between the organization and the Greek Cypriots.[188] There were two types of leaflets, those signed by EOKA and those signed by General Grivas. In the latter, Grivas published his personal thoughts regarding the struggle, replying to and challenging the British on a personal level. In the early phase of the revolt, General Grivas was solely responsible for writing the proclamations under the pseudonym 'Dighenis'. Dighenis was a legendary Byzantine hero who used to guard the borders of the Byzantine Empire from foreign invaders. According to Alexandrou although EOKA's district leaders were allowed to publish leaflets concerning their districts with Grivas's '*a priori* approval', seldom did they produce leaflets for the mass of the people; this task at the beginning of the revolt was reserved for Grivas himself.[189]

Only a small number of EOKA leaflets were being circulated from April 1955 to the beginning of 1956. Alexandrou attributes this to the absence of an editorial team responsible for written propaganda. During this period priority was instead given to so-called propaganda of the deed. Alexandrou further argues that perhaps during that early period of the revolt there was no need for a more systematic mode of leaflet publication, due to the fact that British propaganda against EOKA was almost non-existent as the colonial government lacked specific information regarding the organization's leadership, motives and modus operandi. The few leaflets created by EOKA could arguably achieve their target which, at that point in the revolt before Governor Harding's exiling of Archbishop Makarios in March 1956, was to establish EOKA's presence and to send the desirable message to '"foes and friends"'.[190] Alexandrou also refers to one further reason contributing to the limited production and dissemination of leaflets at that period. This was Archbishop Makarios's presence in the island, whose political messages given through his sermons and public speeches covered the need for propaganda. Therefore, during the early months of the revolt, EOKA was mostly limited to the military aspect of its campaign.[191]

After EOKA's proscription in September 1955 and Harding's arrival into Cyprus in October of the same year, with which he placed the island under emergency regulations, leaflet production increased. EOKA had to refute the colonial government's accusations about 'terrorism'. After negotiations between Governor Harding and Archbishop Makarios broke down and after Makarios was exiled, after the colonial government jammed Radio Athens in May 1956, and after the first hangings of EOKA fighters took place, General Grivas had to find another medium that would boost the people's morale, that would continue and further Makarios's work, but would also keep the Archbishop's image alive in the Greek Cypriots' minds. PEKA, the Political Committee of the Cypriot Struggle, took up this role.

PEKA was established in August 1956 and was to be the political arm of EOKA.[192] It was responsible for leaflet production and dissemination in Cyprus. These leaflets were meant to boost the Greek Cypriots' morale but were also essentially instructing them how to behave against the colonial forces and to continue in their anti-colonial struggle for independence and *enosis* with Greece. In a secret telegram of 15 September 1956 from Harding to the Secretary of State for the Colonies, Harding wrote about this 'new subversive organisation PEKA'. From a series of PEKA leaflets made available to him after confiscation, Harding came to the realization that PEKA's views and aims were identical to those of EOKA. Therefore, PEKA was also to be banned, making the reproduction by any newspaper of a PEKA leaflet illegal, as it was the case with EOKA's leaflets. The Cyprus Intelligence Committee had advised Harding that the emergence of this new organization 'probably represents an attempt to establish a political wing of EOKA in readiness to continue dominating the political scene, even after terrorism is abandoned or crushed'.[193] This was arguably a fair and accurate prognosis, as many EOKA and PEKA members dominated Cyprus's political scene after independence and indeed continue to do so until this day.

EOKA's and PEKA's first printing facilities were found at the Theological College in Nicosia. A duplicating machine/mimeograph printed the leaflets in batches, and these were then sent to EOKA's cells. When Constantinos Lefkosiatis, the College Director, was arrested in June 1956, the process of reproduction had to be decentralized and therefore EOKA's cells took over. Decentralization created problems, as it became increasingly difficult to find typewriters and duplicating machines. This problem was solved by acquiring new machines from schools, unions and offices. There were cases when these were 'stolen' in agreement with the school's principal. Until this problem was solved hundreds of leaflets were handwritten and typed for dissemination.[194]

Dissemination of leaflets was the most dangerous part of the mission. At the beginning, 'couriers' fly-posted the leaflets on walls or slid them under doors. When the colonial police started the arrests for leaflet possession and dissemination, leaflet 'couriers' limited their method of dissemination by dropping them in the streets, in public spaces such as the cinema, coffee shops and sport stadiums.[195] In this way people could pick them up, read them and pass them on by hand, all done very carefully and in total secrecy, as couriers were aware that they were being watched by the police and informants. Even more interestingly, they dropped them from the *gynaekeion* (part of the church assigned to women separating them from the men, from the pulpit (*bema*) or the precinct of the church. Archbishop Makarios had not denounced

EOKA and it was well known that there were several clergymen supporting and aiding the revolt. The Church therefore, in which British soldiers were not present, was a useful space wherein EOKA could effectively disseminate its messages.

As Alexandrou aptly observes, leaflets were transported throughout the island and this gave the people the sense that EOKA was everywhere.[196] PEKA's role in EOKA's campaign boosted the Greek Cypriots' morale during the conflict. PEKA's leaflets often mocked and ridiculed Governor Harding and his regime, diminishing him and his team in the eyes of the Greek Cypriot people. Very often they were humorous and witty. This concept of ridiculing the enemy was an important aspect of the Greek Cypriot propaganda campaign and a powerful weapon for those who used it, as it effectively discredited the colonial government in the eyes of local public opinion.

General Grivas wrote in his *Memoirs* that the reason for PEKA's establishment was 'to coordinate the political and the military struggle, to keep the internal front coherent, to raise the morale of the people and to fight off enemy propaganda'.[197] Furthermore, 'My task, as leader, would be to give them [the people] that faith'.[198] Harding's callous decisions had led the Greek Cypriots to humorously name his government's Security Services 'In-security Services'.[199] In PEKA's leaflets, as in Athens Radio broadcasts, the governor was adorned with all kinds of imaginative adjectives. Some of them were witty, amusing and playful. Others exemplified unbelievable fits of choler, hatred and rage, and very often were a combination of the two. A few examples: 'Fanfaron Field Marshall' (from 'fanfare' and 'baron', EOKA leaflet), 'the anti-Christ satrap of Cyprus' (PEKA leaflet), 'Harding, Eden and Selwyn-Lloyd, the three-headed Cerberus of Hades. The unending anathema of the Cypriot people will forever remain on him' (PEKA leaflet).[200] Mark Twain's aphorism about the powerful 'assault of Laugher' is therefore particularly relevant here:

> Will a day come when the race will detect the funniness of these juvenilities and laugh at them – and by laughing at them destroy them? For your race, in its poverty, has unquestionably one really effective weapon – laughter. Power, Money, Persuasion, Supplication, Persecution – these can lift at a colossal humbug, – push it a little – crowd it a little – weaken it a little, century by century: but only Laughter can blow it to rags and atoms at a blast. Against the assault of Laughter nothing can stand.[201]

However, putting too much emphasis on PEKA's leaflets' 'medicinal' effects of laughter would be unfair as these leaflets served other purposes as well.

According to General Grivas the leaflets also did 'good work rebutting British claims and arguments'.[202] A representative specimen is a PEKA leaflet produced on 14 October 1956, after the organization was proscribed. The leaflet thanked 'the unbalanced dictator' for this 'honour'. The translation is provided below by the author of this book:

> PEKA is obliged to thank the unbalanced dictator, Sir John Harding, because he has declared it an illegal organisation. In a country where laws are passed speedily and sent to the Government printing office without those for whom the laws are enacted even being consulted, where the laws are made to serve the interests of the Imperialists in London, ... where the law is carried out according to the interests of Colonialism, where justice is absolutely laughed at since the travesty of trials held by aged, paralysed judges brought from England, it is a title of honour for PEKA to be considered illegal in such a miserable country. PEKA would have failed its duty, had it been not proclaimed illegal. Such waste papers which are called British laws, are written by the Cyprus people under their old boots. It is not law but LAWLESSNESS for the love of liberty to be considered a crime, and for every authority to be given to a mad murderer to torture with collective punishments a whole people because our bosses are in need of petroleum!! (which will burn them). ... Like EOKA, it [PEKA] will fight for a free Cyprus where then law will not be a mockery as it is now, but will regulate the rights of a Free People.[203]

The Greek Cypriots were urged by EOKA to fight not only for *enosis*, but also against "'international colonialism'". In this way EOKA was not merely a nationalist movement but an anti-colonial one as well. In this anti-colonial frame EOKA did not hesitate to attack the British government over its 'piratic raid' on Suez, calling every people under foreign rule to revolt. The anti-colonial spirit of the struggle served a crucial purpose: to show the Cypriots that they were not alone in this battle against colonialism and that other peoples revolted as well when they faced unjust colonialism.[204]

In mid-1957 Strong Youth of EOKA (ANE) was formed, comprising of secondary and elementary school students and controlled by EOKA's district leaders. ANE also issued its own leaflets that had as their primary target the Greek Cypriot student community. When two subversive magazines, *Clarion Call* (*Egertirio Salpisma*) and *Youth Education* (*Agwgi twn Newn*) appeared, ANE's leaflet publication decreased.

At the end of 1957 Harding left Cyprus and Sir Hugh Foot became the island's new, and last, governor. The beginning of 1958 signalled the beginning of passive resistance. Along with this came the climax of EOKA's leaflet campaign. Several factors contributed to the increase of leaflets. Arguably, two of the most important ones were intercommunal clashes between Greek Cypriots and Turkish Cypriots intensifying during the summer of that year and the Macmillan plan.[205] Passive resistance as a form of propaganda under Governor Foot will be investigated in the following chapter.

EOKA's, PEKA's and ANE's leaflets were a source of information for the Greek Cypriot public, as people read them in order to know how the revolt progressed. They also put forward EOKA's case which, according to EOKA, was manipulated and deformed by the London and colonial governments, many times leading to accusations of downright lies and misinformation. At the same time, these leaflets were a source of, and cause for, laughter as they were humorous and entertaining, arguably alleviating the people's anxiety. PEKA and by extension EOKA, through the dissemination of these leaflets, boosted the people's morale, keeping them under EOKA's belt, ensuring their collaboration, either through active support and/or through passive resistance. At the other end of the scale, they were a source of worry and often intimidation for the British, as the banning of PEKA proves.

British pseudo-EOKA leaflets

Some files containing information on British propaganda leaflets produced during the counter-insurgency campaign in Cyprus have become accessible to the public since 2013. Tellingly, one of these files is titled 'Cyprus: Psychological Warfare; Leaflets' and contains information on the British pseudo-leaflet counter-campaign in Cyprus during the revolt.[206] Furthermore, in the 1959 report 'Practicabilities for Psychological Warfare in Cyprus – January' by Leslie Glass first discovered during this research, there is mention of a '"leaflet album"', which contained all British efforts in leaflet propaganda.[207]

In August 1955 D. Stephens, the Director of Intelligence in Cyprus, in correspondence with J. W. Sykes, the Acting Colonial Secretary, with the agreement of Government House, was about to embark on a counter-propaganda campaign, through which he was to pursue two parallel aims: to undermine EOKA by all possible means and to build up a positive alternative.[208] He wrote: 'In the covert manipulation of these two themes I visualise a leafleteering campaign in the form of pseudo Eoka [*sic*] leaflets in presenting the fist, and in the form of leaflets purporting to have been issued by a new party aiming at an Independent Cyprus in the second.'[209] The plan was set out in general terms by the Director of Intelligence before Harding arrived in Cyprus. At that early point the mechanics of preparation, reproduction and distribution had not yet been worked out. However, Stephens was planning to obtain different Greek script typewriters so that the two different classes of leaflets (pseudo EOKA leaflets and leaflets by the imaginary new party) could not be attributed to the same source and to ensure that the leaflets would not be traceable to any other typewriter used by the government for other purposes. Distribution was expected to be more complicated than reproduction, as official channels could not be used in the process.[210]

In this attempt at reactive propaganda, the colonial government started dropping leaflets from the air as an answer to EOKA's and PEKA's leaflets, in an effort to contain and regulate local public opinion, but also to manipulate it.[211] Leaflets were made in the same layout and typeface as the EOKA leaflets, either printed or mimeographed (using a duplicating machine that reproduced copies from a stencil, what the British called 'cyclostyled' at the time) and some even forging EOKA's signature. Leaflets were dropped by air and distributed by hand. It was estimated that between March 1956 and September 1957, ninety-five leaflets totalling over 7.5 million copies were issued.[212] As Leslie Glass, Director General of Information wrote, 'Seven or eight million leaflets were dropped and the Island was knee-deep in paper.'[213]

Correspondingly, SGM Herbert A. Friedman (Ret.) and Brigadier General Ioannis Paschalidis in their online article 'Cyprus 1954–1959' cite Tom Driver of the Glider Pilot Regiment, who in the June 1963 *Falling Leaf* publication of the Psywar Society wrote about the propaganda campaign in Cyprus. Driver claimed that an average run of leaflets was 120,000 copies. Of those, generally, 105,000 were airdropped and the remaining 15,000 were distributed by hand. The number of leaflets dropped on a specific community was not fixed. If there was guerrilla action in a certain area the leaflets dropped there would be increased. In addition, certain important themes like surrender leaflets were often printed in greater numbers than average. Driver gave an example of the city of Famagusta that normally would receive a drop of 2,500 leaflets, but received 8,000 surrender leaflets. In a case where a special leaflet was prepared, the number of villages targeted might be doubled. Friedman and Paschalidis explained that, as a rule of thumb, the number of leaflets was decided by the number of people in the village.

> How their politics were perceived by the British (was it a hotbed of EOKA support?), and how accurately the leaflets could be dropped. Where the villages were on level ground and the drop could be controlled, less might be

disseminated. If the village was on the side of a mountain, where many leaflets could be lost or blown away, more would be dropped.[214]

EOKA often publically responded with more leaflets to British forged leaflets in order to inform the public about British 'black propaganda' tactics and to restore EOKA's 'truth'. An example of a leaflet follows, translated by the author of this book:

'The Forgers' The British have always, when their interests demanded it, apart from other dishonesties, resorted to forgery. The famous Intelligence Service, which is only good for inhumane torture, have in their possession special script typewriters which long ago made an impression with the famous 'Grivas diaries' that they themselves fabricated. Many times they forged orders or published leaflets supposedly by EOKA. Lately the snakes, desperate because people do not even stoop to pick up their silly leaflets, resort to their usual trick. They [Intelligence Service] display them allegedly as EOKA leaflets, in the same shape and typeface. Certainly the People, as soon as they glance at them, immediately understand the situation, and shred as many as time allows them to. This prosperity, that their leaflets advertise every now and then, people know it well. They have exhausted us with all this prosperity. The people due to their prosperity are imprisoned for weeks now, due to prosperity their life has become unbearable [...]. Hence the British forgers are very clumsy. So far they were forging Greek History by saying that we are not Greeks. Now they forge the name of those who write new golden pages of history. The whole wide world knows them [the forgers]. And appreciates them as he appreciates a common counterfeiter. With these actions the British once again stand trial. Their judge will be the Cypriot People. PEKA[215]

Other, more detailed leaflets responded to British 'pseudo EOKA leaflets' point by point. Alexandrou convincingly argues that British 'pseudo EOKA leaflets', as the Director of Intelligence called them, by mimicking EOKA's leaflet style admitted that EOKA's leaflets had a positive reception among Greek Cypriots. If the people dismissed EOKA's leaflets then the colonial government would not use the same method to reach them by forging EOKA's signature.[216]

The majority of these government leaflets were safe conduct passes, surrender leaflets and leaflets offering rewards for information on the insurgents or weapons caches.[217] There were also consolidation leaflets that supported the British colonial government and attempted to convince the Cypriot public that 'a legal government is better than a rebel government'.[218] Friedman in his article 'Cyprus 1954–1959' reproduces a part of his correspondence with former Corporal Ken Major who served in Headquarters Company, 1st Battalion, the

King's Own Yorkshire Light Infantry Regiment of the British Army, whose regiment had served in Nicosia in 1956. This is worth citing here, as it serves as primary evidence for the use of leaflet propaganda on the part of the British in Cyprus:

> I was sent overseas in May of 1955. I was in Kenya, Aden, then deployed to Cyprus. I left Cyprus 1 February 1957 [...]. I recently read your article about the 'troubles' in Cyprus. I have some leaflets that we used to hunt for the EOKA members, a white and grey propaganda leaflet that our people printed to attack the EOKA, and one that is black and purports to be from the EOKA. Conditions in Cyprus were pretty rough. We were only allowed out on the streets in groups of four and had to be armed at all times.[219]

Another example of forgery on the part of the British colonial government is the so-called confiscation of 'the Grivas diaries'. In two instances during Harding's rule, in December 1955 and June 1956, parts of Grivas's diaries were recovered during military operations. The colonial government decided to use excerpts for propaganda purposes.[220] The risk of losing track of Grivas's whereabouts, as he was hunted down by the security forces, was considered worthwhile because of the certainty of demolishing the government's opponents in Britain and abroad. The Colonial Secretary duly unveiled the diaries because they proved that Makarios was, as he said, 'up to his neck in terrorism'. PEKA declared that the documents were in fact forged and were made to cover imperialistic schemes. The valid question PEKA posed was: 'How could a man like Grivas, experienced in resistance work, write his diary in his usual handwriting and refer to people by their correct names?'[221] To this day, there is no evidence to show whether the diaries were fake.

Regarding the pseudo-EOKA leaflets, these were perceived by EOKA and its sister organizations, primarily PEKA, as a desperate attempt on the part of the colonial government to be heard.[222] General Grivas would later write in his memoirs, 'Forged letters attacking us purporting to come from anonymous priests, sorrowing mothers, bereft widows and "true patriots" were constantly broadcast. We countered this poisonous rubbish by leaflet and word of mouth. [...] They could find no other way to make people read their opinions. What greater confession of failure could there be than this?'[223] (Figures 4 and 5).

Cartoons: 'Getting a simple idea across with simple people'?

In his attempt to reach the Greek Cypriot public, Governor Harding became interested in using cartoons produced by the Psychological Warfare Division.[224]

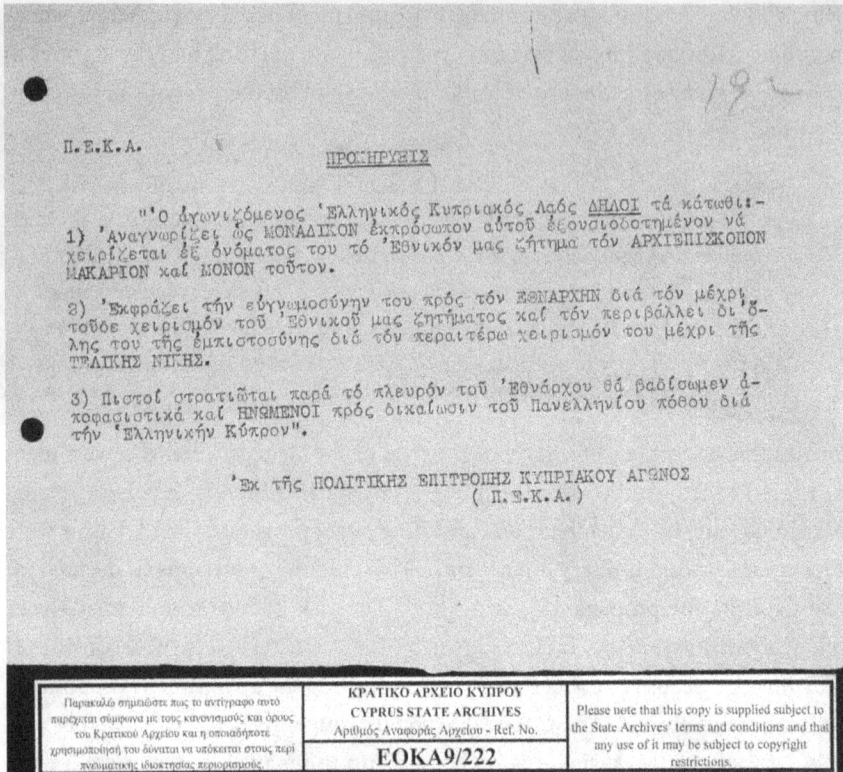

Figure 4 'Announcement', PEKA leaflet, reminding the Greek Cypriots that their sole representative was Archbishop and *Ethnarch* Makarios III and expressing gratitude for what he had done so far for them.

Lawrence Durrell, while in Cyprus and in his role as Director of Information Services (before Leslie Glass's arrival), was the middleman between the colonial government and cartoonists. During this research a few cartoon samples were discovered in a file titled 'Cyprus: Psychological Warfare; Leaflets'.[225] This fascinating, newly accessible material includes visual evidence of the colonial government's efforts in psychological warfare. In a personal and confidential letter sent to Durrell by D. Stephens, Director of Intelligence, dated August 1955 (a few months before Governor Harding's arrival), Durrell is requested to contact some of the 'local cartoonists' to draw 'anti-terrorist cartoons' purporting to have been issued by a new party aiming at an Independent Cyprus, as Stephens had planned.

Along with the letter there is also a list of ten 'suggested subjects'. For example, two of them are the following: 'A butcher's van on the way to the slaughter house.

Π.Ε.Κ.Α.

ΠΡΟΚΗΡΥΞΙΣ

'Ο ἀγωνιζόμενος 'Ελληνικός Κυπριακός λαός δηλώνει τά κάτωθι:

1. 'Αναγνωρίζουν ὡς τόν μόνο ἀντιπρόσωπό τους τόν 'Αρχιεπίσκοπον Μακάριο, πού ἔχει ἐξουσιοδοτηθῆ νά χειρίζεται τά ἐθνικά τους συμφέροντα, ἐξ ὀνόματός των.

2. 'Εκφράζουν τήν εὐγνωμοσύνην των, ἀπέναντι τοῦ 'Εθνάρχου διά τόν μέχρι τοῦδε χειρισμόν τῶν ἐθνικῶν των δικαίων, καί δηλώνουν τήν τυφλήν των ὑπακοήν εἰς αὐτόν εἰς τό μέλλον, ὁτιδήποτε νέες καταστροφές καί ἐάν τούς φέρη.

3. Μέ τό νά εἴμεθα πιστοί στρατιῶτες θά βαδίσωμεν ἀκαφασιστικά στό πλευρόν τοῦ 'Εθνάρχου, καί θά εἴμεθα ἡνωμένοι εἰς τήν ἐκτέλεσιν τῆς πανελληνικῆς ἐπιθυμίας διά μίαν 'Ελληνικήν Κύπρον - ἀκόμη καί ἐάν εἰς τό τέλος θά εἶναι μόνο ἕνα ἥμισυ τῆς Κύπρου 'Ελληνικόν (Εἰς ποιό ἥμισυ θά εἶσαι ΕΣΥ;)

4. Πιστά προχωροῦμεν, βαθύτερα εἰς τόν βάλτον, πάντα ἐμπρός πρός τήν τελικήν καταστροφή εἰς τήν προσταγήν τοῦ 'Εθνάρχου μας.

5. Εἴμαστε βέβαιοι ὅτι τά ἀνωτέρω ἐκφράζουν καί ἀντιστοιχοῦν μέ τάς ἀπόψεις κανενός ἀπό τούς 'Ελληνας Κυπρίους ἐκτός ἀπό τήν ....

Π.Ε.Κ.Α.
ΠΟΛΙΤΙΚΗ ΕΠΙΤΡΟΠΗ ΚΥΠΡΙΑΚΟΥ ΑΓΩΝΟΣ

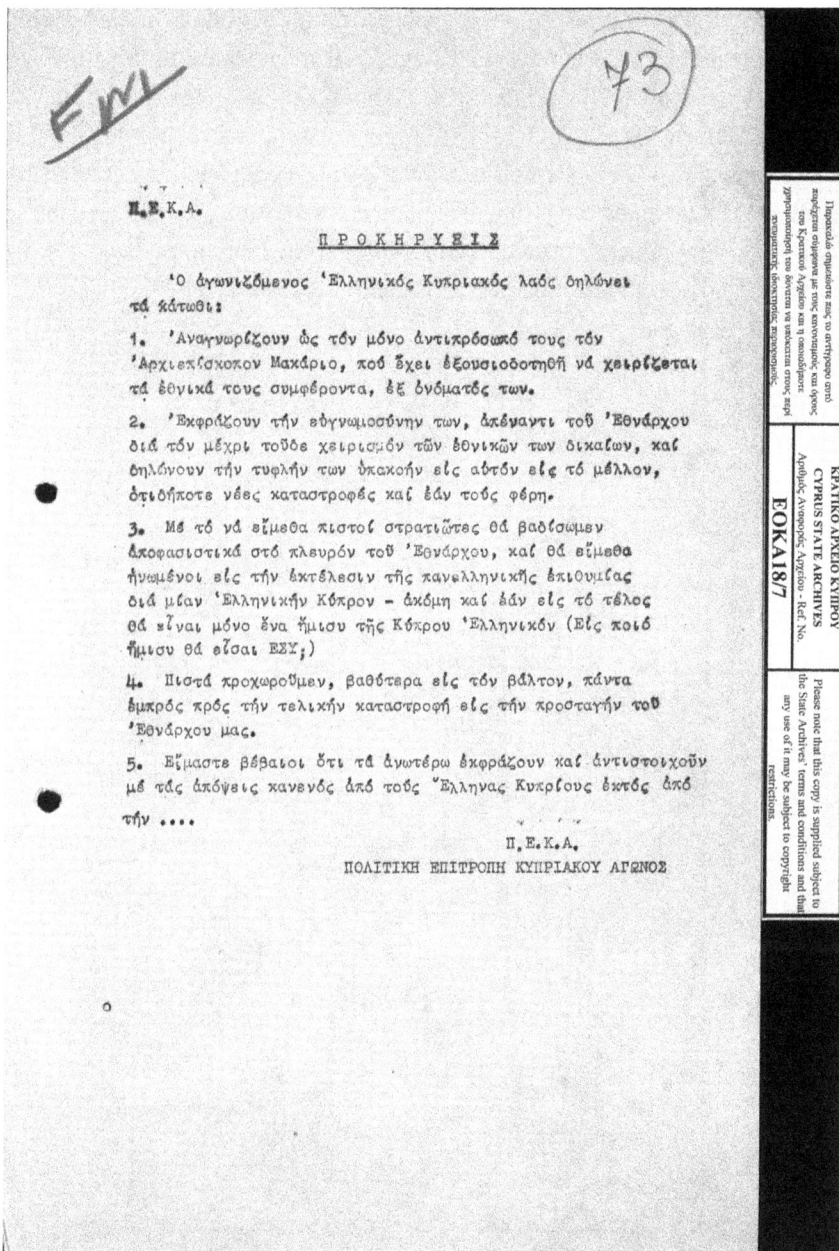

Figure 5 'Announcement', forged leaflet, colonial government. In a deeply sarcastic tone this leaflet was 'thanking' the Archbishop for his disastrous handling of the Cyprus issue and warning the Greek Cypriots against partition.

A number of unprepossessing sheep, goats and pigs with their heads hanging over the tailboard. One bearing a striking facial resemblance to the Mayor of Nicosia, Dr. Themistoklis Dervis O. B. E. An inscription on the side of the van reading "Dhigenis & Co., Butchers." Caption – "We are all EOKA here.'"; and 'The entrance to a Greek Orthodox club for young men. Over the doorway the word AGAPE (love). Issuing from the door a group of young thugs armed to the teeth with sten guns, pistols and hand grenades. No caption.' Several of these ideas were made into cartoons and distributed (Figures 6 and 7).

Figure 6 British propaganda cartoon. 'The entrance to a Greek Orthodox club for young men. Over the doorway the word AGAPE (love). Issuing from the door a group of young thugs armed to the teeth with sten guns, pistols and hand grenades. No caption.'

ΕΚΔΙΔΕΤΑΙ ΥΠΟ ΤΟΥ ΚΥΠΡΙΑΚΟΥ ΑΝΕΞΑΡΤΗΤΟΥ ΚΟΜΜΑΤΟΣ

ΣΦΑΓΕΙΟΝ

ΔΙΓΕΝΗ και ΣΙΑ

ΚΑΣΑΠΗΣ

EOKA

ΕΙΜΕΘΑ ΟΛΟΙ **EOKA** *ΕΔΩ*

Figure 7 British propaganda cartoon. 'A butcher's van on the way to the slaughter house. A number of unprepossessing sheep, goats and pigs with their heads hanging over the tailboard. One bearing a striking facial resemblance to the Mayor of Nicosia, Dr. Th. Dervis O. B. E. An inscription on the side of the van reading "Dhigenis & Co., Butchers." Caption: "We are all EOKA here."'

Information on the cartoonists remains scant. Some evidence has been discovered on a cartoonist named 'Vicky'. Victor Weisz 'Vicky' was born in Berlin and began drawing caricatures freelance in 1928 after his father committed suicide. 'Vicky' was working as a cartoonist for the journal *12 Uhr Blatt*, which took a strongly anti-Hitler stance, when the Nazis took over the magazine in 1933. 'Vicky' arrived in Britain as a refugee in 1935. He drew for a whole variety of publications, including the *Evening Standard*, *News Chronicle*, *Daily Mail*, *Daily Mirror* and the *New Statesman*. Vicky's famous portrayal of Harold Macmillan as 'Supermac' first appeared in the *Evening Standard* in November 1958. Randolph Churchill described 'Vicky' as a genius and Michael Foot thought him 'the best cartoonist in the world'.[226] 'Vicky' was brought to Cyprus in November 1958 to join the *Cyprus Mail* team, which was believed to have an attentive audience among Greek Cypriots.[227] Before Vicky's arrival, and while Durrell was still in Cyprus, Durrell was discontented because he could not 'find anyone capable and trustworthy.[228] Nevertheless, the Cyprus Director of Intelligence was 'sure that the cartoon is a most effective method of getting a simple idea across with simple people – and those are the Cypriots whom we most want to reach'.[229]

In late 1956 John Reddaway, who always had a leading role in propaganda affairs in Cyprus, requested copies of cartoons and leaflets the Psychological Warfare, Allied Forces Headquarters for Egypt produced during the Suez Crisis.[230] These, even at first glance, look very similar to the pseudo-EOKA cartoons. The cartoons portrayed President Nasser either as a sinister Nasser grooming teenagers to become soldiers for the cause or as a defeated Nasser on his knees, hands on head, shaken by the sound of explosions (Figures 8 and 9). Similarly,

قال جمال عبد الناصر: على كل واحد ان يعتبر

NO. 2

Gamal Abdul NASSER said: "Let each one of you be a soldier in the Armed Forces so that we may defend our honour, dignity and freedom".

NASSER

November 1956

ناصر

نوفمبى ١٩٥٦

Figures 8 and 9 In late 1956 John Reddaway, propagandist in the Cyprus government, requested copies of cartoons and leaflets which were produced by Psychological Warfare, Allied Forces Headquarters for Egypt during the Suez Crisis. The above two depicting President Nasser were to serve as examples for the cartoons attacking General Grivas.

General Grivas was often depicted in cartoons as being defeated, afraid and weak or menacing like Nasser. The colonial government was more apprehensive in using Archbishop Makarios in these cartoons, as he was a religious and a political figure, not a guerrilla leader, and reducing him to a caricature would possibly cause negative reactions among certain audiences, not only the obvious, hostile reaction of the Greek Cypriot audience, but an international reaction, from the opposition in London as well. Opinions differed however, further confirming the argument about personal temperaments shaping policies. Revealingly, in a letter from the governor's office to the Colonial Secretary one reads: 'Whether one would ever be well-advised, as a matter of psychological tactics, in taking the Archbishop as the target is infinitely arguable [...]. I do not myself see how one can create resistance to extremism without challenging and condemning its titular head.'[231]

Vision

Television: 'Compelling the belief of the Cypriots' or 'a provocation against national pride and elementary logic'?

Ian Aitken in his book *The British Official Film in South-East Asia: Malaya/ Malaysia, Singapore and Hong* Kong (2016) argues that during the late 1950s, television was still felt to be a new and tentative medium with an uncertain market value.[232] In regard to the British colonies, at that time it remained unclear to what extent television would become as significant as radio and film. This attitude was partly formed out of the belief that television would primarily become a medium of entertainment, not information. Aitken writes that even though this perception would change in the 1960s, 'as the propaganda value of the medium became more apparent', in the 1950s several colonial governments remained dismissive towards this medium.[233] There was also a degree of uncertainty as to what was happening in the colonies regarding the overall development of television there.

In June 1957 the Colonial Office had sent out a circular (Circular 680/57, 18 June 1957) to all colonial governments, on the matter of the development of television services in the colonies, requesting their answer to several questions on the issue, for example if there were any plans to introduce the medium in the respective colony. Out of the twenty-eight colonies where the circular was sent, only three reported on an existing television service on their grounds. These were Hong Kong, Cyprus and Bermuda (although the Bermuda station was operated by a US military base). Singapore was preparing plans for the creation of a station, and some of the Caribbean colonies were also considering the possibility of television. Malaya and the rest of the colonies were contemplating no such thing. Aitken concludes there was 'very little television broadcasting taking place within the colonies, and very little interest in developing such broadcasting'.[234]

No academic research has been published to date on Cyprus Television Service. Very short references to this subject are included in Ian Aitken's book mentioned above and in Elihu Katz and Eberhard George Wedell's *Broadcasting in the Third World: Promise and Performance* (1977).[235] What follows is the first study to date on the Cyprus Television Service, based on primary material found in the Migrated Archives collection. The study traces the television service's history, from its inception in 1952 to its inauguration in 1957, and debates around its closing in 1959. It also explores EOKA's and PEKA's responses to the service through the Greek-to-English translation and analysis of leaflets. In this way, the reader gains access to the Greek Cypriot viewpoint, through material that is directly produced by the organization and not through the material's interpretation, for example, in the British colonial reports and correspondence.

The Cyprus Television Service: 'The most effective medium'?

The Cyprus Television Service was the first colonial government-operated wireless television service to be founded, and the first government-sponsored, directly state-controlled television service in the British Commonwealth.[236] It was also, with the exception of a similar experimental service in Bagdad, the first television service in the Eastern Mediterranean and the Middle East.[237] In Katz and Wedell's book one reads that 'television was introduced in Cyprus by the British [...] to help keep the people off the streets – as a tranquilizer, so to speak'.[238] The possibility of setting up in Cyprus cinema vans which would play British propaganda films was quickly dismissed as it was believed that they would be ignored by the local public. The Cypriots were perceived to be 'blasé' about the cinema, too aware of its propaganda effects due to its use in the island since the years of the Second World War. In 1941 the Press and Information Office's Film Section was set up in Cyprus 'to show propaganda films to the villagers'.[239] After the end of the war the vans continued touring the villages and giving shows in schools, in British Institutes and clubs, even in prisons, as part of the activities of the Education Department and the British Council. Village

shows were particularly popular. In 1950 the Public Information Officer had
written to the Colonial Secretary: 'Invariably, the greater part of the village turns
up and – starved of information and entertainment as Oliver Twist was starved
of porridge – they invariably ask for more.'[240] Arguably, another important
reason for not setting up cinema vans was because there were fears that if the
vans were used, they would serve as ideal targets for stone throwing, as this was
a particularly beloved pastime of Cypriot children during the revolt.

However, setting up a television service was seen in different light.[241] During
this research a document was discovered, dated January 1952, three years before
EOKA's armed campaign. The author's name is missing but its title is intriguing:
'Where there is no vision, the people perish.' It is a 'fantastic suggestion', as its
author calls it, arguing for the establishment of a Television Service in Cyprus. It
would be useful to give an excerpt here:

> That Government should be investing nearly £90,000 in a Broadcasting Station,
> plus some £38,000 yearly to run it, at a time when the Island is notably lacking
> in facilities for technical education, in adequate measures to combat soil erosion
> and in any systematic provision for the care of the poor and aged is evidence
> of the importance which it attaches to securing means of reaching the Cypriot
> people in their homes and social centres and of providing them there with
> entertainment, instruction and a truthful presentation of Government's record
> and point of view. And indeed no one with any knowledge of the cheerless
> monotony of life in the villages of Cyprus, or of the Cypriot people's eagerness
> and capacity for instruction or of the evil effects which a malicious and dishonest
> Press has already had on the common people of Cyprus could have much doubt
> about the justification for the proposed Broadcasting Service if it will, in fact,
> achieve what has been claimed for it.[242]

The author of the proposal believed that television was 'a medium with which
neither Press nor Church, Athens radio nor coffee-shop demagogy could
contend for the attention and favour of the people of Cyprus'.[243] He believed
that television could provide 'entertainment, instruction, information' in a
considerably more efficient manner than radio. He was so optimistic that he
went a step further to claim that a Television Service in Cyprus would be 'the
answer to all those problems of public administration in Cyprus which arise
from the need to reach the ordinary Cypriot man and woman in their own
homes and to persuade them to change their inherited and ingrained habits'.[244] A
local Television Service would limit the reach and effect of local newspapers and
Athens Radio, as Cypriots would turn to television as a source of information
on Cyprus affairs. This, he believed, could 'attract the attention and compel the

belief of the Cypriot public at large', thus securing public interest. As 'affection and respect for the Television grew, distrust would decline and truth prevail', after all 'seeing is believing'.[245] There is no evidence showing the colonial government's reaction to this 'fantastic suggestion'.

It was three years later, in June 1955 that the issue of a Television Service reappeared in the official correspondence regarding Cyprus affairs. This time it was in the form of a suggestion for an experiment, coming from John Proud, the Controller for the Cyprus Broadcasting Service. Proud's proposal for setting up an experimental television service in Nicosia, the island's capital, was based on his conviction that, given the political situation in Cyprus, 'a television service would be the complete answer to the propaganda war with Athens'.[246] Based on the premise that 'some time in the distant future television will become the main medium of broadcasting in every country', he believed that television would provide 'the most effective educational medium', for the people residing in the villages of Cyprus. Proud was echoing the 1952 proposal. Proud's argument comes in contrast to the evidence provided by Ian Aitken in his book about television as a predominantly entertainment medium.[247]

The Cypriots therefore could be informed about 'the progress which has been made in all fields of activity in the island and counter the propaganda of the *Ethnarchy* regarding the alleged failure of the British Administration to carry out its obligations to the people'.[248] In this fashion, 'over a period of 10 years I believe we could re-orientate the minds of the people'.[249] Furthermore, Proud believed that it would give 'enormous prestige' to the colonial government if it were to initiate it and it would give to the Cypriots great pride in the progressiveness of their island, particularly if Greece and the Middle East countries had yet to acquire such a service, and it would also boost their morale. Although he acknowledged that the cost of setting up a television service in Cyprus, covering ideally most parts of the island, was 'extremely high', 'it may not be high if it would secure us a permanent base in the Middle east [*sic*] indefinitely'.[250]

In October 1955, shortly before Governor Harding's arrival into Cyprus, colonial Administrative Secretary John Reddaway confidently stated that 'television seems to be the answer' to the streams of hostile propaganda coming from Greek and Greek Cypriot media.[251] Reddaway, after Proud's prompting, had made a strong case to the War Office and the Colonial Office, for the necessity of a television service in the colony. 'A television service might prove a most powerful medium for getting ideas and accurate accounts of government policies and activities across to the public of Cyprus.'[252] Even though 1955 was admittedly early for a colonial government to be thinking about introducing television in a colony, as it was only taking off in the dominions, Australia and Canada, nevertheless, Reddaway in agreement with Proud was convinced that television could have a significant impact on public opinion throughout the island, and this was because it was both a new and attractive medium.[253]

When Harding arrived that month, he embraced the proposal, making immediate arrangements. He arranged for Robert McCall, C. M. G., Assistant Director of Television at BBC Television Centre, an Australian who played a significant propaganda role at the BBC during the Second World War, to come to Cyprus for a reconnaissance trip in order to offer its expert and urgent advice and finalize the proposals for a television service. During his visit to Cyprus, McCall had meetings with the governor, the deputy governor, other Government House officials, the head of the Information Service, the chief of police, Commander Proud (director of the CBS), the director of Forces Broadcasting, and others, ensuring that he was adequately briefed on the situation in Cyprus and how this informed the ambition for the creation of a Television Service.[254] McCall also produced a report evaluating the conditions in the island for the creation of a television service, as branch of CBS.[255] In his report, sent to Harding on 20 October 1955, McCall estimated that such a venture would be 'fraught with difficulties, and, like all television, certain to be costly'.[256] It was perceived to be nevertheless a worthy addition to the British propaganda machinery in the island.

During the months that followed, John Proud, the CBS Controller, was sent to London to have a meeting with the responsible parties for the venture and a BBC Working Party was sent to Cyprus to study the problems associated with the creation of a television service in Cyprus and after this to carry out field tests and design the buildings.[257] Although Harding regarded 'the installation of such a service as one of the most important features in our publicity and propaganda campaign', he also thought that such a service should be established only when the emergency situation in the island was resolved.[258] This because it was estimated that there were more chances for the venture covering the whole area of Cyprus to be successful when the political front was more stable. In early 1956 it was considered vital to British interests that under self-government in Cyprus the Broadcasting Services would remain under British control. By March 1956, almost a year since the beginning of EOKA's liberation campaign, Harding had postponed the television project 'until we are in a position to see our way more clearly'; 'television would not be practicable under emergency conditions'.[259] The security risk, which involved in carrying out field strength tests in remote parts of the island, was thought to be too high, and this would make the Working Party's operation extremely difficult.

Given the emergency circumstances, it was decided to implement Proud's alternative suggestion: to embark on a pilot scheme which would bring a limited television service to Nicosia and its surrounding suburbs. Proud therefore asked for a preliminary budget of £5,000 to be allocated in 1956 for research purposes. During this experimental phase the government would deny that it was conducting such experiments officially and, if questioned, would state that they were purely experiments conducted personally by the Chief Engineer.[260] This brings to mind the government's denials concerning the jamming of the signal of Athens Radio and, even before that, its secret arrangements for restructuring Cyprus's Information Services. This is therefore one more example confirming the government's policy of secrecy, at times amounting to dishonesty as seen previously. By running this pilot scheme the reaction of the public to the new medium of television would be tested before heavy expenditure was incurred on an island-wide service. Furthermore, a pilot scheme would give the chance for the political situation in the island to stabilize.

It was anticipated that television in Cyprus would be welcomed enthusiastically, as was the case in other countries. This would then provide the justification for investing in a full-scale service. Should the opposite occur, in other words if local reception was not strongly favourable, a more restricted development would take place.[261] The Television Service was to be a section of the Cyprus Broadcasting Service, itself a Department of the colonial government. Furthermore, in the future, advertising material would be accepted in order to defray the high costs of the service while remaining under government control. It was envisaged that in the future under self-government, a Cyprus Broadcasting Corporation was to be created and was to be a public monopoly service broadcasting in sound and television. This was included in Lord Radcliffe's Constitutional Proposals for Cyprus, even though these were rejected by Archbishop Makarios.[262]

Governor Harding, in putting forward the proposition to the Colonial Office, stressed the advantages of such a move. In Cyprus, the main object of a television service would be to engage the attention of the Greek Cypriots. The BBC would extend its Greek-language broadcasts for local consumption, and these would focus on the validity of the British position: that Britain was willing to give Cyprus a form of self-government when and if negotiations with Archbishop Makarios came to a positive conclusion. Harding stressed the fact that from a strategic point of view it was essential for Britain to retain full control of the island, as Cyprus had great strategic importance as a staging post, a command centre and a base of operations.[263] This position was of course vague, and far from convincing, arguably reflecting the British government's difficulty in coming up with a viable scenario that would be accepted by the interested parties, Britain, Greece, Turkey and, lastly, the Cypriots.

Even operating to a limited extent, television in Cyprus was to have its effects on Cypriot opinion as evidence of a forward-looking, progressive administration. The scheme would run as an entertainment service with the possibility of incorporating news bulletins and commentaries if the personnel could be found to carry this out.[264] It would include films and telerecording from the BBC, films from the Library of the Central Office of Information on social services, cultural subjects and educational films. Importantly, it would include children's programmes which 'if successful it would have obvious value' in the education of the young generations, as McCall tellingly wrote. Moreover, the scheme would incorporate films from industrial firms (such as Imperial Chemical Industries) for instructional and public relations purposes, films produced by commercial television stations in England, feature films produced for cinema exhibition and shown once a week as the week's highlight, news programmes. Sports was also an important highlight of the scheme, even though 'the Church controls the Stadium and is non-cooperative'.[265] Lastly, the advantages of the Commonwealth connections would be projected via films of local interest that were to be produced by CBS in order to demonstrate the development of the country, as well as from imported films from the Commonwealth countries.[266]

Furthermore, except for BBC programmes in Greek, 'some interest, naturally, must be paid to the Turks', as well as to the English-speaking Cypriot and expatriate population and British servicemen.'[267] One particularly 'Cypriot' problem, as McCall had identified ('This is a Cyprus problem ... '), was the problem of non-cooperation. 'Speakers, actors and entertainers may be frightened to be identified with the CBS. Some take the risk because they only write a script or only their voices are heard. If they are seen they will be known and this may dry up some of the "talent". This is an occupational risk.'[268] The source of fear was once again EOKA and its reprisals targeting Greek Cypriots who collaborated with the British, as well as British servicemen and government organs. In light of television's expansion into the overseas territories in the next decade, Harding urged that immediate steps to be taken in order to establish the first television service in the British colony.[269]

By the end of 1956 therefore, a proposed provision in the 1957 development estimates of £30,000 for capital and £45,000 for recurrent expenditure on a television service was approved by the Secretary of State for the Colonies.[270]

In February Harding wrote to the Colonial Office that he was 'anxious to get the television service operating as rapidly as possible' and that it was 'essential that [...] any unnecessary delays in getting the Marconi [Marconi's Wireless Telegraph Co. Ltd.] equipment shipped' were avoided.[271] Then, in October 1957, Cyprus Television Service was finally inaugurated, shortly before Governor Harding's departure from Cyprus. In his speech he proclaimed that the service was 'essentially experimental', run by a team of 'pioneers': it would eventually 'enable the people in Cyprus to get a clearer idea than is possible through any other medium of the problems and point of view of their fellow countrymen in different parts of the island and of the outside world'.[272] This 'exciting medium of culture, entertainment and education', as he called it, aimed at contributing directly towards 'better understanding and closer cooperation between everyone'.[273]

Nevertheless, merely a month into the operation of the Television Service, Controller Proud gave warning that 'it is quite clear that we have to revise very considerably our projected programme for 1958'.[274] Although there was hope that the service would be expanded the equipment in the pilot scheme was found 'very inadequate'. The original plan therefore was to change radically. The colonial government considered to provide 'the minimum equipment for putting out the minimum programme acceptable to the public'.[275] In February 1958 Proud wrote to the financial secretary that outstanding accounts from the Crown Agent coming up for payment were making the financial position 'extremely critical'.[276] Estimates were made for the second year of the service's operation based on the assumption that the service would have a bright future ahead of it, and therefore a long-term policy had to be designed.

However, given the circumstances, with Harding gone, with Governor Foot replacing him, and with the island moving fast towards independence, no such decision was reached. Due to this, Proud warned that unless provision is made in the estimates from other sources the television service would have to be discontinued by the end of 1958. With the situation being deeply 'unsatisfactory', and since it was not possible to speculate on the future financial pattern if constitutional changes occurred, Proud did not 'feel like spending even a small amount of money on the purchase of new equipment when the future is so obscure'.[277] He proposed that the service was either 'abandoned entirely in 1959' or 'to accept that as a first charge at least £100,000 has to be found from the Ordinary Budget in 1959 to keep it going at its existing level'.[278]

John Reddaway, Cyprus's Colonial Secretary and by now the unofficial go-to person for propaganda in Cyprus, tried to convince the Colonial Office of the importance of the Television Service in Cyprus, attempting to persuade the Executive Council to consider the future of the broadcasting service. He claimed that the broadcasting service was 'now the only really effective weapon we have for putting over the British point of view and for exerting some Anglicising influence on the community as a whole, as a counterweight to the very powerful Hellenising and "Turkising" influences that are work here'.[279] In attempting to gain the support of the Foreign Office, Reddaway tried to make the idea of the service's expansion appealing by saying that if expanded the service should be able to reach the Levant coast or beyond (the colonial government had reports of reception in Beirut with the pilot installation).[280]

In late 1958 it was estimated that 175 licences were issued by September, out of which fifty-seven went to Greek Cypriots, fifty-four to Turkish Cypriots, fifty-one to Armenians and thirteen to English. These numbers however were not absolute, as it was also known that several television sets were being operated without licenses: 'probably as many as again' as Hedley Chambers, the Controller of Cyprus Television was reported saying.[281] Chambers also reported that although Greek Cypriots were the principal audience, the reason for the low rate of purchase by them was because 'the terrorists have tried to enforce a boycott of the service'. He claimed that many Greek Cypriots owners of television sets told him that they had their houses broken into and their sets destroyed. There was no further evidence of this claim in the archival material. Television, Chambers reported, was regarded as a target for damage and sabotage by EOKA in a similar manner that roadworks and government financed schemes to help vine growers and farmers were. Chambers was not the only one to acknowledge this.

In the official correspondence regarding the progress of the Television Service in Cyprus and the issue of marketing certain television receivers, there was a discussion on the ways 'the political boycott of the televisions services by the Greek citizens' could be overcome.[282] This 'political boycott' is examined in the following chapter. There was the suggestion of permitting some advertising by Greek traders in some of the programmes. Furthermore, it was believed that the boycott was partly due to the high cost of a receiver, and this could be amended by introducing rental facilities and a reduction in retail price. According to Chambers, these measures were effective because when they were applied a number of Turkish Cypriots had bought sets and with the introduction of the rental system 'a large increase in sales has been taking place'.[283] As Proud had mentioned one of the service's problems was that the Greek dealers were 'not pushing the receivers'.[284] At the same time, Chambers noted that lately there were indications of a strong counter-feeling against the boycott of television and that both open and clandestine viewing by Greek Cypriots continued.

Chambers claimed that television was received with enthusiasm by all the island's communities. One year into the service's operation it was decided that a part of the service was to target at the British Community in Cyprus, particularly the armed forces and their families. If the Greek boycott were to continue the service would continue providing entertainment to servicemen and their families, as they were confined to barracks and quarters in off-duty hours.[285]

EOKA criticism: 'A useless thing we call it'

During this time, the EOKA/PEKA criticism on this new medium of television was severe. Although PEKA's leaflets were customarily undated, those that were about the Cyprus Television Service have to be placed chronologically sometime between late 1957 and late 1958, as the station was inaugurated in October 1957.[286] Below two examples of leaflets are translated from the original Greek into English by the author, showing how the service was received by PEKA, and therefore by EOKA as their views were aligned, and then how PEKA presented this new medium to the Greek Cypriot people.

> 'Cyprus Television Service' Many [stratagems] the colonial Government of Cyprus devises daily. So that it shows ... how much it loves us!! How much ... it cares for our spiritual growth and most importantly ... for our entertainment! For this purpose it established long ago the Cyprus Broadcasting Service, which it didn't take long to prove as the best medium for disseminating local and international news twisted according to the interest and commands of its shameful imperial propaganda. And it silenced with disruptive interferences all the Greek radio stations so that Cypriots can't listen to the truth, [so that the Cypriots] can't listen to the voice of their Country, to listen only and solely to the voice of their master.
>
> Hence the heavily taxed Greek Cypriot painstakingly pays several thousands of pounds! – so that he listens to the news as is being served by his Master, so he enjoys the music that his masters want, so that he listens to propaganda, which is suitably prepared in their sinister laboratories [by] all the devil agents of the Intelligence Service. Those who try every means possible to poison the souls of the Cypriots without being able to, to divide the Greeks without being able to, to incite the Turks into disorder against the Greeks in every way they are able to. And for all these [he] pays, willing or not, the brutally oppressed wretched Greek of Cyprus.
>
> Now a new expression of ... love has been promised! The television station!! But Cyprus, a small place, what does it need television for, when big European

states do not have it? Why should the Cypriot budget, which already shows a huge deficit and has reached incredible heights, be burdened with a useless thing? What does the Cypriot need this luxury for, this extra entertainment, since his brother, his father, his child, his relatives, his fellow villagers are kept in the overcrowded prisons, the Bastille of the Cypriot People, and in the inhumane concentration camps of the little GAULEITER of Cyprus?

A useless thing we call it. For the fascist colonisers these stations are the most powerful weapon in their hands. Or so they believe and this is the only reason for its establishment.

We are therefore called to react. And since we cannot do anything else for the time being, let us practice boycotting. Only in this way we will show that we are not aiding the deceitful plans of the enemy with our submission. We implore all the honest Greek Patriots. NO ONE TO BUY A TELEVISION SET. The Cypriot People is once again asked to give a lesson to colonialism.[287] PEKA, undated.

'Television' We give notice to the Greek Cypriot people that the establishment of the television service in Cyprus has first and foremost a propaganda purpose. Through television the Cyprus Government will be doing its vile propaganda at the expense of the national sentiment of our people. The aims and ambitions of the Government are well known to us and we will react, because our national interest requires it.

We suggest to the public to abstain from this kind of entertainment and to boycott the Government's television. Television today is not a necessary [form of] entertainment due to the current conditions we are traversing.

Today that which comes first and must RULE inside our souls is the national issue and help toward those who are affected, those who suffer and those who are kept in prisons and in the concentration camps of the Gauleiter, and not entertainment and [offering] assistance to Government propaganda. Greek Cypriots, Our national duty imposes [that we keep] our distance from television. Boycott television.[288] PEKA, undated.

The leaflets encouraged the Greek Cypriots to 'abstain' from this form of entertainment and to boycott television. Boycotting was used as an act of collective resistance against 'shameful imperial propaganda'. In these leaflets there is a pervasive sense of disgust and contempt towards the colonial government and its attempts in propaganda through the new medium of television, but also against other methods, such as the jamming of the signal of Athens Radio. There is also a sense of resentment towards the government for making the Greek Cypriot pay 'several thousands of pounds' for this 'useless' service. Lawrence Durrell had mentioned this 'tedious wrangle', as he called it, in regard to the

Cyprus Broadcasting Service. When in his village he was often reminded by 'the village wiseacres that the Cypriot taxpayer is paying for it'.[289]

In PEKA's leaflets, there is also the reference to boycotting as a moral act. PEKA's rhetoric highlighted the Greek Cypriots' national duty to resist and not to aid 'the deceitful plans of the enemy' by submitting to 'vile propaganda at the expense of the national sentiment of our people'. The first leaflet given here is a fine specimen of PEKA's typical use of irony. PEKA called television a 'new expression of ... love'. In the first leaflet there is also strong religious imagery, presenting propaganda as something malevolent, created in 'sinister laboratories' by 'all the devil agents of the Intelligence Service'. This imagery was arguably exciting the Greek Cypriots' imagination in a similar way that the reference to their national duty was creating the need to serve it, in this case by boycotting television.

In another leaflet, titled 'Faulty Luxury', PEKA used considerably more emotive language to evoke the Greek Cypriots' national feeling, 'national pride and perseverance'.[290] At the same time the language was much harsher against the island's 'Nazi Government' which, according to PEKA, was doing 'disgusting English propaganda' through its Cyprus Broadcasting Station. With the Broadcasting Station having 'miserably failed', the 'English colonisers fumed and asked for a new way through which to display their plans and their expanding propaganda', and this was the Television Service. However PEKA, claiming to be talking on behalf of the whole Greek Cypriot people, 'laughed at and pitied' these new attempts. The use of irony is again strong:

> They [...] have built a Television Service: What do they care? Is it from the English pocket that thousands of pounds are going to be extracted to construct and conserve this station? These thousands [of pounds] burden for once again the Cypriot tax payer.[291]

PEKA then directly asked the Greek Cypriot reader, 'Is there a Cypriot who will now want to help the Tyrant in succeeding in his plan and in bankrupting his [the Cypriot's] country? Undoubtedly no one'. Only those who were 'naïve' and 'xenomaniac nouveau riche' would dare to buy a television set. PEKA attacked Governor Harding's promises that television was an 'exciting medium of culture, entertainment and education'.[292] PEKA refuted this by proclaiming that 'television is not Culture, nor is it what our land needs. This is rather taunt and ridicule for those who fought and spilled their blood to bring to this island Freedom the A to Z of Culture'. Ending with a statement that aimed to bring the Greek Cypriot to his senses, if by any chance he had any doubts about the evils of the Television Service, PEKA reminded him that 'it is a provocation against National pride but also against every Greek's elementary logic who comprehends his country's needs'.[293]

PEKA leaflets were not the only medium of resistance against the television service. Private letters of Greek Cypriots were sent to the colonial administration expressing disagreement with and problematizing over the new colonial venture. Some months before the inauguration of the television station a letter from an H. Constantinou, whose address suggests that he was living in London, was sent to the Administrative Secretary in Nicosia. This letter supported the view that

> the expense incurred to [*sic*] the taxpayer in the Television Service is not justified considering the so many other vital and immediate needs in development. A Television Service in Cyprus would be an unnecessary luxury [...]. The money could more beneficially be spent in building decent roads in the rural areas, where, even by British standards of roads, they are disgraceful.[294]

The colonial government was well aware that even before the inauguration of the Television Service there had been 'reasoned criticism' of this 'item of Government policy'.[295] In a report from June 1957 Nicosia's commissioner considered it 'perhaps natural' that those who did not reside in and around the capital were criticizing the expenditure on such a service as the service would benefit only the residents of Nicosia and its suburbs. What is interesting is that the Commissioner had acknowledged that some of the service's critics, who were thought to be supporters of the *Ethnarchy*, were negatively inclined towards it. This was because it was feared that television could also become another strong propaganda weapon against the *Ethnarchy* and EOKA in a similar manner that the Cyprus Broadcasting Service was the government's most effective instrument of propaganda. Nevertheless, what he also acknowledged was that criticism of the service had to be accepted 'with as much equanimity as a certain amount of other Government wastefulness which has crept in while more urgent matters received attention, as long as there is also enough money to go round for more necessary purposes'.[296] In this way he expressed his own reservations about the introduction of this promising, yet expensive, communication medium.

The Corporation finally came into being in January 1959, whereas commercial sound broadcasting was introduced in April 1958. In January 1960 the Cyprus Television Service was still a pilot project giving reception in the area of 15 miles radius of the capital Nicosia. Up until January 1960 advertising had not yet begun for the television service, while further development was to be left in the hands of the newly formed government of the Republic of Cyprus after the transfer of power.[297]

Conclusion

This chapter was structured around three case studies on the use of propaganda media during the revolt in Cyprus: sound, print and vision. The study on sound media has reconstructed and examined the history of radio broadcasting and radio jamming on the island during the 1950s, looking at the ways Athens Radio and the Cyprus Broadcasting Service competed for the Greek Cypriots 'hearts and minds', with Athens Radio finally winning the race. Here, the use of other sound media, such as voice aircraft and public address vans, was also introduced, showing why these media were less popular with the Cypriot audience. The study on print media explored how newspapers and leaflets, publications and even literature were assigned a significant role by the opposing sides, as these did not only have a role of primary importance in reaching out to a Cypriot local audience, but also in affecting international public opinion. The establishment of the first television service in Cyprus has been also investigated in this chapter for the first time, making use of previously inaccessible archival material. Television was intended to take the lead in British propaganda efforts when the service first operated in 1957; however as the analysis has shown, it was too late to present the Cypriot people with a convincing message that would eventually serve the colonial government's efforts against EOKA. EOKA and PEKA soon branded this medium as another propaganda instrument.

'No one should expect dramatic results from propaganda', November 1957–March 1959

Introduction

Hugh Foot became Cyprus's last governor and presided over the island's transition from a British colony to an independent state. He was characterized as a 'British diplomat who led British colonies to their independence'.[1] He arrived in Cyprus on 3 December 1957 and stayed for almost three years, until 16 August 1960. As it was aptly phrased in the 1964 short newsreel *Cyprus – Bone of Contention* 'Sir Hugh Foot succeeds to the governorship and tries the personal approach'.[2] Unlike his predecessor John Harding who stayed in history more as a field marshal and less as a governor, diplomat Foot was to try a more 'personal approach' in order to appease public opinion about Cyprus and find an acceptable solution for all interested parties. It was not Foot's first time in Cyprus. In 1943 during the Second World War the island was considered to be susceptible to Communist propaganda and even takeover, as it was dangerously near to German-occupied Greece, Rhodes and Crete. During this time Foot was Cyprus's colonial Secretary.[3]

Back then one of Foot's main worries was the issue of propaganda for Cypriot audiences. Upon taking the reins in Cyprus in the late 1950s this issue would once again trouble him. Propaganda designed for Cypriot audiences was a thorn in the British colonial government's side. During the Second World War, Foot thought that colonial strategies taken from other empire outposts would be useless in Cyprus where

> politics are delicate, complex and peculiar […] it would be disastrous to transfer staff from, say, Eritrea to Cyprus, in the belief that the experience they had gained there would qualify them to tackle problems here […] it would be necessary for a cut and dried plan to be put up to the Governor [of Cyprus] on a ministerial level, or by the head of our propaganda department in the Middle East.[4]

This chapter will argue that Hugh Foot's considerations about propaganda for Cyprus during the Second World War were also relevant more than ten years later, during the Cyprus revolt. This will become evident through the study of Governor Foot's intentions for a renewed psychological offensive in the second half of the emergency and eventually his actions/policies given the international circumstances affecting the future of Cyprus in relation to the future of the British Empire. Foot's methods in persuasion differed from Harding's hard-line tactics. The field marshal's methods were not supported by the diplomat Foot, and this is proven in Foot's more subtle, more persuasive line of action when trying to untangle the Cyprus mess, after Harding was effectively dismissed. By the end of the Cyprus Emergency and upon reaching a political agreement for the future of Cyprus, the Conservative government in London was to pay tribute in the House of Commons to Foot's 'unfailing imagination, courage and leadership' in regard to the treatment of 'certainly the most obstinate of Mediterranean problems', as Lawrence Durrell had called Cyprus.[5]

This chapter investigates the considerations surrounding the use of propaganda in Cyprus under Governor Hugh Foot's rule. At the same time, it explores EOKA's policies in propaganda and the general state of affairs in the colony after Harding's departure. This chapter strengthens the argument being made throughout, that personal attitudes, such as Harding's and Foot's, inevitably affected policy-making and, consequently, the development of events, in Cyprus in particular, but also on a grand-scale within the empire project. More importantly however, it argues that although propaganda was one significant aspect of Foot's policy, as it was of Harding's, the speed of decolonization under Macmillan's government cut short a renewed initiative for psychological operations in Cyprus and therefore Foot and his advisors' plans did not materialize.

Boycott and passive resistance: 'A public conditioned and encouraged by EOKA'

In November 1957, a month before Hugh Foot's arrival, EOKA launched a campaign to boycott British goods. This was discovered by the British administration after a 22 November leaflet was recovered by an EOKA member instructing the Greek Cypriots to stop buying English cigarettes and government lottery tickets and also forbidding them from gambling on Football Pools. In a leaflet of February 1958 General Grivas addressed to 'The People of Cyprus', urging them to fight …. TOTAL WAR! [… to] fight the occupant wherever we find him – in his economy and in his administration. There will be passive resistance on the part of the population and everyone will contribute what he can. TOTAL WAR will not only mean sacrifices in blood but also in money. […] those business men who have trade relations with British firms and factories should give up or at least reduce their trade. […] the people should confine their needs and their demands to only those goods which local industry may provide […] The present leaflet should be considered in the light of a simple warning in order that all concerned should be prepared and aware of their duties. Both the date and the declaration of TOTAL WAR and the nature of what we shall demand from the Greek Cypriot people of Cyprus will be communicated by us in due time … […] Whatever happens, the poor are not going to suffer.[6]

Arguably Greek Cypriot passive resistance during the Cyprus revolt was a form of revolt against the colonial ruler that not only aimed to disrupt 'normality', 'law and order' in the colony, but also aimed to disturb Britain's goals 'in the commercial field'. Cyprus may had been a small island, yet it was an island and a transport hub between three continents (Europe, Africa and Asia). British Oversea Information Services, active in the various countries of the world through the commercial field, had as their aim to increase knowledge and understanding of Britain's economic and commercial policy and promote a disposition to cooperate with it; to publicize individual British products and classes of products, so as to stimulate demand for them; and to increase knowledge and appreciation of British economic, scientific and cultural achievements in the belief that prestige in such field will increase the demand for British goods. In this way, 'they are reinforcing Britain's effort to place her balance of payments on a secure footing'.[7]

Passive resistance could therefore be considered as a means for propaganda, as boycotting British products in a British colony during emergency conditions was effectively affecting public opinion and was a further blow to the crumbling empire's prestige. In his memoirs General Grivas explained that passive resistance in Cyprus took the form of widespread minor sabotage backed by boycott of everything British. In his preparatory plan he explained how important sabotage and boycotts were as a tactic, to be used by EOKA and the general Greek Cypriot public. Grivas believed that the real value of the boycott was in that it heightened patriotic feeling and brought the public and EOKA even closer together. 'Every man, woman and child could feel that he was doing something to help the fight.'[8] A prerequisite for the success of the campaign was that public morale was kept high and that Cypriots continued to trust EOKA and Archbishop Makarios.[9]

PEKA was responsible for introducing this form of resistance to Cypriots, who up until that point were not familiar with it, through the production and subsequent dissemination of several leaflets. PEKA was coordinating, giving guidelines and arguing for passive resistance's necessity at this point in EOKA's campaign. The leaflets proclaimed that the boycott deprived British industry of a market and thus discouraged the continuation of British rule. At the same time, they claimed that the boycott created local employment, that it helped the sale of Cypriot products and that it improved the economic position of the Greek Cypriots. Importantly, they claimed that it won publicity for the struggle abroad.[10]

A secret report by the Special Branch discovered during this research reveals how the colonial government understood the boycott. In the report the two phases of the boycott were fleshed out. Based on several leaflets confiscated since the beginning of the boycott, the Special Branch understood that the boycott was falling into three categories. Firstly, economic, affecting imported goods or local produce from certain sources and British services such as banks. Secondly, ethnic, affecting the English language, 'British persons and culture' and thirdly, government and other services, affecting the spheres of education, health, broadcasting and television, postal, telegraph and telephone services.[11] The first phase covered the period between November 1957 and April 1958. During this time the boycott affected British goods of a type that could be manufactured in Cyprus, for example cigarettes and tobacco, sweets, alcoholic drinks, shoes, soap and detergents, paper napkins and tissues.[12]

In March 1958 passive resistance's flag was raised next to the flag of the liberation struggle. PEKA's proclamation was 'Cyprus is for the Cypriots'. Many other leaflets followed urging Cypriots to boycott British clothing; British insurance companies; British cars, motor types and agricultural tools. A few days later British banks, shops and airlines were included in the boycott. English-language advertisements on shops, vehicles and hoardings were banned; English street signs, traffic signs and shop signs were removed; and the people were told to replace them with Greek ones. In May, Greek Cypriots were ordered to refrain from buying toilet articles and cosmetics, shoe polishes, furniture and tinned food. By June pupils were told to stop attending British government schools, listening to Cyprus Radio Service and watching British cinema films and television. More importantly they were ordered to stop appealing to British 'justice'.

British administrators were complaining in their correspondence that government activities, such as government public events, were 'boycotted by order of the ecclesiastical authorities', meaning the Church through its various organizations and representatives. PEKA's pen was, as always, dipped in irony and drama. 'The Conqueror is trying to set up evening classes in the villages in order to dish out his propaganda stuff to the pure peasants of the countryside. These classes must be boycotted because they serve the tyrants' objects'.[13] The rationale of passive resistance was that 'the Cypriot people would go without today to thrive tomorrow'.[14]

The youth of Cyprus, the main disseminator of leaflets, was also the backbone of passive resistance. ANE, EOKA's Youth Movement was responsible for enforcing the boycott.[15] As explained in the Special Branch's report, ANE's members kept 'surveillance on purchasers of British goods, set fire to British cars, destroy televisions sets and where necessary take inventories in the shops under the eyes of their terrified owners'.[16] Governor Foot, in a letter to the Secretary of State for the Colonies on 6 December 1958, informed him about EOKA's activities in schools.[17] Information was based on the translation of 'terrorist documents', as they were called, recovered during a government operation. These documents underlined the importance attached by EOKA to 'the subversion of youth' and included instructions for ANE to supervise EOKA's orders for the boycotting of British goods. Orders were being sent to youth group leaders regarding the waving of flags and also bulletins to be broadcast with the aid of loudspeakers in the Church during doxology hymns. Another example was that orders were sent by EOKA to youth leaders regarding school strikes and mass demonstrations. A captured document said that 'youth must take part in Demonstrations even if the ladies [possibly meaning, soldiers] of Harding intervene'.[18]

In the extract below, taken from the captured documents, a clear connection is made linking propaganda and passive resistance. This arguably shows that passive resistance was a result of propaganda, but also that passive resistance was a form of propaganda in itself.

> Our youth must not only propagandize in the schools, and at home everywhere for Passive Resistance, but supervise. For this reason young people at home must ask their parents not to use anything British, at school they must [....] make use of local products. [... they must] observe those who make use of British products and report them to their superiors [...]. Also the continual writing of Passive Resistance slogans to keep reminding the public [...]. ANE [...] should see to the faithful execution of my orders for Passive Resistance and make propaganda.[19]

In comparing the report by the Special Branch and Grivas's memoirs one cannot help but notice that their accounts of passive resistance differ. Grivas's over-optimism is questioned by the Special Branch's report. The report mentioned that there were certain violent methods used by EOKA in order to enforce the boycott. For example:

Irresponsible members of terrorist groups were using violent methods to enforce the boycott against the orders of its leader, brutal intimidation was widely reported. Youthful thugs of ANE force smokers of English cigarettes to swallow them in public, Greek Cypriots were stopped in the street and searched, shops were entered and English goods destroyed, Greek Cypriots visiting shops were kept under observation and on leaving their purchases were checked and articles of English origin destroyed in the street.[20]

Upon examining PEKA's leaflets it becomes evident that the organization was replying to Greek Cypriot reactionaries, for example 'moderate' merchants whose interests were affected by the boycott, but the leaflets make no reference to violent methods used by EOKA; instead they speak of propaganda by the British administration. The Special Branch's report claimed that in mid-1958 several leaflets were produced naming and shaming individual Greek Cypriot shopkeepers for not willingly complying with the boycott and having failed to observe EOKA's orders. The leaflets branded the individuals as 'traitors' to the national cause. Not only that, many of these individuals were obliged to publish 'confessions' in Greek-language newspapers, such as *Ethnos*. An example is given below:

> I, the undersigned, Manolis Manoli of Varosha [southern quarter of Famagusta city], hereby express my regret for importing soap of British origin. In future I will follow the orders of Passive Resistance. I also declare that I have given the said soap to the charitable brotherhood of Varosha. (Signed) M. Manolis, Grocer, Municipal Market, Varosha.[21] *Ethnos*, 31 December 1958.

Several Greek Cypriot shopkeepers holding stock of British products were affected by the boycott. Furthermore, AKEL, Cyprus's Left Wing Party, only supported the boycott in May 1958, ignoring EOKA's orders before that. However, EOKA's threats disseminated through leaflets possibly made them refrain. As Special Branch's report aptly commented 'To be branded a "traitor" is considered a heavy price to pay for buying English', the same applied for the terms 'pro-Government' and 'collaborator'.[22] It is worth mentioning here that, as in other cases of propaganda and counter-propaganda, during the boycott of British goods the British security forces unofficially replied by boycotting Greek Cypriot products, for example KEO beer. However, the official line coming from the colonial administration was that 'any counter boycott activity by Government is likely to encourage EOKA to press forward with its campaign'.[23]

It was therefore amidst a general Greek Cypriot insurgency, and not due a few 'isolated terrorist incidents', that Governor Foot was called to design a new propaganda policy. His and others' considerations on this issue are examined below.

EOKA's 'smear campaign' and reassessing British 'psychological warfare'

Research has showed that in mid-1958, under Hugh Foot's governorship, there was once again a wish to revive British propaganda efforts on 'the Cyprus problem'. In a letter sent by Lt. General Bower, Commander-in-Chief, GHQ MELF [Middle East Land Forces] to Governor Foot on 28 May 1958, Bower suggested to Foot (as he had done several times in the past) 'that good dividends might be expected from an intensified psychological approach to the inhabitants of this Island'.[24] Interestingly he acknowledged that until there was 'a definite policy on which to work no approach on these lines was worth making'.[25] This however had now changed, a firm policy was introduced and Foot should 'drive home in every possible way the advantages which such a policy will have for the Cypriots'.[26]

Lt. General Bower offered to lend Governor Foot military resources to help him to put across his policy. The content of propaganda was left to Foot and his staff. Propaganda was to be transmitted via loudspeaker, voice aircraft, leaflets or poster, in conjunction with any operation of the security forces, or as a separate operation if Foot wished to. Bower also offered to help him organize the physical aspect of the 'psychological operation', as he called it, by lending him Colonel Davy and his General Service Officer for a few months. They would help with the loudspeaker and printing facilities, ensuring that the governor's point of view 'was shouted from the house-tops (if you wish, quite literally) and drummed into an appropriate audience, wresting the psychological initiative from EOKA, exploiting the mistakes which they make almost daily, and forestalling criticism from irresponsible and hostile quarters. I cannot imagine a more opportune moment for a vigorous psychological approach'.[27]

Colonel Davy was finally lent to the Director of Operations, Cyprus, from June 1958 to January 1959 to advise on psychological warfare.[28] At this point, the objective remained to destroy EOKA through military operations. Military operations were to be supported by propaganda. Davy considered propaganda as one of the many weapons that had to be used in an emergency. He also believed that propaganda was often ineffective in proportion to the time and effort spent on it. However, it could not be ignored. He emphasized that 'we could not afford to neglect any weapon available'.[29] In a revealing minute titled 'Psychological Warfare', prepared by Cyprus's deputy governor, he considered the possibility of the resumption of psychological warfare, as suggested above by General Bower.[30] He explained that in mid-1958 the new feature of the Cyprus situation was that the British government was to have very soon 'a declared policy which we are determined to stick to'.[31] Their biggest problem remaining was the application of this policy to an international frame, but also the problem of making 'a maximum effort to get it put across locally'.[32] There was a strong belief from the Army side, in the potential of organized propaganda (a term again used here as a synonym for 'psychological warfare'); the most striking example was the success of measures taken in Malaya under Gerald Templer. This time the deputy wanted to get it right, with an organized, efficient propaganda campaign.

It was not only the problem of Greek Cypriot passive resistance that was making the British administration crave a new propaganda policy for Cyprus. Greece's 'smear campaign' was perhaps a more significant problem as this was shaming the colonial, and by extension the British, government in front of the whole world. On 17 July 1957, shortly before the beginning of passive resistance in Cyprus, the Greek government appealed to the Human Rights Committee (the first appeal was on 7 May 1956), alleging the abuse of forty-nine Greek Cypriots by the British security forces.[33] The British House of Lords, the UN and the European Civil Rights Commission all criticized the methods used by the British colonial authorities in Cyprus, and in January 1958, a team from the European Court of Human Rights conducted an enquiry to determine whether the situation in Cyprus justified British emergency measures.[34]

Susan Carruthers in her book chapter '"Mischief in the Air": Cyprus: EOKA and the Struggle for Enosis, 1955–59' (1995) argued that the main aim of British counter-propaganda was to create a critique of the smear technique, which would deflect criticism from the British forces and focus on the insurgents.[35] Although this is a valid argument, nevertheless as a result of the research conducted here, it could also be suggested that EOKA's 'atrocity stories' were not fabrications in their entirety and that instead they were based on facts. There is currently a small but significant number of academic studies, examining the brutal response of the British security forces in Cyprus during the Emergency, the violent and coercive way of counter-insurgency, giving thus validity to the above claim, for example Brian Drohan's chapter 'A Lawyer's War: Emergency Legislation and the Cyprus Bar Council' in his book *Brutality in an Age of Human Rights: Activism and Counterinsurgency at the End of the British Empire* (2018); Martin Thomas's broader chapter on 'The United Nations, Decolonization and Violence against Civilians in the French and British Empires' in the book *The Civilization of War: The Changing Civil-Military Divide, 1914–2014* (2018); Charlie Standley's chapter 'The British Army, Violence, Interrogation and Shortcomings in Intelligence Gathering during the Cyprus Emergency, 1955–1959' in *Interrogation in War* and *Conflict: A Comparative and Interdisciplinary Analysis* edited by Andrew Christopher and Simona Tobia (2014).

Moreover, an interesting international discussion discovered between K. J. Neale of the Cyprus Administrative Secretary's Office, A. S. Aldridge of the Colonial Office and F. A. Vallat of the Foreign Office gives further validity to the claim on the use of violence. Neale had claimed that 'in the early days he [Grivas] was urging his followers to organise riots and demonstrations for the purpose of provoking counter measures which could be exploited before world opinion'.[36] Also that EOKA's captured documents evidently demonstrated how a special effort had been made by the guerrilla organization to collate material for 'an atrocities campaign'.[37] Aldridge of the Colonial Office, on replying to Vallat, argued that Neale's letter was not entirely convincing and that there was a distinct difference 'between organising riots to provoke counter measures and organising a campaign of falsehoods about the torture of single individuals'.[38] In fact:

> I have seen nothing in the captured documents or the EOKA leaflets which calls upon the Greek Cypriots to fabricate atrocity stories. It might plausibly be argued that it is perfectly reasonable to organise the collection of genuine reports of ill-treatment. However, there is so much errant nonsense in so many EOKA leaflets and in so much of the Athens radio material that there should be little difficulty in showing the Sub-Commission the hysterical state of mind that the Greeks and the Greek Cypriots were in at the time that the torture stories were produced.[39]

In April 1958, a resurgence of EOKA's propaganda campaign to discredit the security forces was observed. It was believed that this resurgence, which was based on 'familiar planned lines' had a four fold aim: to denigrate security forces in the eyes of international public opinion, to break the morale of the security forces which would weaken their ability to carry out their tasks, to provide justification for specific acts of violence by EOKA and to divert the police from taking violent measures.[40] The media used by EOKA and its political groups such as PEKA and the local 'Human Rights Committee' to achieve this were leaflets and the local press such as articles condemning the brutal behaviour of military police and security forces in *Eleftheria*, *Ethnos* and *The Times of Cyprus*.

At the same time, the colonial government was 'doing its best' with the overseas press in Cyprus and was in contact with the press in London in order 'to present this campaign of denigration in its true perspective'.[41] Foot was very careful in the written instructions he gave to his team, to follow the legal, dutiful path. For example, 'In planning our campaign we shall, of course, keep to the principle and practice, which we have followed for the last 2.5 years, namely that if a properly supported complaint is made against the Security Forces it will be carefully investigated and those concerned will either be cleared or have the matter brought home to them.'[42] At the same time, he ventured to show his support to the security forces by talking personally to soldiers and police. His skills in diplomacy and persuasion are evident here:

> You have to put up with a lot. On top of everything else you have to put up with the organised campaign of abuse directed against you by EOKA. This propaganda has now over-reached itself. [...] EOKA is doing its utmost [...] to create ill-will between you and the people of Cyprus. It is up to us to see that this effort fails. [...] It is our duty to save the people from the tyranny of violent intimidation and evil propaganda.[43]

Inciting the soldiers, building up their confidence and courage, and faith in their task, 'we played the game according to the rules. We must be able to say that neither vicious propaganda nor violence prevented us from pursuing an honourable cause by honourable methods. We must be proud of what we do and the way we do it.'[44]

Leslie Glass in one of his reports explained that in 1957 the psychological warfare effort was less intense than in 1956, and in 1958 'not much' of it was performed.[45] He justified this with reference to EOKA's quiescence and said that there was not much in the way of military operations in the first part of the year. 'The announcement of the new policy in June made it essential not to prejudice reaction by any provocative propaganda; that the intercommunal riots made it even more important not to put a foot wrong in the way of exacerbating either the Greeks or the Turks. A flow of non-controversial government publicity, of course, continued, publicising Government activities in the fields.'[46]

By mid-1958 therefore, the need to convince international circles of the rectitude of the British policy in Cyprus became increasingly urgent. This realization arguably resulted from a number of factors, such as the impact of the Suez crisis, Macmillan's post-Suez 'audit of empire' in which officials considered which colonies were ready for independence and whether Britain would gain or lose by their departure, the changing overall British view about decolonization under Macmillan's government.[47] From London's end, Charles Peake, formerly Britain's Ambassador to Athens, became responsible for coordinating the propaganda effort for Cyprus and collaborating with the Colonial and the Foreign Offices. This venture however soon proved unsuccessful, as many officials from both departments believed that strenuous propaganda at that stage 'would do far more harm than good'.[48] The result was that many of the propaganda pamphlets prepared 'never saw the light of day', and the full stream of propaganda material they provided 'ceased to flow when it got absorbed in the sands of doubt lying between the Colonial Office and the Foreign Office'.[49]

Not 'blowing the gaff': Special Investigations Group and 'non-attributable propaganda'

Under Hugh Foot's governorship the Special Investigations Group (SIG) was set up in the field 'as a defensive counter-measure to the propaganda campaign mounted by Greece and EOKA to discredit our administration in Cyprus'.[50] 'The European Commission of Human Rights investigation into Greece's first (1956) application demonstrated that the Cyprus government might not be able to stop an inquiry into the second (1957) application concerning torture. Recognizing this situation, administrators shifted tactics from trying to prevent investigations into torture allegations to trying to control the tenor of public discussions on those allegations.'[51] The group was effective from June 1958 to March 1959 for a period of nine months. Its aim and purpose was to 'counter misrepresentation' not only within Cyprus, but also in international bodies such as the Human Rights Sub-committee at the Council of Europe. Its immediate tactical aim, as defined in its 1959 report, was 'the wresting of the initiative from EOKA in the propaganda and "smear" campaign', with 'an ultimate and overriding aim – the prevention of allegations against the Security Forces and, in any case, to buttress their morale'.[52] Neither the British nor the colonial governments could afford to let EOKA's allegations 'smear' their image further in international fora such as the UN arena, in Britain, and in Cyprus. The Greek government dragging them to the Human Rights Committee was perceived as a low blow and they had to come back as winners to save face. The creation of the Special Investigation Group was an answer to this demand. Based on their experience during the earlier days of the Cyprus Emergency, the group asserted that EOKA's allegations against the conduct of security forces was one of the main features of the subversive organization's campaign, 'waged locally but designed to have its effect equally on the international front'.[53] Retrospectively, the Special Investigation Group had correctly gathered that EOKA's campaign aimed at 'a) discrediting the Security Forces locally, at Strasbourg and in international circles generally; b) engendering hatred locally of the Security Forces; c) diverting and discouraging the Security Forces from their proper tasks'.[54] The group's existence became known to EOKA; however, the press and the Cypriot public 'never became fully aware of its exact composition and methods. This "incognito status" assisted the Group in many of its investigations in the field'.[55] As defined in their final report:

> The duties of the Group were to investigate immediately, and record, the facts [...] with a view to: a) issuing a prompt, positive and accurate denial of any false allegations; b) preparing the ground [... for] legal action [...] against the offenders [such as individuals or newspapers that had published 'smear material']; c) maintaining a record for use [...] before the Human Right Committee [...] d) forestalling subsequent faked or exaggerated allegations.[56]

The group was to perform on-the-spot investigations and planned operations such as cordons and searches of villages, followed by the publication 'of the accurate facts', arguably being those serving the British viewpoint, before the Greeks had time to make any formal allegations. In cases where allegations had already been made, the group had to investigate and make 'a prompt, positive and accurate statement or denial', usually through the press.[57] Handling of the press was one of the Special Investigation Group's significant methods and tactics. This was because it was acknowledged that English and vernacular editions of the local Cypriot press were antagonistic to the colonial government and the security forces throughout the revolt, and therefore the group's imperative was to outrun them by publishing official releases on any allegation complaint, thus winning over public opinion. This attempt, once put into effect, was estimated to tone down the public outcry in the colony. This estimation was based on the understanding that the Greek Cypriots, 'as a race, are sensitive to ridicule'; therefore, the 'effective use of lime-lighting the absurd and improbable allegations carried considerable weight from a propaganda point of view'.[58] Racial stereotypes such as the one here evidently held strong well towards the end of the revolt in 1959.

In studying their report it becomes evident that the Special Investigation Group went to extraordinary lengths to 'counter misrepresentation' and finally to change perceptions. For example, when the group was effective the use of cameras was introduced during searches by the security forces in villages. This tactic was devised when it was discovered that 'villagers were given to "rigging" premises', thus 'denigrating the Security Forces' and 'claiming excessive compensation for damage'.[59] Therefore, security forces were ordered to photograph the premises in the presence of the owners to prevent '"rigging"'. This was also designed to have a psychological effect on the Greek Cypriots; complaints of damage were said to have lessened considerably, leading in this way to 'buttressing morale', as was the group's original goal.

In October 1958 EOKA operations had heightened to such a degree that October became known to the British soldiers as 'Black October'.[60] Grivas's execution groups in the towns fought a war of nerves. A number of street killings took place in the centre of the capital Nicosia. London's newspapers branded it 'Murder Mile'.[61] Andreas Karyos argued that EOKA's harassment was so severe that by late 1958 the British Army had retreated into barbed wire encampments, cut off in almost every way from life in Cyprus.[62] On the other hand, EOKA's assaults resulted in more punitive measures targeting the Greek Cypriot population, such as curfews and searches. This fed into the Greek Cypriots public's antipathy towards the government, as it was the recipient and the scapegoat of this so-called war of nerves.[63] It is therefore highly questionable whether the group's activities actually contributed positively towards the appeasement of local feeling or whether by targeting EOKA they were actually targeting the whole Greek Cypriot population, leading to a 'splitting of sympathy' as Leslie Glass had called it in early 1956. Brian Drohan writes:

> Before SIG's creation, British official were on the defensive. News reports would often appear in the local press two or three days after an incident had occurred. But SIG's immediate on-the-spot investigations meant that the first reports about an event were British reports. [...] SIG reports proactively circulated positive accounts from the very first. SIG officers proved adept at learning how to conduct [...] the 'battle of words' in Cyprus.[64]

The available archival material on the group (final report and some correspondence) shows that during the time the group was effective it functioned productively, successfully executing its tasks and dealing with 191 cases. The arguably somewhat self-validating report went a step further to note that considering that the Greek/Greek Cypriot 'Campaign of Abuse was planned well before terrorism started in Cyprus, and that for three-and-a-half years it was waged relentlessly by a public conditioned and encouraged by EOKA', then the size of the group's mission had to be considered and appreciated.[65]

A sceptical reader may take this as an indirect criticism of Harding's emergency policy in Cyprus. This idea is further encouraged when the group proclaimed that if it had been formed at an earlier stage during the revolt, 'the battle for public opinion would have had greater chances of success', suggesting thus in this way that winning public opinion had been unsuccessful. In a telegram to the Colonial Office from George Sinclair, Cyprus Deputy Governor and founder, along with Reddaway, of SIG, Sinclair claimed that the group's results 'were very well worth the effort we put into it'.[66] Sinclair was so proud of the Special Investigation Group's results that he recommended that the group's report be forwarded to the Ministry of Defence so that it might be of help to other colonial governments facing 'similar campaigns of misrepresentation with the emphasis on the actions of the Security Forces in dealing with terrorist movements and supporting sections of the local population'.[67]

In order to achieve its goals the Special Investigation Group required maximum cooperation from the security forces and the civil administration. In its final report it was mentioned that this support was granted.[68] However, archival evidence also reveals information on an unknown aspect of British propaganda in Cyprus during the revolt that showed a degree of liberty taken on the part of the security forces personnel. This information concerns British paramilitary organizations based in Cyprus, taking vigilante action against EOKA and its supporters, and acting concurrently with the Special Investigation Group. These organizations were 'Cromwell' and 'AKOE' (Anti-Killers Organisation of Expatriates, EOKA reversed spelling). Both of these organizations generated propaganda supporting the British point of view. Cromwell and AKOE's activities included preparing and distributing propaganda leaflets against EOKA killings, threatening with retributions, calling for British passive resistance by boycotting Greek Cypriot goods. AKOE was to be renamed Anti-EOKA, allegedly for anyone who was anti-EOKA, not only expatriates, to join.[69] 'The EOKA Haters' (TEH), as they also called themselves, allegedly included Orthodox, Muslims, Armenians, Maronites and British of the Commonwealth. AKOE was to unite anyone who shared a common interest: their hate towards EOKA.[70] AKOE's creation is estimated around mid-1958. On 9 May 1958 a letter was sent from the Administrative Secretary's Office in Cyprus to London, in regard to the appearance of the first two anti-EOKA leaflets by AKOE, which seemed to had been run off on a mimeograph machine, and calling for all Britons to boycott Greek Cypriot stores where the English signs had been removed (Figure 10).

Information regarding Cromwell is even more limited and uncorroborated; the individual's identity and nature remains a mystery until today (Figure 11). SGM Friedman writes in his article that in 2013 he received a letter from a former British RAF sergeant who wished to remain anonymous. The soldier's letter provides some information on Cromwell:

> If a British civilian were murdered, Cromwell demanded swift retribution by killing two or more Greeks. Should Grivas bomb a British establishment, Cromwell wanted to destroy the equivalent amount of Greek property. British Intelligence Officers discovered several British soldiers were in league with Cromwell. They had duplicated his pamphlets on military duplicating machines

```
A.K.O.E.                                                     178/58


EXPATRIATES, what are YOU going to do about it?


     One hundred and six of your comrades, husbands, sons and
brothers have been murdered - shot in the back - by EOKA'S
dastard gunmen.

     No Greek Cypriot, be it barman or businessman, chemist or
cafe proprietor, hairdresser or hotelkeeper, sewing girl or
shopkeeper, has ever "seen" an expatriate murdered, even when
the outrage was perpetrated in broad daylight and in a crowded
street. This proves the contention of DR DERVIS, Mayor of
NICOSIA, that all Greek Cypriots are EOKA. Why not take the
Doctor at his word?

     The braggart GRIVAS and his EOKA poltroons have threatened the
Government with "total war". Why not take them at their word too?

     In war "trading with the enemy" is a crime. Government
cannot be expected to pass the requisite legislation, but YOU
and your friends can stop dealing with Greek Cypriot shops, firms
or establishments and give your custom to Moslems, Maronites,
Armenians or expatriates, and as far as possible refrain from
buying goods manufactured by Greek Cypriots. In this way you can
hit back at these gutless yellow-bellies in the place where it
hurts them most - their pockets.

                              "Anti-Killer" Organisation of
                                   Expatriates.

Please read this and pass it on to a friend of BRITAIN.
```

Figure 10 AKOE leaflet urging the expatriates to boycott Greek Cypriot shops.

and scattered them while on patrol. To avoid bad publicity in the press back at home, those service personnel found to be co-operating with this clandestine organization were quietly and quickly shipped back to the UK.

Both the British colonial government and General Grivas were aware of the existence of AKOE and Cromwell. Grivas mentions it in his memoirs.[71] David French mentions Cromwell and AKOE in a paragraph in his book on the British counter-insurgency in Cyprus. French writes that Governor Foot

was alarmed at the possibility of the security forces getting out of control and mounting unauthorized reprisals. Determined to do 'everything possible to put a stop to this damaging nonsense', he instituted rigorous enquiries to find the culprits. They led to the arrest of a Royal Signals Corps Corporal who was the senior member of a group of sixteen soldiers who had helped to compose the 'Cromwell' leaflets. He faced court martial and pleaded guilty to a charge of conduct prejudicial to good order and military discipline.[72]

435/58

CROMWELL

, TO ALL BRITONS
TAKE HEED - WE MUST REMOVE THE BAUBLE

E.O.K.A.WHO FOR THE PAST FEW YEARS HAVE BEEN MURDERING YOUR
COMPATRIOTS BY GANGSTER TYPE ATTACKS ARE NOT WHAT THEY BOAST TO
BE,"FREEDOM-FIGHTERS", BUT LACKEYS OF THE VERY CHURCH, WHICH FOR
GENERATIONS BATTENED ON THE RUSSIAN PEOPLE, AND EVENTUALLY PRODUCED
THE MOST HIDEOUS REVOLUTION IN HISTORY, AND AN ANTI)GOD REGIME WHICH
NOW THREATENS CHRISTIANITY. THIS SAME GROUP OF MISGUIDED CLERICS
ARE PRODUCING IN CYPRUS A CAULDRON OF HATRED WHICH IS LIABLE TO
DESTROY FOREVER THE FRIENDLINESS WHICH WE HAVE FOR THE GREEK PEOPLE.

UNLESS E.O.K.A. STOP THEIR SENSELESS BUTCHERING OF THE INNOCENT,
AND INTIMIDATION OF THE PEOPLE.I INTEND TO STRIKE BACK AT THE MEN
WHO "GUIDE THE ASSASSINS BLADE".

TO HELP BRING THESE MEN TO THEIR SENSES YOU ARE TO :-
(A) BUY BRITISH ONLY FROM "FRIENDLY"CYPRIOTS.
(B) WRITE TO YOUR MEMBERS OF PARLIAMENT EXPRESSING "YOUR VIEWS".
(C) INSIST ON THE EXPULSION OF ALL GREEK CYPRIOT BROTHEL KEEPERS
FROM BRITAIN (THEY CANNOT HAVE IT BOTH WAYS, IF THEY ARE NOT
   (D) BE ALERT AT ALL TIMES - ARMED AND READY.
(E) PROTECT THE INNOCENT -DESTROY THE GUILTY.
(F) ASK YOUR GOVERNMENT TO INTRODUCE MILITARY COURTS OR REMOVE
THE RIGHT OF ADMITTED GUNMEN TO APPEAL AGAINST THE DEATH PENALTY.
(G) WITHDRAW GRANTS FROM THE U.K. GOVERNMENT TO THE ISLAND'S
ECONOMY.

I CAN WAIT A LITTLE LONGER BUT MY PATIENCE IS RUNNING OUT.

IF ANY MORE BRITONS ARE MURDERED MY "MEN OF IRON" WILL STRIKE
BACK HARD AND MERCILESSLY - NOT AT THE GREEK CYPRIOT VILLAGER BUT AT
THE MANGLIS'S, DERVIS'S, LANITIS'S WHO BY THEIR GREED FOR POWER HAVE
REDUCED THIS ISLAND TO THE LEVEL OF POST-WAR GREECE.

TAKE NO HEED OF GREEK PROPAGANDA. FOR TEN YEARS THOUSANDS OF
MEN HAVE ROTTED IN THE GAOLS OF ATHENS, THEIR ONLY CRIME BEING OPPOSI-
TION TO THE RIGHT WING GOVERNMENT. THE MEN GAOLED IN CYPRUS ARE ALL
KNOWN E.O.K.A. SYMPATHISERS, BACKERS, AND KILLERS WHO IN ATHENS WOULD
HAVE BEEN EXECUTED LONG AGO.

"FEAR NOT FOR I AM WITH YOU".   CROMWELL
    TO ALL BRITONS

Figure 11 'Cromwell' leaflet titled 'To all Britons' and giving them directions on
how to 'help to bring those men [EOKA] to their senses'.

Charles Foley and W. I. Scobie also briefly mention AKOE and 'Cromwell' in their 1975 book *The Struggle for Cyprus*.[73]

It seems that some British soldiers serving in Cyprus during the revolt, either via propaganda or violence, attempted to take matters in their own hands, perhaps in a move of exasperation due to the conditions on the island, to take revenge and strike back on EOKA, and, by association, the Greek Cypriot public. 'Black' and 'grey' propaganda were being used by the British colonial government throughout their counter-insurgency campaign. Some of this information is included in Leslie Glass's final report on psychological warfare for Cyprus, produced in January 1959, to be examined more closely in the following section of this chapter. In this report Glass wrote:

> When there is a great deal of resistance to overt propaganda from Government sources, it is only sensible to use 'grey' (unattributable [*sic*]) propaganda and 'black' propaganda (i.e. ascribed to specific sources from which they do not emanate or using terms and arguments we certainly could not use openly. A certain amount of propaganda of this sort, e.g. through forged leaflets, postal campaigns, appeals from 'notional' organisations and individuals, whisper and rumour campaigns, was carried out in the past through the Operational Propaganda office. The flow has never been large partly because of the difficulty in getting absolutely secure Greek Cypriot assistance, partly because anything of this sort has to be meticulously planned and executed [...], and partly because too frequent repetition would blow the gaff. In the last 18 months some responsibility for production and distribution of this material has been passed to another organisation, which has also taken a hand in the drafting of the material.[74]

It remains unclear whether this other organization was AKOE, but it is possible. It also remains unknown whether Hugh Foot was involved in setting up Cromwell.[75] Glass had also stated in his enlightening report that 'one of the most important and effective ways [...] of carrying out psychological warfare is through non-attributable propaganda'.[76] This excerpt is also significant as it confirms the use of clandestine, 'intangible' propaganda as Freya Stark called it, in Cyprus during the revolt. Leslie Glass had also written that it was not possible to explain British counter-insurgency efforts 'on the non-attributable side for obvious reasons except to the very highest officers such as C.-in-C. MELF [Commander-in-Chief, Middle East Land Forces]'.[77] This is yet another case where the argument about the British government's common practice of secrecy is further reinforced.

'Practicabilities for psychological warfare' and an 'unreceptive target'

In November 1958, Leslie Glass, then Head of Information Services in the United States, was called to Cyprus for 'an early advisory visit' with the purpose of redesigning and resuming psychological warfare in the island.[78] This issue, as seen above, was already being discussed as soon as Hugh Foot arrived on the island. Foot, like Harding before him, was eager to get Glass's personal opinion. Although he did not know him personally, he knew of him and his fine reputation as an expert in psychological warfare.[79] Foot was also aware of the fact that Glass 'had no very high opinion of the possibilities of psychological warfare' in Cyprus; however, he thought that during his visit Glass could help with 'some new ideas on information and publicity policy generally'.[80] In keeping up with his earlier assessment that colonial strategies taken from other empire outposts were to be useless in Cyprus and that 'it would be disastrous to transfer staff from, say, Eritrea to Cyprus, in the belief that the experience they had gained there would qualify them to tackle problems here', in one of his letters to the Secretary of State for the Colonies, Foot wrote that he 'certainly prefer[red] to have someone like Glass who knows Cyprus rather than anyone who comes with preconceived ideas formed in Malaya or Kenya'.[81]

Although Governor Foot was willing to explore the possibilities of a renewed psychological campaign for Cyprus, at the same time his letters did not hide his pessimism on the issue. In a letter of 19 November 1958 to the Secretary of State for the Colonies he was quite frank in saying that although

> we do not want to neglect any possible action which may be fruitful [...] I am bound to say that in our unique circumstances I feel doubtful if psychological warfare methods can do much to help. They might usefully supplement a flat-out publicity campaign designed to convince the Greeks of the advantages of our policy to them but we are at present precluded from making such an open campaign and I frankly have not much hope that we can achieve much by more peculiar methods.[82]

When Glass finally visited Cyprus he produced a report aptly titled 'Practicabilities [*sic*] for Psychological Warfare in Cyprus' where he suggested a revised course of action in the current circumstances of Cyprus. This was sent to the governor of Cyprus, the Colonial Office and the Foreign Office, keeping, as usual, all interested parties, in the loop. The report was to be considered by all and then a renewed plan was to be put into action. Glass believed that at this point there was scope for a postal campaign in Cyprus which would exploit grievances against the economic boycott, largely fanned by PEKA. At the same time, a postal campaign originating in London should support the idea of independence for Cyprus, in this way assisting in the formation of a Greek Cypriot national group in London which would correspond with the Greek Cypriots in Cyprus. Furthermore, forged EOKA, PEKA and AKEL leaflets, being produced during the revolt for counter-propaganda purposes, were intended to worry EOKA and cause dissension within its ranks.[83]

Although Foot was largely in agreement with Glass, these recommendations did not materialize as the situation for Cyprus changed in the early months of 1959, with the interested parties arriving to a political agreement. In April 1959, Governor Foot wrote to the Colonial Office that 'the recommendations which Glass made have been overtaken by events – and the proposals he made can no longer arise'.[84] Foot, although grateful to Glass, was at this point also quite sceptical about the efficiency of psychological operations in Cyprus. This scepticism, although carefully concealed in his public appearances, under his diplomatic, evasive rhetoric, nevertheless could still be discerned in his private correspondence. For example: 'It was good to have someone [Glass] to advise us on this who was under no delusions about "psychological warfare". As you say this is a subject about which a lot of nonsense is talked – not least amongst the High Priests who claim to be experts in the cult.'[85]

In a discussion between Glass and John Vincent Prendergast, Head of the Cyprus Special Branch and formerly the Director of Intelligence in Kenya, the latter assured Glass that at this point there were not any propaganda techniques used in Kenya which were not being used in Cyprus and which could be effectively used.[86] Prendergast's reply was immediate and definite: in Kenya a large section of the population were supporting the colonial government and were 'pre-disposed to receive' government material and also to facilitate the preparation of it. In addition, important bodies of Mau Mau were in known stretches of jungle; these could be addressed by voice aircraft and leaflets. Contrastingly, in Cyprus the number of 'mountain gangs' was small, each gang consisting of a few men, and these were not 'good propaganda targets'.[87]

Prendergast's perception of the Greek Cypriot population is even more interesting, as it provides yet another admission that most of the Greek Cypriots 'were' EOKA. 'Even if they did not always approve of EOKA methods, were in general sympathy with EOKA aims and at least those under 24 were passionate supporters of what they believe to be a national liberation movement.'[88] Prendergast also came to the conclusion that roughly the same arguments could be used when comparing the emergency in Cyprus to the emergency in Malaya. Even more so, at this late point in the revolt, when Cyprus had become 'an international problem', 'any error in propaganda' in Cyprus could affect negotiations on the future of the island. As a result, on the eve of 1959, government propagandists were 'severely limited in what they can say', 'as far as the Greek population goes [they] have an exceptionally unreceptive target pathologically disinclined to believe anything from official sources'.[89]

In the same vein, in having identified the limitations of psychological warfare in his report, Leslie Glass did not support 'do[ing] nothing but rather that no one should expect dramatic results from propaganda'.[90] Even though Glass's recommendations could not be put into effect because they were 'overtaken by events', the report nevertheless contains some interesting points which considerably enlighten the reader's understanding on what 'psychological warfare' and 'propaganda' actually meant for the empire's propagandists.[91] Glass offered a very useful definition of the problematic term 'psychological warfare', so often used in official correspondence, so often used in practice, but rarely defined and therefore, most of the time, remaining obscure. It is worth giving Glass's definition in full:

1. […] 'psychological warfare', a loose and unsatisfactory phrase used by
   different people to mean different things and often used to mean different
   things in the same official paper. In World War II [*sic*] 'psychological
   warfare' was adopted as the name in all-out war for all forms of propaganda
   to total populations in enemy, neutral and friendly countries. The
   phrase helped make propaganda acceptable to the fighting Services and
   understanding by them of the value of propaganda as a fourth arm. The
   phrase has been retained by Services' forward planners looking ahead to the
   needs of another war, and has, perhaps, some special charm for the Services
   since the word 'warfare' implies that they are entitled to a proper interest
   in the subject. The phrase 'psychological warfare' has now been officially
   adopted by the British and United States Services and must be accepted for
   what it is worth.
2. There is still some confusion as to what the phrase means in peacetime.
   In the uneasy peace following World War II [*sic*] our armed forces have
   found themselves from time to time in limited wars and in fierce conflicts
   with armed rebels in British colonial territories. They have felt the need for
   special propaganda to support the military efforts, and fairly rough and
   ready definition has been reached in Whitehall that 'psychological warfare'
   is propaganda in support of military operations.

3. This definition recognises a genuine military requirement for a limited,
intensive and specialised propaganda campaign: (a) To demoralise and
disrupt the enemy against whom military operations are being deployed.
(b) To counteract enemy propaganda. (c) To split civil populations from the
enemy.[92]

At this late point in the Cyprus revolt and two months before the official
end of the emergency in March 1959, there was still an admitted confusion
on the part of the colonial government and its collaborators, as to the course
that psychological warfare should take in Cyprus. Colonel Davy, Director of
Operations, attempted to offer some clarification between 'political propaganda
and psychological support', something that could have been usefully done
early in the emergency. 'Political propaganda is applied in support of H.M.G.
policy when the time is ripe, e.g. after UNO, and adjusted to any changes
which there may be in government policy. The object might, for example, be
the "selling" of the partnership plan.'[93] This propaganda was not connected
to the psychological campaign, except in so far as the latter could, and only if
required, assist by putting across the political propaganda with the resources
at its disposal.

The psychological campaign shared the same objectives as the military
campaign, and the object of the military campaign in Cyprus was, from the start
of the British counter-insurgency, to destroy EOKA. The director explained
that political propaganda was at its most effective when 'a plan can be made'
and when 'the time is ripe'.[94] However, as long as the objectives remained the
same for the military operations, including the psychological offensive, then 'the
time must therefore be always ripe'.[95] At the same time, 'there cannot [...] be a
cast-iron boundary between political propaganda and psychological support for
military operations when both are operating. But there seems to be no reasons
why a moratorium on the former should prohibit the operations and planning of
the latter, which is a military requirement and over which there would, of course,
be full political control'.[96]

A fascinating finding which arises from Glass's report is that British
propagandists were, usually, not aware of the content of Greek Cypriot
propaganda, especially the content of EOKA and PEKA's leaflets. Glass, in his
1959 visit to Cyprus, met with the island's Director of Operations, who had
told him that 'since EOKA themselves in one of their recent leaflets expressed
such belief in the value of propaganda, they might well be sensitive to a well-
conceived propaganda attack from us'.[97] 'Might' is the operative word here, as it
reveals the uncertainty, if not ignorance, that surrounded the British Services

regarding (much of) the propaganda pursued by the Greek Cypriot and Greek agencies and targeted against them. The problem arguably lies in the fact that propaganda by the Greek and Greek Cypriot sides was, to its largest extent, created in the Greek language. EOKA and PEKA's leaflets were in Greek. These, very often, criticized British techniques in propaganda targeting Cyprus. However, as supported by the evidence here, most probably the majority of these leaflets remained undiscovered, or if discovered, it is not certain whether most of them were translated into English. Therefore, what is being argued here is that, at various instances, British propaganda for Cyprus, especially targeting the local Greek Cypriot audience, was shooting in the dark, this automatically making it weak.

Lastly, another point in Glass's report, further contributing to the argument made in this book about British propaganda's weak effects on the local audience, is that of the limited quantity of psychological warfare in Cyprus. Glass wrote that 'at recurring intervals the question is raised of whether enough use is being made of "psychological warfare" in the Cyprus Emergency'.[98] Throughout this book, the analysis of the archival material has proved that psychological warfare/propaganda for Cyprus was an issue worrying the colonial government throughout the revolt's duration. Here Leslie Glass's statement reconfirms this finding. Having experienced the Cyprus Emergency, since almost its beginning, Glass's estimations in this report are particularly pertinent, as they were in his earlier reports. One cannot fail to observe how considerations in the Cyprus colonial government in early 1959 remained the same to the issues preoccupying it in the mid-1950s early into the revolt, and at points, even before then, during the early 1950s.

Conclusion

This chapter examined Governor Foot's considerations surrounding the use of propaganda in Cyprus during his rule in the second half of the emergency, after Harding's departure. EOKA's propaganda policies of passive resistance and boycotting have also been investigated, demonstrating the Greek Cypriots' collective struggle against the British colonial ruler and Foot's difficulty in designing effective propaganda measures that would reverse the situation on the island in which Harding had contributed considerably with his coercive measures. This chapter has shown that even though Foot knew that by this time propaganda could not persuade the Cypriots into renouncing EOKA, he was nevertheless eager to get Leslie Glass's advice on the next steps British propaganda should take in Cyprus. However, negotiations on 'the future of Cyprus' and the speed of decolonization under Macmillan's government cut short a renewed initiative for propaganda and psychological warfare in Cyprus, leaving Foot's and Glass's plans unmaterialized.

Conclusion and avenues for further research

This book is a study about propaganda's crucial role in the Cyprus revolt (1955–1959) and more broadly on propaganda's role during the last decade of British rule in Cyprus. Up until this point, historians have given emphasis on other aspects of the British counter-insurgency campaign. They have given much less attention on aspects of the Greek Cypriot insurgency, whereas research on the aspect of propaganda as used by both British and Greek Cypriot/Greek sides during the revolt has been very limited altogether. This study, based primarily on previously inaccessible, untranslated or unpublished archival material (such as the Migrated Archives and primary sources in the Greek language), but also on recent historical debates about propaganda during the British Empire's 'small-wars' of decolonization, has attempted to establish propaganda as a vital aspect of the conflict in Cyprus at the end of empire. The overarching argument of this study has been that propaganda was an aspect that significantly contributed to, even shaped to a large extent, the development of events in Cyprus during the years of the revolt until, and after, the island's independence in 1960.

The abundance of archival evidence discovered and investigated in repositories in the UK and Cyprus has revealed a fierce battle of propaganda raging between the belligerent sides during the period in question. 'Secret and confidential', as they were categorized, discussions between British colonial officials, and between leading members of EOKA and the Cyprus *Ethnarchy*, have demonstrated propaganda's prominence in the Greek Cypriot and British ways of insurgency and counter-insurgency. This material has so far been inaccessible and/or obscured by other considerations. Access to this has created the need to bring to the foreground of academic research the issue of propaganda's catalytic role in this episode of colonial conflict at the sunset of the British Empire. This is because reconstructing the history of propaganda in Cyprus during decolonization leads to wider implications for the history of other colonial emergencies, for the British 'ways' in counter-insurgency, for the history of previously colonized nations and for the history of the British Empire. For this reason, the aspect of propaganda during the empire's 'small-wars' of decolonization needs to resurface, to be examined and to instigate future research.

Before fleeing Cyprus, Lawrence Durrell had warned John Reddaway, the head of propaganda who was staying behind to assist Governor Harding in his effort to restore law and order in the rebellious colony, that

> clumsy propaganda tends to widen the gap between government and the people - and create the impression that we are at war, not with Athens, but with the people of Cyprus. This is really playing EOKA's game: they want us to be as harsh, repressive and irritating etc. as possible in order to increase the peasantry's annoyance with us and recruit sympathy for themselves.[1]

'Clumsy' is arguably a fair description of the British efforts in propaganda, information and psychological warfare for Cyprus during the anti-colonial revolt.

The British propaganda effort in Cyprus during the 1950s, and especially during the emergency attempting to affect, shift, change local Greek Cypriot feeling, or 'public opinion' (a preferred term within the British and colonial governments), was deemed ineffective, slow, often even unavailing, by the very same people that were responsible for it. The propaganda organization was permanently underfunded, usually disorganized and seldom 'aggressive' as it was intended by British propagandists. Propaganda and psychological warfare staff for Cyprus was coming and going. Strategy formulation was left to military men such as Governor Harding. Recommendations designed by experts in psychological warfare, such as Leslie Glass, were overruled by officials in London who did not have immediate experience of the conditions in Cyprus.

Although information on British propaganda techniques was being requested by the colonial government, especially at the beginning of the Cyprus Emergency, very often this information came with the excuse that there was 'no guarantee that what has been tried with success in one part of the world will succeed in another'.[2] Throughout the 1950s, British officials aired their grievances in secret and confidential correspondence regarding the issue of access to information. They felt that in order to deal efficiently with the emergency conditions in Cyprus the colonial government had to have access to information on British counter-insurgency practices during the empire's 'small-wars'. Some London officials believed that the general course of British counter-insurgency operations in the various territories of the empire followed a similar pattern and that Cyprus was no exception to this rule.

Others however had the exact opposite opinion. For example, K. J. Neale, Secretary for the Interior and Local Government, wrote: 'We usually drew a blank or had to rely on failing memories' during activities for Cyprus.[3] As a result, the colonial government, even though desperate to draw on previous experience in other settings, could not do this to the extent it wanted to because it rarely had the information needed in a readily available form. Instead, this hypothetically valuable information got 'buried in dormant files' in London, and familiar problems in different operating theatres were being treated *de novo*. For example, as was admitted:

> When the Emergency was declared in Kenya, that Government [the Kenya colonial government] set about its problems of detention, propaganda, rehabilitation, etc. as if they were new and strange phenomena. Cyprus in turn did much the same thing. I do not think that this was the fault of either Government. It was merely that the experience gained in Malaya was nowhere summarised in a form available for reference. Cyprus, in turn, suffered from lack of any systematic collation of experience gained in Kenya.[4]

Even when useful information was exchanged Governor Harding's regime failed in making effective use of this previous experience.[5] Halfway into the revolt, what was perceived as lacking was a distillation of the British experience gained in Malaya, Kenya and Cyprus on matters such as intelligence organization, information machinery, interment and rehabilitation problems, so that this experience was 'digested' for 'future use in similar situations'.[6] As seen through this study, applying several borrowed propaganda methods from other colonial settings such as voice aircraft and leaflet dissemination did not have the desirable effect on the Greek Cypriot audience.

From the archival evidence gathered for this study, it becomes evident that despite the current vogue for transnational history, in the case of the Cyprus episode, there were clear limits on borrowing and flows of ideas between different colonial settings. Therefore it is attested here that decolonization was less 'connected' than some of the recent historiography might lead us to believe. Nevertheless, more detailed, comparative studies on the Cyprus Emergency and other emergencies should be performed in the future, using the archival material that has become accessible (e.g. Migrated Archives) but also material of the colonized in its native language, in order to better test and better inform the above statement, open new pathways for research and produce new knowledge.

Foreign Office and Colonial Office administrators who were often in disagreement with those in the field had usually the upper hand in the decision-making process regarding issues in the colony even though these issues were not experienced at first hand. Even more than that, Cyprus officials were often in the dark about the future of the island, often staying out of the loop, inadequately getting informed by the metropole, such as Governor Harding, the strongest of examples. Harding, in a constant debate on the future of the island, between Cyprus, London, Athens, Ankara, Washington, in a whirlwind of diverse opinions from people in the field, from the metropole and abroad, from people representing various departments of the crumbling empire, such as the Colonial Office, the Foreign Office, his own colonial government, and British embassies, and while battling with his own preconceived notions of the Greek Cypriots and his experiences of other foreign rebellious populations in faraway lands, while carrying the baggage of the sins of previous colonial governments of Cyprus, while being constantly worried about what people were going to say (international public opinion) and constrained by decisions of men in higher places and by the confusion and insecurity of his collaborators on the ground, was in no position to re-impose order 'in a place where the law had ceased to function'.[7] The efforts of the colonial government therefore were uncoordinated, decentralized and were lacking effective and site-specific direction from London.

Importantly, British propaganda in Cyprus had no message, no attractive political alternative to the possibility of and desire for *enosis*. This is explained by the fact that the British government was, for the most part of the 1950s, undecided about the future of the island. More often than not, colonial propaganda policy was based on half-truths and suppositions rather than on a solid plan for the future of Cyprus. Therefore, the British/colonial government had nothing convincing to say to its Cypriot target audience or indeed to the 'world' that could appear credible or appealing. In conjunction to this, the British venture to project Britain's national image in Cyprus arguably offered too little too late. In belatedly acknowledging propaganda as a significant instrument of colonial policy, the British colonial government could not succeed in persuading the Greek Cypriots that their future lay with Britain when armed conflict finally stepped into the breach.

Local public opinion was geared towards EOKA and its liberation struggle. Furthermore, as it was understood by some colonial officials in Cyprus, 'the gimmicks of what is termed psychological warfare are ineffective against a people which is well accustomed to conventional mass communications media and which in any case has already decided what it wants and what it wants to know'.[8] A report on propaganda for Cyprus noted: 'To a tropical savage the *deus ex machina* might well be an awe-inspiring ju-ju, but not to the comparatively sophisticated Cypriot'.[9] On the contrary, as it was admitted in official correspondence 'EOKA's grip over the population has never been loosened'.[10] Their overarching conclusion: 'In Cyprus itself the battle for men's minds was lost before the British really entered it.'[11]

Propaganda was a significant aspect of the pro-*enosis* coalition between EOKA, Archbishop Makarios and Greece. For example, this can be seen in General Grivas claim in his memoirs, where he took pride in the fact that he had a 'deep understanding of Cypriot psychology' and a '"sense of war" – the quality of judgment that brings correct decisions in moments of crisis'.[12] What was also fascinating to discover during this research is that during the war of propaganda for Cyprus, even though the propaganda methods used by General Grivas and Archbishop Makarios were more basic than those used by the British colonial government, in the sense that the Greek Cypriot side did not use modern technology in contrast to the colonial government (television, voice aircraft etc.), in their simplicity, methods such as PEKA's leaflets and word of mouth were highly effective given the specific conditions and infrastructure of the Cypriot society.

The colonial government, in realizing that it was losing the propaganda war, could not act efficiently in order to suppress it as quickly and effectively as possible. More often than not it reacted spasmodically, for example by producing forged leaflets, by jamming Athens Radio, by censoring the local press or through undiplomatic moves, such as exiling the Greek Cypriot political leader, Archbishop Makarios. However, it was not only because of reactive propaganda measures that a negative result was brought upon British attempts in persuading the Greek Cypriot audience and to a large extent the international audience as well.

It has been a main argument of this study that coercion in conjunction to propaganda jointly contributed to the Greek Cypriots' mounting feeling of dissatisfaction and frustration against the colonial government. A 'crisis of trust' as Robert Holland called it, or the 'splitting of sympathy' in Leslie Glass's words, was the result of a policy of coercion and violence in Cyprus, under the auspices of Governor Harding, targeting EOKA and by extension the Greek Cypriot people. David French and other historians' argument of 'wholesale coercion' has been debated here, and its refocusing has been suggested as archival evidence shows that propaganda, and its more aggressive name in times of conflict 'psychological warfare', was also a significant factor adjunct to coercion.[13]

As Martin Thomas aptly writes: 'Violent decolonization was always as much a struggle for minds as for territory.'[14] In Cyprus, 'hearts and minds' were being coerced as much as they were being courted. This discovery further challenges the pervasiveness of the 'winning hearts and minds' doctrine and further de-mythologizes it. Recycled violent and repressive tactics from the Malaya and Kenya emergencies, from Ireland and Palestine (curfews, incarcerations, interrogation etc.), resulted in the gradual and complete alienation of the Greek Cypriot public, leading to open hostility.[15] However, it was not only British measures that instigated the people's reaction against the colonial government. This research has shown that 'the split[ting]' came gradually and well before armed conflict erupted. Before the commencement of the revolt, Athens Radio, the Greek press and the *Ethnarchy*'s persuasive rhetoric were decisively paving the way towards a collective rebellion.

After three years in the revolt, British propaganda considerations of 1955 remained considerations and did not turn into 'lessons-learned' as colonial propagandists hoped. Instead, the official correspondence on the issue of propaganda for Cyprus was replete with the usual rhetoric of 'considering and recommending', stressing on the 'paramount importance' of external briefing in modern times, where international fora such as the UN and the Council of Europe were habitually resorting to 'for the ventilation of views', for example on popular topics such as colonialism.[16] Britain's prestige and reputation, as highlighted by the country's Oversea Information Services throughout the 1950s, depended on colonial perceptions of British rule, in other words what people thought of Britain.

International public opinion was formulated based on an image of Britain and of her relation to her colonies, exported by the media, the press and by word of mouth. In secret official correspondence it was discussed over and over again that external briefing of international fora was inadequate. This was attributed to the London government's 'innate aversion to propaganda and shrink from publicity'.[17] Propaganda was considered a 'dirty game' that the government was not willing to play publically.[18] Although publicity material was prepared for use abroad and in Cyprus, this was repeatedly being 'pigeon-holed' or ineffectually released in London, whereas in Cyprus it did not find the desirable response or effect in its attempt to win over the Greek Cypriot public.

The British government, therefore, was losing the support of international public opinion in regard to the issue of Cyprus, largely because of its own fault, and not solely because of the success of the propaganda mounted by the enemy side (Archbishop Makarios's 'enlightenment campaigns' abroad etc.). For example, for most of the time during the Cyprus revolt, the colonial government's, and in extension the British government's, public image was also being affected by a vocal, even aggressive British opposition opposing to their policies. Governor Harding's ways in counter-insurgency were heavily criticized in Britain, but also in the United States and elsewhere, finally obliging him to resign from the position of the governor on 22 October 1957.

The primary and secondary material dealing with the four-year period of the Cyprus revolt is replete with allegations, accusations and incriminations exchanged between EOKA and the colonial and British governments. It has been challenging, but rewarding to cross-reference the available archival evidence, which to its largest extent has not been seen before. Much of it has only recently become available through the declassification of many colonial files pertaining to the modern history of Britain's colonies, in this case Cyprus. More information on propaganda in Cyprus during the revolt was also found, not in the historiography, but in private accounts of people who were in Cyprus during the period in question and later decided to publish their experiences, for example Martin Bell's autobiography *The End of Empire: The Cyprus Emergency: A Soldier's Story* (2015) and Costas Montis's novella *Closed Door* (1964). These are only two examples of non-academic publications that contain primary evidence for academic analysis. Therefore, there is abundance of material that waits to be explored.

What also emerges from this research is the issue of 'parallel monologues' found not only in the primary material as observed above, but also in the Greek/Greek Cypriot and British historiographies on Cyprus at the end of empire.[19] 'Parallel monologues' is a term coined by the Greek Cypriot historian Paschalis M. Kitromilides. Kitromilides emphasizes 'the partitocracy that shapes the historiography' on the topic. The existing, though limited, academic research dealing with propaganda and counter-propaganda in Cyprus during the EOKA campaign is often limited to the analysis or often the mere identification and referencing of either British archival sources, or Greek and Greek Cypriot accounts. In doing so, two polarized perspectives are created, the one largely dismissing the other. One of course cannot underestimate language barriers which render them unable to delve into comparative studies of the available untranslated material of both sides. However, in future research, this barrier should be openly acknowledged as a limitation, rather than consciously or obliviously, being brushed under the carpet.

Therefore, accepting the existence of a different or an expanded narrative should be the first step towards an attempt to write a more informed history, through a collaborative, bi-level, if not multi-level, investigation.[20] For example, as established in this book, David French's recent argument on the use of 'wholesale coercion' instead of 'hearts and minds' during the British counter-insurgency campaign pre-exists in the Greek Cypriot/Greek primary material of the 1950s and also in some of the secondary material, both in the Greek language. This material in Greek has been largely missing from the historiography on the topic in English due to language barriers in the research process. Consequently, comparative studies on the Cyprus revolt/emergency are needed in order to produce more accurate historical knowledge.

This book has reconstructed the history of propaganda in Cyprus at the end of empire, focusing on the Greek Cypriot anti-colonial revolt against the British ruler, 1955–1959. It has analysed the propaganda deployed by both the British and the Greek Cypriot/Greek sides and has argued that propaganda played a catalytic role in the development and final outcome of the revolt. The book has identified the propaganda media used by the two rivals, who each intended to persuade their respective local Greek Cypriot and international audiences that they offered a better future for Cyprus. It has analysed the use of sound (radio, voice aircraft), print (newspapers, publications, leaflets), vision (television, cinema) and clandestine propaganda media. At the same time it has looked at the perceived importance of 'public opinion' and at the issue of what one contemporary called 'the splitting of sympathy' between the Greek Cypriots and the British due to the use of coercion by the colonial regime and the EOKA guerrilla organization. The significance of personal agency has been emphasized by focusing on the various protagonists involved in the conflict and examining the ways in which these individuals and groups shaped policy through their ambitions, plans and expectations about propaganda for the future of Cyprus. Propaganda has been established as a vital aspect of the history of the Cyprus revolt. The study has intervened in wider debates about propaganda and the end of empire. Through an investigation of bilateral uses of propaganda it brought new insight into British counter-insurgency tactics and into the Greek Cypriot response to the revolt. It also drew attention to the ways in which those tactics were successfully undermined by the Greek Cypriot/Greek side and, even more interestingly, unintentionally weakened by the British themselves. Finally, it has aimed in shifting the focus of the current historiography away from an overwhelming emphasis on the use of 'wholesale coercion', by arguing that propaganda was, along with coercion, the joint driver of the conflict for Cyprus.

Notes

Chapter 1

1   The 'Cyprus Emergency', as it is most commonly called in the Anglophone historiography, or the 'Cyprus struggle' as it is called in popular Cypriot and Greek histories, or the 'Cyprus revolt', a more moderate term used by a diversity of researchers, came to an end in March 1959 shortly before the island's independence. Independence was a result which ran contrary to the goal of EOKA, the National Organization of Cypriot Fighters, which was liberation from British rule but also *enosis* (political union) with Greece.

2   John M. MacKenzie, *Propaganda and Empire: The Manipulation of British Public Opinion 1880–1960* (Manchester: Manchester University Press, 1984), p. 3.

3   Simon J. Potter, 'Propaganda and Empire', in *The Encyclopedia of Empire*, ed. by John M. MacKenzie (New Jersey: John Wiley & Sons, Ltd., 2016), 1–6 (p. 5) (http://onlinelibrary.wiley.com/doi/10.1002/9781118455074.wbeoe086/full) [26 March 2019].

4   Potter, 'Propaganda and Empire', p. 5.

5   Lawrence Durrell, *Bitter Lemons of Cyprus* (London: Faber & Faber, 1957), p. 157.

6   Erik Linstrum, *Ruling Minds: Psychology in the British Empire* (Cambridge, MA; London: Harvard University Press, 2016), pp. 217–218.

7   Linstrum, *Ruling Minds*, p. 218.

8   Susan Carruthers, '"Mischief in the Air": Cyprus: EOKA and the Struggle for Enosis, 1955–59', in *Winning Hearts and Minds: British Governments, the Media and Colonial Counter-insurgency 1944–1960* (London; New York: Leicester University Press, 1995), pp. 194–259. Although Carruthers's interest in the 'Cyprus Emergency' was confined to her 1995 book chapter, her book *The Media at War: Communication and Conflict in the Twentieth Century* (Basingstoke: Palgrave Macmillan, 2000) is also noteworthy as it provides an exploration on how wars have been reported, interpreted and perpetuated from the dawn of the media age to the present digital era.

9   Ian Cobain, 'Britain's Secret Wars', *The Guardian*, 8 September 2016 (https://www.theguardian.com/uk-news/2016/sep/08/britains-secret-wars-oman) [26 March 2019].

10 David French, *The British Way in Counter-insurgency, 1945–1967* (Oxford; New York: Oxford University Press, January 2011) (https://www.worldcat.org/title/british-way-in-counter-insurgency-1945-1967/oclc/751726089) [3 April 2017].

11 Robert F. Holland, *Britain and the Revolt in Cyprus, 1954–1959* (Oxford: Clarendon, 1998), p. 70.

12 Andrew Mumford, *The Counter-insurgency Myth: The British Experience of Irregular Warfare* (Milton Park, Abingdon, OX; New York: Routledge, 2012), p. 2.

13 See for example Simon J. Potter's journal article 'Strengthening the Bonds of the Commonwealth: The Imperial Relations Trust and Australian, New Zealand and Canadian Broadcasting Personnel in Britain, 1946–1952', on the flow of media professionals moving back and forth between Britain, Canada, Australia and New Zealand subtly influencing the shape of journalism and broadcasting around the British world during the mid-twentieth century. *Media History*, 11:3 (2005), 193–205.

14 The phrase 'law and order' is used extensively in the official colonial correspondence, most prominently in Governor Harding's correspondence with other colonial officials such as John Reddaway and Lawrence Durrell. For example, TNA FCO 141/3794, Lawrence Durrell, letter to John Reddaway, 10 November 1955. The phrase 'British connection' is used in the reports of the Committees for the British Oversea Information Services, for example: TNA CAB 129/87/41 "Oversea Information Services", 18 June 1957, Introduction, point 5. It is also used by John Reddaway, Cyprus's head propagandist during the revolt, in his book *Burdened with Cyprus: The British Connection* (London; Nicosia; Istanbul: Weidenfeld & Nicolson, 1986).

15 Although one can find in the academic literature comparative studies between other Emergencies, usually Cyprus is absent from the list. It is absent even from recent publications such as *British Propaganda and Wars of Empire: Influencing Friend and Foe 1900–2010*, ed. by Greg Kennedy and Christopher Tuck (Surrey, UK; Burlington, VT, USA: Ashgate, 2014). A notable exception is Brian Drohan's chapter "'A Litigious Island": Law, Rights, and Counter-insurgency during the Cyprus Emergency', in *Decolonization and Conflict Colonial Comparisons and Legacies*, ed. by Martin Thomas and Gareth Curless (London: Bloomsbury Academic, 2017), pp. 99–114.

16 Potter, 'Propaganda and Empire', p. 5.

17 Imperial War Museum, *Harding Papers*, Francis Noel-Baker to Lady Harding, 29 May 1956.

18 For example: Alexis Rappas, 'The Transnational Formation of Imperial Rule on the Margins of Europe: British Cyprus and the Italian Dodecanese in the Interwar Period', *European History Quarterly*, 45:3 (2015), 467–505; Rappas, 'The Elusive Polity: Imagining and Contesting Colonial Authority in Cyprus during the 1930s', *Journal of Modern Greek Studies* 26:2 (October 2008), 363–397; Rappas, 'Greeks under European Colonial Rule: National Allegiance and Imperial Loyalty', *Byzantine and Modern Greek Studies*, 34:2 (2010), 201–218; Panayiotis Persianis, 'British Colonial Higher Education Policy-making in the 1930s: The Case of a

Plan to Establish a University in Cyprus', *Compare: A Journal of Comparative and International Education*, 33:3 (2003), 351–368; Persianis, 'The British Colonial Education "Lending" Policy in Cyprus (1878–1960): An Intriguing Example of an Elusive "Adapted Education" Policy', *Comparative Education*, 32:1 (1996), 45–68; Antigone Heraclidou, 'Politics of Education and Language in Cyprus and Malta during the Inter-war Years', *Journal of Mediterranean Studies*, 23:1 (2014), 75–89.

19 Mumford, *The Counter-insurgency Myth*, p. 3.

20 Linstrum, *Ruling Minds*, p. 1.

21 Linstrum, *Ruling Minds*, p. 1.

22 Linstrum, *Ruling Minds*, p. 2.

23 Robert Holland and Diana Markides, *The British and the Hellenes: Struggles for Mastery in the Eastern Mediterranean 1850–1960* (Oxford: Oxford University Press, 2006). This book includes the chapter 'Mastery and Despair: Cyprus, 1931–1960'. The book offers an expanded view on the modern history of the region, by developing a comparative overview of Britain's engagements with the modern Hellenic experience, looking at the interaction between internal and external forces that shaped the futures of divided island societies, such as Cyprus. The authors provide an original insight into the political and social morphology of the eastern Mediterranean in relation to British authority overseas and its limits, identifying it as a region that has been traditionally neglected; however, it has also been traditionally significant in world power politics. Holland revisits and expands on this topic in the article 'Patterns of Anglo-Hellenism: A "Colonial" Connection?' where he explored the issue of the ambiguity of Britain's involvement in Cyprus and argued that this was crucial to the eventual erosion of Britain's leading position in the Mediterranean region. 'Patterns of Anglo-Hellenism: A "Colonial" Connection?' *The Journal of Imperial and Commonwealth History*, 36:3 (2008) 383–396 (p. 391).

24 Persianis, 'British Colonial Higher Education Policy-making in the 1930s'; Persianis, 'The British Colonial Education "Lending" Policy in Cyprus (1878–1960)'.

25 Linstrum, *Ruling Minds*, p. 5.

26 Linstrum, *Ruling Minds*, p. 217.

27 Harry Luke, *Cyprus: A Portrait and an Appreciation* (London: Roy Publishers, 1957); TNA BW 26/1, British Council's Activities in Cyprus, 1946.

28 For example, how it dealt with the realities of the Cold War and growing tension in the Middle East, by briefly offering to concede self-determination for the Cypriots, however, 'without really meaning it, at least not for the foreseeable future'. Diana Markides, 'Britain's "New Look" Policy for Cyprus and the Makarios–Harding Talks, January 1955–March 1956', *The Journal of Imperial and Commonwealth History*, 23:3 (1995), 479–502 (p. 482). Also see Diana Markides, *Cyprus*

1957–1963: From Colonial Conflict to Constitutional Crisis: They Key Role of the Municipal Issue (Minneapolis, MN: University of Minnesota, 2001). Here Markides examines the issue of separate municipalities during the process of decolonization. The practical difficulties of the prescribed arrangements and the pressures of intracommunal domestic politics, which were exacerbated by an injection of Cold War priorities and misleading diplomatic initiatives, contributed to the failure to find a mutually acceptable formula. A series of attempts to do so exposed the more substantial differences regarding sovereignty and the limitations on the political power of the majority. Markides argued that the failure to resolve the municipal issue was bound to contain the seeds of the unravelling of the Zurich and London Agreements by which Cyprus had gained its precarious independence.

29 Markides, 'Britain's "New Look" Policy for Cyprus', p. 501.

30 Rory Cormac, *Confronting the Colonies: British Intelligence and Counterinsurgency* (London: Hurst Publishers, 2013). See especially his chapter 'Turf Wars and Tension: Cyprus, 1955–1995' which focuses on the example of Cyprus. Cormac's earlier article, 'Organizing Intelligence: An Introduction to the 1955 Report on Colonial Security', *Intelligence and National Security*, 25:6 (2010), pp. 800–822, published selected extracts from chapter one of the Report on Colonial Security, which dealt specifically with intelligence organization both in London and overseas. Written by General Sir Gerald Templer in 1955, Cormac supported that the report, particularly the intelligence aspects, is significant for the following reasons: it highlights the centralized and colonial intelligence failures in a particularly frank and candid manner, it details channels of communication and liaison between London and the colonies which remain classified elsewhere, and it had a substantial impact on the subsequent reorganization and reform of intelligence in Whitehall and across the British Empire.

31 Rory Cormac, *Disrupt and Deny: Spies, Special Forces, and the Secret Pursuit of British Foreign Policy* (Oxford: Oxford University Press, 2018), p.126.

32 Cormac, *Disrupt and Deny*, p. 142.

33 Evanthis Hatzivassiliou, 'Cold War Pressures, Regional Strategies, and Relative Decline: British Military and Strategic Planning for Cyprus, 1950–1960', *The Journal of Military History*, 73:4 (October 2009), 1143–1166 (p. 1166). In this article he focuses further on the aspect of strategy, placing the London government's post–Second World War military requirements in Cyprus within the wider context of British security policy in the eastern Mediterranean. He further deals with this in his 2006 book chapter 'British Strategic Priorities and the Cyprus Question, 1954–1958' in the collective volume *Britain in Cyprus: Colonialism and Post-colonialism 1878–2006*, ed. by Hubert Faustmann and Nicos Peristianis (Mannheim and Mohnesee, GER: Bibliopolis, 2006). Also see Hatzivassiliou, *Britain and the International Status of Cyprus, 1955–59* (Minneapolis: Minnesota Mediterranean and East European Monographs, 1997); Hatzivassiliou, *The Cyprus Question, 1878–1960: The Constitutional Aspect* (Minneapolis: Minnesota Mediterranean and East European Monographs, 2002).

34   Panagiotis Dimitrakis, *Military Intelligence in Cyprus: From the Great War to Middle East Crises* (London: Tauris Academic Studies, 2010). See also: Dimitrakis, 'British Intelligence and the Cyprus Insurgency, 1955–1959', *International Journal of Intelligence and Counter Intelligence*, 21:2 (2008), 375–394 (p. 377 and p. 390).

35   Dimitrakis, 'The Special Operations Executive and Cyprus in the Second World War', *Middle Eastern Studies*, 45:2 (2009), 315–328. Another contribution to the study of British intelligence in Cyprus is Richard J. Aldrich's book chapter 'Cyprus: The Last Foothold', in *The Hidden Hand: Britain, America and Cold War Secret Intelligence* (London: John Murray, 2002), where he presents information on covert action, mainly from secondary sources.

36   TNA FO 371/123898, Governor to Allen Lennox-Boyd, Secretary of State for the Colonies, 24 May 1956.

37   In several PEKA leaflets and also in Costas Montis, *Closed Doors* (Nicosia: Cypriot National Youth Board, 1964, in Greek).

38   Holland, a historian of the British Empire focusing on decolonization in the eastern Mediterranean, and particularly on Cyprus and Greece, has significantly expanded the historiography of modern Cyprus. Also see R. Holland and Hubert Faustmann, 'Independence Day through the Colonial Eye: A View from the British Archive', *The Cyprus Review*, 22:2 (Fall 2010), 49–60. Holland has also trained (for example as a PhD Supervisor) and collaborated with a number of historians who now belong to a new generation of Cypriot and foreign researchers. Andreas Karyos, Antigone Heraclidou, Diana Markides and Hubert Faustmann, whose work is referenced here, are some of them.

39   Robert F. Holland, *Britain and the Revolt in Cyprus, 1954–1959*. Next to this is Holland's article 'Never, Never Land …', a meticulous study of the breakdown between British administration and the majority of the Greek Cypriot population, sliding eventually into the four-year emergency. 'Never, Never Land: British Colonial Policy and the Roots of Violence in Cyprus, 1950–54', *Journal of Imperial and Commonwealth History*, 21 (1993), 148–175.

40   Holland, 'Patterns of Anglo-Hellenism: A "Colonial" Connection?' p. 394; Holland, *Britain and the Revolt in Cyprus, 1954–1959*.

41   Aaron Edwards, *Defending the Realm: The Politics of Britain's Small Wars since 1945* (Oxford: Oxford University Press, 2012), p. 145.

42   Hatzivassiliou, *Strategies of the Cyprus Struggle: The 1950s* (Athens: Patakis, 2004; in Greek), p. 244; Andreas Karyos, 'Britain and Cyprus, 1955–1959: Key Themes on the Counter-insurgency Aspects of the Cyprus Revolt', in *Great Power Politics in Cyprus: Foreign Interventions and Domestic Perceptions*, ed. by M. Kontos, S. C. Theodoulou, N. Panayiotides, H. Alexandrou (Newcastle upon Tyne: Cambridge Scholars Publishing, 2014), pp. 33–53 (p. 48).

43   Martin Thomas, *Fight or Flight: Britain, France, and Their Roads from Empire* (New York: Oxford University Press, 2014), p. 269.

44 French, 'Nasty Not Nice: British Counter-insurgency Doctrine and Practice, 1945–1967', *Small Wars & Insurgencies*, 23:4–5 (October–December 2012), 744–761; French, *The British Way in Counter-insurgency 1945–1967*.

45 David M. Anderson, 'Policing and Communal Conflict: The Cyprus Emergency, 1954–60', *Emergencies and Disorder in the European Empires after 1945*, ed. by Robert Holland (Oxford: Frank Cass, 1994), 177–207 (pp. 202–203).

46 Andrew R. Novo, 'Friend or Foe? The Cyprus Police Force and the EOKA Insurgency', *Small Wars & Insurgencies*, 23:3 (2012), 414–431 (pp. 428– 429). Novo wrote his PhD thesis on the history of the Cyprus Emergency, titled *On All Fronts: EOKA and the Cyprus Insurgency, 1955–1959* (Oxford University, 2010). Also, the journal article 'The God Dilemma: Faith, the Church, and Political Violence in Cyprus', *Journal of Modern Greek Studies*, 31:2 (October 2013), 193–215.

47 Michael Crawshaw, *The Evolution of British COIN by Colonel (retd) Michael Crawshaw* (London: Ministry of Defence and Joint Doctrine Publication, 21 December 2012) (https://www.gov.uk/government/publications/the-evolution-of-british-coin) [26 March 2019]; Robert Holland, Carl Bridge, H. V. Brasted, 'Counsels of Despair or Withdrawals with Honour?: Partitioning in Ireland, India, Palestine and Cyprus, 1920–1960', *The Round Table: The Commonwealth Journal of International Affairs*, 86:342 (1997), 257–268 (p. 261).

48 Mumford, *Puncturing the Counterinsurgency Myth: Britain and Irregular Warfare in the Past, Present, and Future* (Carlisle, PA: Strategic Studies Institute, U.S. Army War College, 2011), p. 13.

49 Thomas, *Fight or Flight*, p. 269.

50 French, 'British Intelligence and the Origins of the EOKA Insurgency', *British Journal for Military History*, 1:2 (2015), 84–100 (p. 85); Anthony Badger, 'Historians, a Legacy of Suspicion and the "Migrated Archives"', *Small Wars and Insurgencies*, 23:4–5 (September 2012), 799–807.

51 TNA FCO 141/3727, Draft Note on Propaganda, Information and Publicity, author and date unknown [possibly c.1958].

52 TNA FCO 141/3727, Draft Note on Propaganda, author and date unknown [c.1958].

53 TNA FCO 141/3727, Draft Note on Propaganda, author and date unknown [c.1958].

54 French, 'Nasty Not Nice: British Counter-insurgency Doctrine and Practice, 1945–1967', p. 756.

55 French, 'Winning Hearts and Minds', in *The British Way in Counter-insurgency, 1945–1967* (Oxford; New York: Oxford University Press, January 2011), p. 198.

56 Thomas, *Fight or Flight*, p. 271.

57 Freya Stark, *Letters. Vol. 7 Some Talk of Alexander, 1952–1959*, ed. by Caroline Moorehead (Salisbury: Michael Russell, 1982), pp. 64–65.

58 Holland, Preface, *Emergencies and Disorder in the European Empires after 1945*, ed. by Robert Holland (Oxford: Frank Cass, 1994), p. ix.

59 French, 'Nasty Not Nice'.

60 Mumford, *The Counter-insurgency Myth*, pp. 3–4.

61 Karyos, *EOKA 1955–59: A Study of the Military Aspects of the Cyprus Revolt* (PhD thesis, Institute of Commonwealth Studies, University of London, 2011); Karyos, 'Britain and Cyprus, 1955–1959: Key Themes on the Counter-insurgency Aspects of the Cyprus Revolt'.

62 Karyos, 'Britain and Cyprus, 1955–1959', p. 48.

63 Karyos, 'The Political Committee of the Cypriot Struggle (PEKA), 1956–1959: An Introductory Approach' ('*H Politikh Epitroph Kypriakou Agwna (PEKA), 1956–1959: Mia Eisagwgikh Proseggish*'), *National Guard & History* (*Ethniki Froura & Istoria*), 34 (July–December 2014), 66–77. In Greek.

64 Karyos, 'PEKA', p. 68 and p. 75.

65 Karyos, 'PEKA'; Karyos, 'Britain and Policing of the Revolt in Cyprus, April 1955–March 1956' ('*H Vrettania kai h astynomeush ths Epanastasis sthn Kypro, Aprilios 1955–Martios 1956: To Prooimio ths Klimakwshs tou Kypriakou Agwna*'), *National Guard & History* (*Ethniki Froura & Istoria*), 33 (January–June 2014), 34–51. In Greek; Karyos, 'British Archival Sources and Individual Aspects of the Cypriot Struggle: The Case of Markos Drakos' ('*Oi Vretanikes Arxeiakes Phges kai oi Epi Merous Ptuxes tou Kypriakou Agwna: H Periptwsh tou Markou Drakou*'), *National Guard & History* (*Ethniki Froura & Istoria*), 31 (January–June 2013), 74–85. In Greek.

66 Linstrum, *Ruling Minds*, p. 217.

67 Holland et al., 'Counsels of Despair or Withdrawals with Honour', p. 261.

68 Hubert Faustmann, *Divide and Quit? British Colonial Policy in Cyprus 1878–1960. Including a special Survey of the Transitional Period: February 1959 – August 1960* (Mannheim: Mateo, 1999), p. 450. Faustmann's conclusions are a very interesting diversion from the conventional academic unwillingness to deal critically with this issue, or the readiness to arbitrarily brand it as a 'conspiracy theory', or the hesitance to admit some logical extrapolations that suggest that 'divide and rule' methods were indeed used, especially during the Cyprus Emergency, due to the supposed absence of 'hard evidence'. Also see William Mallinson, *Cyprus, A Modern History* (London: I.B. Tauris, 2005); Robert Holland, 'Reviewing *Cyprus: A Modern History*. By William Mallinson', *International Affairs (Royal Institute of International Affairs 1944–)*, 81:5 (October 2005), 1152–1153; William Mallinson, 'Spies, Jolly Hockeysticks and Imperialism in Cyprus', *Journal of Balkan and Near Eastern Studies*, 3:2 (2011), 263–268.

69 Contested views on the 'divide and rule' argument do not come only from non-Cypriot researchers. An example can be found in Demetris Assos and his article

'Conspiracy Theories and the Decolonisation of Cyprus under the Weight of Historical Evidence, 1955–1959' (2011). Here, the author somewhat superficially brands Greek Cypriot popular beliefs/histories as 'conspiracy theories' in an eager and passionate, but ultimately unconvincing and limited, attempt to refute them. Calling these theories 'naïve' backfires, as his analysis at various points can also be characterized as such, for example when he claims that 'essentially the end point of independence was not the result of a British conspiracy but a case of a political strategy that went wrong resulting in unintended consequences'. A brief counterargument here could put forward the fact of the creation of the Sovereign Base Areas of Akrotiri and Dhekelia, which can hardly be characterized as 'unintended consequences'. Demetris Assos, 'Conspiracy Theories and the Decolonisation of Cyprus under the Weight of Historical Evidence, 1955–1959', *The Cyprus Review*, 23:2 (2011), 109–125 (p. 117).

70 Faustmann, *Divide and Quit? British Colonial Policy in Cyprus 1878–1960*, p. 451.

71 Markides, 'Britain's "New Look" Policy for Cyprus', p. 500.

72 Faustmann, *Divide and Quit? British Colonial Policy in Cyprus 1878–1960*, p. 451. Along with Nicos Peristianis, Faustmann also co-edited *Britain in Cyprus. Colonialism and Post-colonialism 1878–2006* (Mannheim and Mohnesee, GER: Bibliopolis, 2006), a comprehensive study in English, of the British Colonial period in Cyprus and a systematic assessment of the post-independence relations between the island and its former ruler. This collection hosted more than thirty contributions by experts providing analysis of British-Cypriot relations throughout the modern history of Cyprus. In this volume, one also finds Holland's chapter on 'The Historiography of Late Colonial Cyprus: Where Do We Go from Here?'.

73 Holland et al., 'Counsels of Despair or Withdrawals with Honour', pp. 257–268.

74 Holland et al., 'Counsels of Despair or Withdrawals with Honour', pp. 257–268.

75 Ronald Hyam, *Britain's Declining Empire: The Road to Decolonisation 1918–1968* (Cambridge: Cambridge University Press, 2006), Preface, xiii–xiv.

76 Hatzivassiliou, 'Blocking Enosis: Britain and the Cyprus Question, March–December 1956', *The Journal of Imperial and Commonwealth History*, 19:2 (1991), 247–263.

77 Thomas, *Fight or Flight*, p. 270.

78 Christopher Hitchens gives a more damning account on Britain's policy in Cyprus in his provocative book *Hostage to History: Cyprus from the Ottomans to Kissinger*, where he examines power-misconduct and the events leading up to the partition of Cyprus and its legacy, arguing that the intervention of four major foreign powers, Turkey, Greece, Britain and the United States, turned a local dispute into a disaster, namely the Turkish invasion of 1974. *Hostage to History: Cyprus from the Ottomans to Kissinger* (London; New York: Verso, 1997).

79 Rebecca Bryant, 'An Aesthetics of Self: Moral Remaking and Cypriot Education', *Comparative Studies in Society and History*, 41:3 (2001), 583–614.

80 Bryant, 'An Aesthetics of Self', p. 584.
81 Bryant, 'An Aesthetics of Self', p. 605. Also by Bryant: 'Justice or Respect? A Comparative Perspective on Politics in Cyprus Ethnic and Racial Studies', *Ethnic and Racial Studies*, 24:6 (2001), 892–924. Here she further develops this argument, using the case of Cyprus to demonstrate that in this divided island democracy has been imagined as a freedom defined ethnically – as freedom for a particular group, the Greek Cypriots and Turkish Cypriots respectively. Furthermore, in her co-edited book with Yiannis Papadakis *Cyprus and the Politics of Memory: History, Community and Conflict* (London; New York: I.B. Tauris, 2012) one finds 'A Critical Comparison of Greek Cypriot and Turkish Cypriot Official Historiographies (1940 to the Present)'. Also, her book chapter 'Disciplining Ethnicity and Citizenship in Colonial Cyprus', in *Manufacturing Citizenship: Education and Nationalism in Europe, South Asia and China* (Oxford: Routledge, 2005), pp. 104–126.
82 Petros Papapolyviou, *Propaganda – Counterpropaganda: Liberation Struggle 1955-1959*, ed. by Charalambos Alexandrou (Nicosia: Cyprus State Archive, 2013, Greek edition, Catalogue) p. 8. Original Greek text translated to English by Maria Hadjiathanasiou.
83 *Archbishop Makarios III Foundation – Cultural Centre* (http://www.makarios foundation.org.cy/13.html) [28 March 2017].

Chapter 2

1 TNA FCO 141/4168, Armitage to Secretary of State for the Colonies, 12 August 1955.
2 Some examples of the historiography on the Church of Cyprus and Archbishop Makarios III include Andrekos Varnava and Michalis N. Michael, 'Archbishops-Ethnarchs since 1767', in *The Archbishops of Cyprus in the Modern Age: The Changing Role of the Archbishop-Ethnarch, Their Identities and Politics*, ed. by Andrekos Varnava and Michalis N. Michael (Newcastle upon Tyne: Cambridge Scholars Publishing, 2013), 240–293; Sia Anagnostopoulou, 'Makarios III, 1950–77: Creating the *Ethnarchic* state', ibid.; Demetris Assos, *Makarios: A Study of Anti-colonial Nationalist Leadership, 1950–1959* (PhD thesis, Institute of Commonwealth Studies, University of London, 2009); P. N. Vanezis, *Makarios: Faith and Power* (London: Abelard-Schuman, 1971); Also by P. N. Vanezis, *Makarios: Pragmatism v. Idealism* (London: Abelard-Schuman, 1974) and *Makarios: Life and Leadership* (London: Abelard-Schuman, 1979); Theodore Papadopoullos, 'Orthodox Church and Civil Authority', *Journal of Contemporary History*, 2:201 (1967), 201–209.
3 TNA FCO 141/4168, Top Secret report, 'The Application of Psychological Warfare to the Cyprus Question', Cyprus Intelligence Committee, 3 June 1955.

4   SIMAE E 200/7/2 (TNA CO 926/490), Governor to S. of S., copies sent to M.I.5,
    M.I.6, 1 December 1956. Here Harding gives his considerations on what legislative
    and administrative action had to be taken to diminish the political power of the
    Church. The phrase 'Seditious utterances' in the title of this chapter is taken from
    this telegram.

5   Stark to John Grey Murray, Kyrenia, 2 February 1952, in Stark, *Letters. Vol. 7*,
    pp. 64–65.

6   CSA SA1/567/1931, Director of Education Report 'Education in Cyprus', Red 12–11.

7   The EOKA Oath. 'I swear in the name of the Holy Trinity that: 1. I shall work
    with all my power for the liberation of Cyprus from the British yoke, sacrificing
    for this even my life. 2. I shall perform without question all the instructions of the
    organisation which may be entrusted to me and I shall not bring any objection,
    however difficult and dangerous these may be. 3. I shall not abandon the struggle
    unless I receive instructions from the leader of the organisation and after our
    aim has been accomplished. 4. I shall never reveal to anyone any secret of our
    organisation neither the names of my chiefs nor those of the other members of
    the organization even if I am caught and tortured. 5. I shall not reveal any of the
    instructions which may be given me even to my fellow combatants. If I disobey
    my oath I shall be worthy of every punishment as a traitor and may eternal
    contempt cover me.' Signed EOKA. The original Greek text was translated into
    English by Lawrence Durrell. The translation given here is included in his book
    Bitter Lemons.

8   TNA FO 371/112871, Savvas N. Rialas to Governor, 18 June 1953.

9   The *Ethnarchy*'s '"enlightenment" campaign'. TNA FO 371/123898, Governor to S.
    of S., 24 May 1956.

10 SGM Herbert A. Friedman (Ret.) and Brigadier General Ioannis Paschalidis,
    'Cyprus 1954–1959', *Psywarrior* (http://www.psywarrior.com/cyprus.html) [26
    March 2019].

11 TNA FCO 141/4280, Report by Superintendent of Police to Senior Assistant
    Secretary, 28 October 1954.

12 TNA FCO 141/4280, Report by Superintendent of Police to Senior Assistant
    Secretary, 28 October 1954.

13 TNA FO 371/123898, Governor to S. of S., 24 May 1956.

14 TNA FO 371/112874, Peake to Young, 4 November 1954.

15 SIMAE E 206, 'The Church and Terrorism in Cyprus: A Record of the Complicity
    of the Greek-Orthodox Church of Cyprus in Political Violence', Secret publication
    for official use only, Author unknown, revised ed. 15 December 1956.

16 SIMAE E 206, 'The Church and Terrorism in Cyprus'.

17 SIMAE E 206, 'The Church and Terrorism in Cyprus'.

18 General George Grivas, *The Memoirs of General Grivas*, ed. by Charles Foley
    (London: Longmans, 1964).

19 Grivas, Preparatory General Plan, *Cyprus Conflict Organisation* (http://www. cyprus-conflict.org/materials/generalplan.html) [14 June 2017].

20 Grivas, Preparatory General Plan.

21 Grivas, Preparatory General Plan.

22 TNA FO 371/112871, Savvas N. Rialas to Governor, 18 June 1953.

23 Grivas, Preparatory General Plan.

24 Grivas, Preparatory General Plan.

25 Grivas, Preparatory General Plan.

26 Grivas, Preparatory General Plan.

27 Grivas, *Memoirs*, p. 47.

28 Grivas, *Memoirs*, p. 47.

29 French, *Fighting EOKA: The British Counter-insurgency Campaign on Cyprus, 1955–59* (Oxford: Oxford University Press, 2015), p. 171.

30 TNA FO 371/112869/1081/814, Request for Glass's possible visit along with Ankara's Information Officer, 11 October 1954; FO 371/112869/1081/844, 15 October 1954; FO 371/117641/1081/606 Personal message for Glass in Beirut. Governor Armitage requests Glass to visit Cyprus to discuss the present situation, 7 July 1955.

31 TNA FO 371/112869/1081/814.

32 TNA FCO 141/4168, Sykes to Peck, 27 June 1955.

33 TNA FCO 141/4168, Act. Deputy Colonial Secretary to Act. Colonial Secretary, 'Psychological Warfare', 18 July 1955, Secret Minute.

34 TNA FCO 141/4168.

35 TNA FCO 141/4168, Sykes to Director of Information Services; Controller, CBS, 25 July 1955.

36 TNA FCO 141/4168, Note to Governor, 16 July 1955.

37 TNA FCO 141/4168.

38 TNA FCO 141/4168, Act. D.C.S. to Act. Colonial Secretary, 'Psychological Warfare', 18 July 1955, Secret Minute.

39 TNA FCO 141/4168, Secret note 'Publicity and Propaganda on the Cyprus Problem' to Governor, 16 July 1955.

40 Cormac, *Confronting the Colonies*, p. 79.

41 TNA FCO 141/4168.

42 Edwards, *Defending the Realm*, p. 129.

43 Unknown author, 'Compromise on Cyprus', *The Spectator,* 18 August 1955, *The Spectator* Online Archive (http://archive.spectator.co.uk/article/19th-august-1955/3/compromise-on-cyprus) [6 March 2017]; TNA FCO 141/4168, Secret note 'Publicity and Propaganda on the Cyprus Problem' to Governor, 16 July 1955.

44 'Compromise on Cyprus'.

45 TNA FCO 141/4168, Governor to Colonial Secretary, 25 July 1955.

46 TNA FCO 141/4168.

47 TNA FCO 141/4168, Armitage to Secretary of State for the Colonies, 12 August 1955.

48 TNA FCO 141/4168, Governor to Colonial Secretary, 25 July 1955.

49 TNA FCO 141/4168.

50 *Enotist* = ενωτικός (GR) / unionist. In this case those who were in support of union with Greece.

51 TNA FCO 141/4168, Governor to Colonial Secretary, 25 July 1955.

52 TNA FCO 141/4168.

53 TNA FCO 141/4168, Act. Colonial Secretary to Governor, 27 July 1955.

54 TNA FCO 141/4168.

55 TNA FCO 141/4168, Governor to Colonial Secretary, 25 July 1955.

56 TNA FCO 141/4168, Act. Colonial Secretary to Governor, 27 July 1955.

57 TNA FCO 141/4168, Act. Colonial Secretary to Governor, 27 July 1955.

58 TNA FCO 141/4168.

59 TNA FCO 141/4168, Armitage to S. of S., 12 August 1955.

60 TNA FCO 141/4168.

61 TNA FCO 141/4168.

62 TNA FCO 141/4168.

63 TNA FCO 141/4168.

64 TNA FCO 141/4168, Armitage to S. of S., 12 August 1955.

65 Cormac, *Disrupt and Deny*, p. 142.

66 TNA FCO 141/4168.

67 TNA FCO 141/4168, Act. Colonial Secretary to Governor, 27 July 1955.

68 TNA FCO 141/4168, Reddaway to Colonial Secretary, 15 August 1955.

69 TNA FCO 141/4168.

70 TNA FCO 141/4168, Reddaway to Colonial Secretary, 15 August 1955.

71 TNA FCO 141/4168, Secret 'General Directive for the Propaganda Services', The Secretariat, October 1955.

72 TNA FCO 141/4168.

73 TNA FCO 141/4168.

74 TNA FCO 141/4168, Secret 'General Directive for the Propaganda Services', The Secretariat, October 1955.

75 TNA FCO 141/4168.

76 TNA FCO 141/4168, Secret 'General Directive for the Propaganda Services', The Secretariat, October 1955.

77 TNA FCO 141/4168, Secret 'General Directive for the Propaganda Services', The Secretariat, October 1955.

78 TNA FCO 141/4168.

79 TNA FCO 141/3727, Draft Note on Propaganda, author and date unknown [c.1958].

80   TNA FCO 141/4168, Act. D.C.S. to Act. Colonial Secretary, 'Psychological Warfare', 18 July 1955.

81   TNA FCO 141/3727, Reddaway to Cruikshank, 26 September 1955.

82   TNA FCO 141/3727, Cruikshank to Reddaway, 8 October 1955.

83   TNA FCO 141/3727.

84   TNA FCO 141/3727, S. Harold Evans, Head of Information Department to Reddaway, 10 October 1955.

85   TNA FCO 141/3727, Evans to Reddaway, 10 October 1955.

86   TNA FCO 141/3727.

87   TNA FCO 141/3727.

88   TNA FCO 141/3727, Reddaway to Evans, 25 October 1955.

89   TNA FCO 141/3727, Reddaway to Cruikshank, 26 September 1955.

90   TNA FCO 141/3727, Reddaway to Evans, 25 October 1955.

91   TNA FCO 141/3727, Reddaway to Glass, 28 November 1955.

92   TNA FCO 141/3727.

93   TNA FCO 141/3727.

94   Durrell to Alan G. Thomas, Belapaix, 14 March 1954, in *Spirit of Place: Letters and Essays on Travel*, ed. by Alan G. Thomas (London: Faber and Faber Ltd., 1969), p. 124.

95   Durrell, 'Letters of Lawrence Durrell to Austen Harrison', ed. by David Roessel. *Deus Loci* magazine, NS3 (1994), p. 22.

96   Hubert Juin, 'Letting the Reader Loose on the Work', in Lawrence Durrell, *Lawrence Durrell: Conversations*, ed. by Earl G. Ingersoll (New Jersey: Fairleigh Dickinson University Press, 1998), p. 40. 'Letting the Reader Loose on the Work' is a translation of the conversation, 'Paroles Avec Lawrence Durrell', that appeared in *Les Lettres Françaises* (Paris) 17 December 1959.

97   Maurice Cardiff, *Friends Abroad: Memories of Patrick Leigh-Fermor, Lawrence Durrell, Peggy Gugenheim, Freya Stark and Others* (London; New York: Radcliffe Press, 1997), p. 25.

98   Durrell to Freya Stark, 1954, Press and Information Office, Nicosia, in Lawrence Durrell, *Spirit of Place*, p. 126.

99   Cardiff, *Friends Abroad*, pp. 28–29.

100 Maria Guadalupe Flores Liera, 'The Writer – British Crown Spy' [in Greek], *Mignatiou.com* (http://mignatiou.com/2014/09/osingrafeaskataskopostouvretanikoustemmatos/) [28 January 2015] in Greek.

101 TNA FCO 141/3794, Durrell, Memo to Heads of Departments, 18 January 1956.

102 Jonathan Stubbs, 'Lawrence Durrell and the Information Services Department in Cyprus', *Deus Loci: The Lawrence Durrell Journal*, 14 (2015), p. 1.

103 Durrell, *Bitter Lemons*, p. 158.

104 TNA FCO 141/4168, Secret note 'Publicity and Propaganda on the Cyprus Problem' to Governor, 16 July 1955; Durrell to Colonial Secretary, 27 July 1955.

105 Durrell, *Bitter Lemons*, p. 158.

106 Rita Severis, '*Although to Sight Lost, to Memory Dear*': *Representations of Cyprus by Foreign Travellers/Artists 1700–1955*, Vol. 1 (PhD thesis, University of Bristol, 1999), p. 233.

107 Durrell to Freya Stark, 31 March 1955, PIO Nicosia, Cyprus, in Lawrence Durrell, *Spirit of Place*, pp. 127–128.

108 Aaron Edwards, *Defending the Realm*, p. 131.

109 TNA FCO 141/3794, Durrell, Memo, 13 December 1954; Stubbs, 'Lawrence Durrell and the Information Services Department in Cyprus', p. 1.

110 Cardiff, *Friends Abroad*, p. 32.

111 Cardiff, *Friends Abroad*, p. 32.

112 Durrell to Alan G. Thomas, 1956, PIO. Nicosia, Cyprus, in *Spirit of Place*, p. 129; TNA FCO 141/3794.

113 TNA FCO 141/3727, Draft Note on Propaganda, author and date unknown [c.1958].

114 TNA FCO 141/3727.

115 TNA FCO 141/3727, Draft Note on Propaganda, author and date unknown [c.1958].

116 TNA FO 371/112869, Selby regarding Wilding's report, 22 November 1954.

117 TNA FO 371/112869.

118 Grivas, *Memoirs*, p. 10.

119 Grivas, *Memoirs*, p. 125.

Chapter 3

1 TNA FCO 141/3727, Draft Note on Propaganda, author and date unknown [c.1958].

2 TNA FO 371/123898, Governor to Allen Lenox-Boyd, Secretary of State for the Colonies, 24 May 1956.

3 TNA FO 371/123898, Governor to S. of S., 24 May 1956.

4 SIMAE E 209/8/1 (TNA FO 371/123899), Peake to Ward, Foreign Office on Harding's letter, 6 June 1956.

5 TNA FO 371/123898, Governor S. of S., 24 May 1956.

6 David Hunt, John [Allan Francis] Harding, first Baron Harding of Petherton (1896–1989), *Oxford Dictionary of National Biography* (http://www.oxforddnb.com/view/article/40129) [26 March 2019].

7 Brian Drohan, *Brutality in an Age of Human Rights: Activism and Counterinsurgency at the End of the British Empire* (New York: Cornell University Press, 2018), p. 20.

8 TNA FCO 141/3727, 31 May 1958.

9 SIMAE E 201/4 (TNA CO 926/546), Governor to S. of S., copies to Athens, Ankara, Washington, 23 December 1955.

10 TNA FCO 141/4168, Leslie Glass, Top Secret report 'Practicabilities for Psychological Warfare in Cyprus – January, 1959', 15 January 1959.

11 TNA FCO 141/3794, Glass to Evans, 22 December 1955.

12 TNA FCO 141/3727, Draft Note on Propaganda, author and date unknown [c.1958].

13 SIMAE E 201/4 (TNA, CO 926/546), Governor to S. of S., copies to Athens, Ankara, Washington, 23 December 1955; TNA FCO 141/3727, Draft Note on Propaganda, author and date unknown [c.1958].

14 Edwards, *Defending the Realm*, p. 131.

15 SIMAE E 201/4 (TNA, CO 926/546), Governor to S. of S., 23 December 1955.

16 TNA FCO 141/3727, Draft Note on Propaganda, author and date unknown [c.1958].

17 TNA FCO 141/3727.

18 A *Times of Cyprus* newspaper cutting retrieved during this research reveals that 'our late Director-General of Information [Leslie Glass], who shook off the dust of this Island nearly two months ago and until now hasn't been heard of since' got married in London and soon was to be appointed Consul-General in Washington, as his plans of joining the Foreign Office before coming to Cyprus came into effect. Press and Information Office Archive (PIO), 'Simple Simon: A Social Scrapbook of the Week', *Times of Cyprus*, 24 March 1957, p. 4.

19 TNA FCO 141/4168, Glass, 'Practicabilities for Psychological Warfare in Cyprus – January, 1959'.

20 TNA FCO 141/4168.

21 TNA FCO 141/4168, Glass, 'Practicabilities for Psychological Warfare in Cyprus – January, 1959'.

22 TNA FCO 141/4168.

23 TNA FCO 141/4168.

24 TNA FCO 141/4168.

25 Grivas, Preparatory General Plan.

26 TNA FO 371/112871, Broadcasts to Cyprus on Athens Radio, 7 September 1954. This is one of several samples of references to 'Cypriot traitors'.

27 TNA FO 371/112871, Broadcasts to Cyprus on Athens Radio, 5 October 1954.

28 TNA FCO 141/4168, Glass, 'Practicabilities for Psychological Warfare in Cyprus – January, 1959'.

29 TNA FCO 141/4168.

30 SIMAE E 200/7/2 (TNA CO 926/490), Governor to S. of S., copies sent to MI5 and MI6, 1 December 1956.

31 SIMAE E 200/7/2 (TNA CO 926/490).

32 SIMAE E 201/4 (TNA CO 926/546), Governor to S. of S., 23 December 1955.

33 John Harding, Imperial War Museum Interview, 1984, Reel 41/50, 08:00 (http://www.iwm.org.uk/collections/item/object/80008532) [26 March 2019].

34 SIMAE E 200/7/2 (TNA CO 926/490), Governor to S. of S., 1 December 1956.
35 SIMAE E 200/7/2 (TNA CO 926/490).
36 SIMAE E 200/7/2 (TNA CO 926/490), Governor to S. of S., 1 December 1956.
37 SIMAE E 200/7/2 (TNA CO 926/490).
38 Ian Cobain, *The History Thieves: Secrets, Lies and the Shaping of a Modern Nation* (London: Portobello Books, 2016); Caroline Elkins, *Britain's Gulag: The Brutal End of Empire in Kenya* (London: Jonathan Cape, 2005); David Anderson, *Histories of the Hanged: Britain's Dirty War in Kenya and the End of Empire* (London: Weidenfeld & Nicolson, 2005); Marc Parry, 'Uncovering the Brutal Truth about the British Empire', *The Guardian*, 18 August 2016 (https://www.theguardian.com/news/2016/aug/18/uncovering-truth-british-empire-caroline-elkins-mau-mau) [26 March 2019].
39 TNA CAB 129/54/9 'Oversea Information Services', 24 July 1952, point 3; TNA CO 1027/69 'Report of the Independent Committee of Enquiry on Overseas Information Services (the Drogheda Report): Recommendations Regarding Colonial Territories', 1954; TNA CAB 129/87/41 'Oversea Information Services', 18 June 1957; Simon J. Potter, 'Webs, Networks, and Systems: Globalization and the Mass Media in the Nineteenth- and Twentieth-Century British Empire', *The Journal of British Studies*, 46:3 (July 2007), 621–646 (p. 622).
40 TNA CAB 129/54/9, 'Overseas Information Services', 24 July 1952, point 8.
41 Cormac, *Disrupt and Deny*, p. 142.
42 TNA CAB 129/54/9, point 3.
43 TNA CAB 129/54/9, 'Overseas Information Services', 24 July 1952, point 3.
44 TNA CAB 129/54/9, point 3.
45 TNA CAB 129/54/9, point 8.
46 TNA CAB 129/54/9, point 3.
47 TNA FO 371/123898, Governor to S. of S., 24 May 1956.
48 SIMAE E 201/4 (TNA CO 926/546), Governor to S. of S., 23 December 1955; Harding, Imperial War Museum Interview.
49 SIMAE E 201/4 (TNA CO 926/546), Governor to S. of S., 23 December 1955.
50 SIMAE E 201/4 (TNA CO 926/546).
51 SIMAE E 201/4 (TNA CO 926/546), Governor to S. of S., 23 December 1955.
52 Glass, *The Changing of Kings: Memories of Burma 1934–1949* (London: Peter Owen Publishers, 1985), p. 19; TNA FCO 141/3727, Draft Note on Propaganda, author and date unknown [c.1958].
53 Glass, *The Changing of Kings*, p. 19; TNA FCO 141/3727, Draft Note on Propaganda, author and date unknown [c.1958].
54 SIMAE E 209/8/1 (TNA FO 371/123899), Peake to Ward, 6 June 1956.
55 SIMAE E 209/8/1 (TNA FO 371/123899).
56 See for example the work of Hubert Faustmann, Evanthis Hatzivassiliou, Diana Markides, Panayiotis Persianis.

57 SIMAE E 209/8/1 (TNA FO 371/123899), Young, 'Turkish Publicity on Cyprus', 6 June 1956.

58 SIMAE E 209/8/1 (TNA FO 371/123899), Note on Young's memo by Ward, 7 June 1956.

59 SIMAE E 209/8/1 (TNA FO 371/123899).

60 SIMAE E 209/8/1 (TNA FO 371/123899).

61 SIMAE E 209/8/1 (TNA FO 371/123899), Ward to Peake, 19 June 1956.

62 SIMAE E 209/8/1 (TNA FO 371/123899), Young, 'Turkish Publicity on Cyprus', 6 June 1956.

63 SIMAE E 209/8/1 (TNA FO 371/123899).

64 TNA FO 371/123885, Glass, Note on 'The Future of Cyprus', 1 April 1956.

65 TNA FO 371/123898, Governor to S. of. S., 24 May 1956.

66 TNA FO 371/123898.

67 Diana Markides, 'Britain's "New Look" Policy for Cyprus', p. 500.

68 TNA FO 371/123885, Glass, 'The Future of Cyprus', 1 April 1956.

69 TNA FCO 141/3727, Reddaway to Glass, 28 November 1955.

70 TNA FO 371/123885, Glass, 'The Future of Cyprus', 1 April 1956.

71 TNA FO 371/123885.

72 TNA FO 371/123885.

73 SIMAE E 209/1, Lloyd, S. of S. for the Colonies to Governor, 25 May 1956: 'I understood that "terrorist" was to be used throughout, but I see that you would now prefer to dub them "outlaws". Although that I realise that there was an earlier outlaws law in Cyprus, the word has unpleasant associations and its use would be unhelpful from the point of view of winning public opinion in this country. Do you attach great importance to the change? [on the issue of Harding wanting general powers] … is there not a risk that publication of the general powers, including the glamour of filling the role of "outlaw", might rather encourage than discourage youngsters to take to the hills? Please understand that these are not intended as quibbling questions. The general concept of outlawry legislation, especially if covering unspecified number of persons, and to a much lesser extent the human rights aspect, present very real difficulties here.' Harding's reply, 31 May 1956: 'I attach no great importance to choice of words. Let us call them terrorists. […] It is evident that the terrorists do not like being hanged or shot. My objection to narrowing the field of "terrorists" to Grivas and his two chief lieutenants is that it will have no deterrent effect on others. It is so well known to everyone in Cyprus that Grivas, Afxentiou and Drakos are public enemies Nos. 1, 2 and 3 that to declare them and them only "terrorists" would be restating the obvious without worrying the other Five Thousand Pounders whom we want almost as much. For this reason I want the general powers.'

74 Harding, Imperial War Museum Interview, Reel 39/50, 25:45.

75 Roel Frakking, '*Collaboration Is a Very Delicate Concept*': *Alliance-formation and the Colonial Defence of Indonesia and Malaysia, 1945–1957* (PhD thesis, European University Institute, Florence, 2017). This thesis takes the concept of local alliance-formation and combines it with theories on territorial control. It investigates why certain individuals or groups cooperated with colonial authorities one moment only to switch to the freedom fighters' side the next. This is a very recent and interesting study that currently remains inaccessible, but it may offer an example for exploring further the issue of cooperation in Cyprus itself during the revolt.

76 Reddaway, *Burdened with Cyprus*, p. 6.

77 Reddaway, *Burdened with Cyprus*, p. 6.

78 TNA FO 371/123885, Glass, 'The Future of Cyprus', 1 April 1956.

79 TNA FO 371/123885, Glass, 'The Future of Cyprus', 1 April 1956.

80 TNA FO 371/123885.

81 Harding, Imperial War Museum Interview, Reel 39/50, 15:04.

82 TNA FO 371/123885, Glass, 'The Future of Cyprus', 1 April 1956.

83 TNA FO 371/123885, Glass, 'The Future of Cyprus', 1 April 1956.

84 Drohan, *Brutality in an Age of Human Rights*, p. 16.

85 Martin Thomas, 'The United Nations, Decolonization and Violence against Civilians in the French and British Empires', in *The Civilization of War: The Changing Civil-military Divide, 1914–2014*, ed. by Andrew Barros and Martin Thomas (London: Cambridge University Press, 2018), p. 290.

86 Holland, *Britain and the Revolt in Cyprus, 1954–1959* (Oxford: Oxford University Press, 1998), p. 197.

87 SIMAE E 206/2a-f (TNA FO 371/123942), Governor to S. of S., 27 December 1956.

88 This was not a new phenomenon. Panagiotis Dimitrakis writes that during the Second World War there was 'a lot of suspicion of the Cypriots in general. SOE officers noted that "it is useless to train Cypriots for a guerrilla role in a pre-occupation period as they cannot be trusted to carry out their tasks. [...]". The SOE did not admit it in writing but the memories of the 1931 Greek-Cypriot revolt that ended up in the burning of the governor's house were still alive. In political terms Cyprus was becoming a hotbed of British colonialism.' Dimitrakis, 'The Special Operations Executive and Cyprus in the Second World War', p. 318.

89 TNA FCO 141/4313, Secret note, author and date unknown.

90 James S. Corum, *Training Indigenous Forces in Counterinsurgency: A Tale of Two Insurgencies* (Carlisle, PA: Strategic Studies Institute U. S. Army War College, March 2006), p. 34.

91 TNA FCO 141/4313, Secret note, author and date unknown.

92 SIMAE E 205/21 (TNA CO 926/201), 'Cyprus: Interest Shown by Francis Noel-Baker MP' (Labour MP), 10 February 1956.

93   Grivas, *Memoirs*, p. 53.

94   Grivas, *Memoirs*, p. 46.

95   SIMAE E 200/7/2 (TNA CO 926/490), Governor to S. of S., 1 December 1956.

96   SIMAE E 206/2a-f (TNA FO371/123942), Governor to S. of S., 27 December 1956.

97   TNA FO 371/123885, Glass, 'The Future of Cyprus', 1 April 1956; FO 371/123885; FO 371/123941, Outward telegram from Commonwealth Relations Office to various Commissioners regarding Cyprus updates, 18 December 1956.

98   TNA FO 371/123941, Commonwealth Relations Office telegram, 18 December 1956.

99   SIMAE E 201/8.

100 SIMAE E 205/3/1 (TNA CO 926/450), 12 July 1956.

101 SIMAE E 200/7/2 (TNA CO 926/490), Governor to S. of S., 1 December 1956.

102 TNA FCO 141/4313, Governor to Colonial Office, 'Cemetery desecration', 2 July 1956.

103 SIMAE E 206/2a-f (FO371/123942), Governor to S. of S., 27 December 1956.

104 SIMAE E 206/2a-f (FO371/123942).

105 SIMAE E 206/2a-f (FO371/123942), Governor to S. of S., 27 December 1956.

106 SIMAE E 209/1/1 (TNA FO 371/123942), Envoys reporting on Makarios's intransigence, 22 December 1956.

107 SIMAE E 206/2a-f (TNA FO371/123942), Governor to S. of S., 27 December 1956.

108 SIMAE E 206/2a-f (TNA FO371/123942).

109 SIMAE E 205/2, Secret D.I.C. report No. 90 for the period 23–29 March 1957, 'Public Opinion', Commissioner's Office, Nicosia, 1 April 1957.

110 Harding, Imperial War Museum Interview, Reel 41/50, 22:00.

111 Harding, Imperial War Museum Interview, Reel 41/50, 22:00.

112 Grivas, *Memoirs*, p. 66.

113 SIMAE E 206/2a-f (TNA FO 371/123942), Governor to S. of S., 27 December 1956.

114 TNA FCO 141/3794, Durrell to Reddaway, 10 November 1955.

115 Harding, Imperial War Museum Interview, Reel 39/50, 25:45.

116 Martin Bell, *The End of Empire, The Cyprus Emergency: A Soldier's Story* (South Yorkshire: Pen & Sword Military, 2015).

117 See for example Andreas Varnava, *A History of the Liberation Struggle of EOKA (1955–1959)*, Series A': Sources and References to the EOKA Struggle, No. 5, translated to English by Philippos Stylianou (Nicosia: Foundation of the EOKA Liberation Struggle 1955–1959, 2004).

118 See for example Alex P. Schmid and Albert J. Jongman, *Political Terrorism: A New Guide to Actors, Authors, Concepts, Data Bases, Theories, and Literature* (New Brunswick; London: Transaction Publishers, 1988), pp. 82–83.

119 TNA FCO 141/4344, Governor's message to Security Forces, 18 November 1956.

120 SIMAE E 209 (TNA CO 926/419), Governor to S. of S., 18 November 1956.

121 SIMAE E 209 (TNA CO 926/419).

122 TNA FCO 141/4344, Larnaca Commissioner to Governor, 20 November 1956.

123 TNA FCO 141/4344.

124 Charlie Standley, 'The British Army, Violence, Interrogation and Shortcomings in Intelligence Gathering during the Cyprus Emergency, 1955–1959', in *Interrogation in War and Conflict: A Comparative and Interdisciplinary Analysis*, ed. by Christopher Andrew and Simona Tobia (London and New York: Routledge, 2014), pp. 153–168.

125 Grivas, *Memoirs*, p. 102; Penelope Tremayne, *Below the Tide* (Boston; Cambridge: Houghton Mifflin Company, BOS; The Riverside Press, CAM, 1959).

126 Carruthers, *Winning Hearts and Minds*, p. 199.

127 Sylvia Foot, *Emergency Exit* (London: Chatto and Windus, 1960), p. 107.

128 Harding, Imperial War Museum Interview, Reel 40/50 [25:45].

129 SIMAE E 209/2, Administrative Secretary to A. Morris, Mediterranean Department, 4 April 1957.

130 TNA FO 371/123885, Glass, 'The Future of Cyprus', 1 April 1956.

131 TNA FO 371/123885.

132 TNA FO 371/123885.

Chapter 4

1 TNA FCO 141/3727, Reddaway to Cruikshank, 26 September 1955.

2 TNA FO 371/112871, Broadcasts to Cyprus on Athens Radio, 20 August 1954. Translated into English for monitoring purposes by a colonial administrator, possibly Lawrence Durrell.

3 TNA FO 371/136401, Neale to Aldridge, 26 February 1958.

4 TNA FCO 141/3727, Draft Note on Propaganda, author and date unknown [c.1958].

5 TNA FCO 141/4168, Secret Minute Reddaway, 25 July 1955.

6 TNA CO 1027/80, Carstairs, Colonial to Clark, Director of External Broadcasting, BBC, London, 17 September 1955.

7 TNA CO 1027/80, Carstairs to Clark, 17 September 1955.

8 Chrysanthos Chrysanthou, 'Broadcasting (Cyprus)', in *Encyclopedia of Postcolonial Literatures in English*, ed. by Eugene Benson, W. Conolly (London; New York: Routledge, 2005, 2nd Revised edition), 155–156 (p. 155).

9 Chrysanthou, 'Broadcasting (Cyprus)', p. 155.

10 Chrysanthou, 'Broadcasting (Cyprus)', p. 155.

11 Chrysanthou, 'Broadcasting (Cyprus)', p. 155.

12 TNA FCO 141/3727, Draft Note on Propaganda, author and date unknown [c.1958].

13 TNA FCO 141/3794, Minute of meeting between Armitage and J. C. R. Proud, 14 July 1955.

14 TNA FCO 141/4168, Secret Minute by the Governor to Colonial Secretary, 29 June 1955.

15 TNA FCO 141/4168, Secret Minute by Reddaway, 25 July 1955.

16 TNA FCO 141/4168.

17 TNA FCO 141/4168, Governor to Colonial Secretary, 29 June 1955.

18 TNA FCO 141/4168.

19 TNA FCO 141/4168.

20 TNA FCO 141/4168.

21 TNA FCO 141/4168, Governor to Colonial Secretary, 29 June 1955.

22 Vangelis Calotychos, *Modern Greece: A Cultural Poetics* (Oxford New York: Berg, 2003), p. 264.

23 TNA FCO 141/3794, Durrell to Reddaway, 10 November 1955.

24 TNA FCO 141/3794.

25 Glass, *The Changing of Kings*, p. 159.

26 TNA FCO 141/3727, Draft Note on Propaganda, author and date unknown [c.1958], Burton Paulu, *Radio and Television Broadcasting on the European Continent* (Minneapolis: University of Minnesota Press, 1967), pp. 17–18.

27 TNA FCO 141/3727.

28 TNA FO 371/117630, BBC monitoring of Athens Broadcasts to Cyprus, 4 April 1955; SIMAE E 201/4 (TNA CO 926/546), Governor to S. of S., 23 December 1955; Harding, Imperial War Museum Interview, Reel 39/50 [12:32].

29 TNA FCO 141/4186, Armitage to S. of S., 26 June 1955.

30 'What Was EOKA? On 1 April 1955 Its Liberation Struggle Begins', *On Alert*, rev. 1 April 2018 (http://www.onalert.gr/stories/poa-itan-eoka/23832) [26 March 2019]. Original Greek text translated to English by M. Hadjiathanasiou.

31 TNA FCO 141/4186, Armitage to S. of S., 22 July 1955.

32 TNA FCO 141/4186, S. of S. to Armitage, 24 April 1944.

33 TNA FCO 141/4186, Armitage to S. of S., 15 April 1955.

34 TNA FCO 141/4186, 'The Jamming of Radio Athens' Memorandum from A. E. Morrison, Major General, Chairman of British Joint Communications for Secretary, 7 October 1955; S. of S. to Armitage, 8 August 1955.

35 SIMAE E 209/1/1, Governor to S. of S., 24 May 1956; E 201/4, Governor to S. of S., 23 December 1955.

36 TNA FCO 141/3716, Durrell to Administrative Secretary, 29 October 1955, Red 58; FCO 141/4280, Red 56.

37 TNA FCO 141/4280, Durrell to Colonial Secretary, 21 January 1955, Red 154–152.

38 TNA FCO 141/4280, Durrell to Colonial Secretary, 21 January 1955, Red 154–152.

39 TNA FCO 141/4280, Durrell to Colonial Secretary, 21 January 1955, Red 154–152.

40 TNA FO 371/123885, Glass, 'The Future of Cyprus', 1 April 1956.

41 TNA FCO 141/3717, A. J. Reddaway, Acting Governor of Cyprus to S. of S., 24 August 1955.

42 TNA FCO 141/3717, Durrell, 'The Case against Athens Radio' in *Extracts from Athens Radio Broadcasts to Cyprus*.

43 TNA FCO 141/3717, Durrell, 'The Case against Athens Radio'.

44 TNA FCO 141/4280, Durrell to Colonial Secretary, 21 January 1955, Red 154–152; CO 1027/43, Note, Information Department, 24 October 1953.

45 TNA FCO 141/4280, Durrell to Colonial Secretary, 21 January 1955, Red 154–152.

46 TNA FCO 141/3716, Durrell to Administrative Secretary, 22 December 1955, Red 72.

47 TNA FCO 141/4186, Major-General A. H. G. Ricketts to Colonial Secretary, 27 September 1955, Red 12.

48 TNA FCO 141/4280, Durrell to Colonial Secretary, 21 January 1955, Red 154–152; CO 1027/43, Note, Information Department, 24 October 1953.

49 TNA FCO 141/4186, Secret extract from minute by Colonial Secretary, 17 September 1955, Red 11.

50 TNA FCO 141/4186, Governor to Colonial Office, 2 January 1956, Red 60.

51 TNA FCO 141/4186, S. of S's proposed reply to Francis Noel-Baker's proposed enquiry in S. of S's telegram to Governor, 27 January 1956, Red 79.

52 Asa Briggs, *The History of Broadcasting in the United Kingdom: Volume 5: Competition 1955–1974* (London: Oxford University Press, 1961–1995), p. 132.

53 TNA FCO 141/4186, S. of S. to Governor, 14 February 1956, Red 96.

54 TNA FCO 141/4187, K. J. Neale to A. S. Aldridge, Colonial Office, 27 August 1958, Red 29.

55 TNA FCO 141/4187, K. J. Neale to A. S. Aldridge, Colonial Office, 27 August 1958, Red 29.

56 Spencer Mawby, for example, in his chapter 'The British Brand of Anti-imperialism: Information Policy and Propaganda in South Arabia at the End of Empire', mentions that 'although [the British government] denied that they ever engaged in jamming operations [...] the colonial authorities had tried to scramble Greek broadcasts after the outbreak of the insurgency in Cyprus. The expense and limited success of this operation was regarded as discouraging' to embark on a jamming operation in Egypt, during the Suez Crisis. In *British Propaganda and Wars of Empire: Influencing Friend and Foe 1900–2010*, p. 183.

57 Carruthers, *Winning Hearts and Minds*, p. 215.

58 French, *Fighting EOKA*, p. 176.

59 'Britain Lowers the Radio Curtain', *New Statesman and Nation*, 4 February 1956, Vol. 51, No. 1300, Editorial, p. 113, referenced in Carruthers, *Winning Hearts and Minds*, pp. 216–217.

60 Grivas, *Memoirs*, p. 34.

61 Grivas, *Memoirs*, p. 125.

62 SIMAE E 209/7/18 (TNA CO 923/1123), Report on 'Activities of Grivas in Cyprus', 8 December 1958.

63 Radio was particularly suited for the creation of an 'imagined [national] community', 'nationalisation project'. Gerd Horten, *Radio Goes to War: The Cultural Politics of Propaganda during World War II* (Berkeley, CA; London: University of California Press, 2002), p. 3.

64 Reginald George Hammond, *Friends and Relations* (http://www.friendsandrelations.com/html/detail.php/id/3227/relations/reginald_george_hammond.html) [13 May 2017].

65 Charles Foley, *Island in Revolt* (London: Longmans, 1962), p. 202.

66 Aldrich, *The Hidden Hand*, p. 575.

67 Foley, *Island in Revolt*, p. 24.

68 Durrell, *Bitter Lemons*, pp. 157 and 172.

69 TNA FCO 141/4186, Governor to S. of S., 31 May 1956, Red 277–276.

70 TNA FCO 141/4186, 'Secret: Greek Radio Anti-British Propaganda Directed on Cyprus', Situation report by Controller John Jones, 2 July 1956, Red 290–289.

71 TNA FCO 141/4186.

72 Montis, *Closed Doors*, p. 3. Original Greek text translated to English by M. Hadjiathanasiou.

73 Montis, *Closed Doors*, p. 3. Original Greek text translated to English by M. Hadjiathanasiou.

74 PEKA leaflet in Alexandrou, *Propaganda – Counterpropaganda*, p. 159. Original Greek text translated to English by M. Hadjiathanasiou.

75 Montis, *Closed Doors*, p. 57. Original Greek text translated to English by M. Hadjiathanasiou.

76 Carruthers, *Winning Hearts and Minds*, p. 214.

77 Montis, *Closed Doors*, p. 57. Original Greek text translated to English by M. Hadjiathanasiou.

78 Montis, *Closed Doors*, pp. 21–22. Original Greek text translated to English by M. Hadjiathanasiou.

79 Montis, *Closed Doors*, p. 22.

80 Grivas, *Memoirs*, p. 111.

81 Grivas, *Memoirs*, pp. 111 and 83.

82 Grivas/EOKA leaflet in Alexandrou, *Propaganda – Counterpropaganda*, p. 121. Original Greek text translated to English by M. Hadjiathanasiou.

83 Grivas, *Memoirs*, p. 83.

84 TNA FCO 141/4186, S. of S. to Governor, 28 March 1957, Red 305.

85 TNA FCO 141/4186, P. J. P. Storrs, Head Information Officer and Director of Public Relations Department, Nicosia to Administrative Secretary, 10 April 1957, Red 307.

86 TNA FCO 141/4186, Governor to Colonial Office, 6 June 1957, Red 318; Foot to Colonial Office, 12 August 1958, Red 328.

87   TNA FCO 141/4186.

88   *Hansard* HC Vol. 582 col. 153, 19 February 1958 (https://hansard.parliament.
     uk/commons/1958-02-19/debates/9762ffe0-2720-49b4-a4fa-33c148abc72f/
     RadioAthens(Jamming)) [26 August 2019].

89   TNA FCO 141/4187, Foot to Colonial Office, 19 September 1958, Red 64.

90   TNA FCO 141/4187, Town-commissioners to Foot, 23/25/27 September 1958,
     Red 65, 72, 74, 76, 76A.

91   TNA FCO 141/4187, Foot to Colonial Office, 26 February 1959, Red 1.

92   Edwards, *Defending the Realm*, p. 143.

93   TNA FCO 141/3727, Draft Note on Propaganda, author and date unknown
     [c.1958].

94   Carruthers, *Winning Hearts and Minds*, p. 91.

95   Mumford, *The Counter-insurgency Myth*, p. 41; Holland, *Britain and the Revolt in
     Cyprus, 1954–1959*, p. 56.

96   Kumar Ramakrishna, *Emergency Propaganda: The Winning of Malayan Hearts and
     Minds 1948–1958* (London: Routledge, 2013), p. 210.

97   Ramakrishna, *Emergency Propaganda*, p. 139.

98   TNA FCO 141/3727, Reddaway to Cruikshank, 26 September 1955.

99   TNA FCO 141/4168, Glass, 'Practicabilities for Psychological Warfare in
     Cyprus – January 1959'.

100 TNA FCO 141/4168, Glass, 'Practicabilities for Psychological Warfare in
     Cyprus – January 1959'.

101 TNA FCO 141/4168, Glass, 'Practicabilities for Psychological Warfare in Cyprus –
     January 1959'.

102 Potter, 'Propaganda and Empire', p. 5. Also see Simon J. Potter, *Broadcasting
     Empire: The BBC and the British World, 1922–1970* (Oxford: Oxford University
     Press, 2012).

103 TNA FCO 141/3727, Draft Note on Propaganda, author and date unknown
     [c.1958].

104 Stubbs, 'Making Headlines in a State of Emergency: The Case of the Times of
     Cyprus, 1955–1960', *The Journal of Imperial and Commonwealth History*, 45:1
     (2017), 70–92 (pp. 70–71).

105 TNA FO 371/112874, Peake to Young, 4 November 1954.

106 SIMAE E 201/4 (TNA CO 926/546), Governor to S. of S., 23 December 1955;
     Harding, Imperial War Museum Interview, Reel 39/50 [12:32].

107 TNA FCO 141/3727, Draft Note on Propaganda, author and date unknown
     [c.1958].

108 Stubbs, 'Making Headlines in a State of Emergency', pp. 70–71.

109 TNA FCO 141/3727, Draft Note on Propaganda, author and date unknown
     [c.1958].

110 Potter, 'Webs, Networks, and Systems: Globalization and the Mass Media in the Nineteenth- and Twentieth-century British Empire'.

111 TNA FCO 141/3727, Draft Note on Propaganda, author and date unknown [c.1958].

112 TNA FCO 141/3727, Draft Note on Propaganda, author and date unknown [c.1958].

113 SIMAE E 206/2a-f (TNA FO 371/123942), Governor to S. of S., 27 December 1956.

114 Stubbs, 'Making Headlines in a State of Emergency'.

115 TNA FCO 141/3727, Draft Note on Propaganda, author and date unknown [c.1958].

116 On 27 January 1958 intercommunal clashes took place in Nicosia between Turkish Cypriot rioters demanding *taxim*/partition and Greek Cypriot rioters demanding *enosis*. British Security Services intervened, several were wounded and a curfew was imposed in Nicosia's walled city. The following day some Turkish Cypriots dismissed colonial orders, headed to the streets and clashed with security forces. Seven Turkish Cypriots died. Efthymios – Mimis D. Vasileiou, *Walking to Freedom EOKA 1955–1959: Its Foundation and Daily Action* (Nicosia: SIMAE publication, 2009, in Greek), pp. 42 and 44.

117 Stubbs and Bahar Taşeli, 'Newspapers, Nationalism and Empire', *Media History*, 20:3 (2014), 284–301 (p. 298).

118 TNA FCO 141/3727, Draft Note on Propaganda, author and date unknown [c.1958].

119 Author unknown, *British Opinion on Cyprus* (USA: Royal Greek Embassy, Information Service, 1956), p. 5.

120 TNA FCO 141/3727, Draft Note on Propaganda, author and date unknown [c.1958].

121 TNA FO 371/123898, Governor to S. of S., 24 May 1956.

122 Stubbs, 'Making Headlines in a State of Emergency', p. 73.

123 TNA FCO 141/3453, Durrell to Colonial Secretary, 4 November 1954.

124 Foley, *Legacy of Strife: Cyprus from Rebellion to Civil War* (London: Penguin Special, 1964); Foley and W. I. Scobie, *The Struggle for Cyprus* (Stanford, CA: Hoover Institution Press, 1975).

125 TNA FCO 141/3727, Draft Note on Propaganda, author and date unknown [c.1958].

126 Stubbs, 'Making Headlines in a State of Emergency', p. 84.

127 TNA FCO 141/3727, Draft Note on Propaganda, author and date unknown [c.1958].

128 Stubbs, 'Making Headlines in a State of Emergency', p. 70.

129 Stubbs, 'Making Headlines in a State of Emergency', p. 71.

130 Stubbs, 'Making Headlines in a State of Emergency', p. 71.

131 Stubbs, 'Making Headlines in a State of Emergency', p. 70.

132 Stubbs, 'Making Headlines in a State of Emergency', p. 82.

133 Stubbs, 'Making Headlines in a State of Emergency', p. 70.

134 Stubbs, 'Making Headlines in a State of Emergency', p. 71.

135 Stubbs, 'Making Headlines in a State of Emergency', pp. 72–73.

136 Stubbs, 'Making Headlines in a State of Emergency', p. 73.

137 Stubbs, 'Making Headlines in a State of Emergency', p. 78.

138 Author unknown, *The Times*, 29 November 1956.

139 Stubbs, 'Making Headlines in a State of Emergency', p. 78.

140 Stubbs, 'Making Headlines in a State of Emergency', p. 78.

141 TNA FCO 141/3727, Draft Note on Propaganda, author and date unknown [c.1958].

142 TNA FCO 141/3727, Draft Note on Propaganda, author and date unknown [c.1958].

143 TNA FCO 141/3727, Draft Note on Propaganda, author and date unknown [c.1958].

144 TNA FCO 141/3727, Draft Note on Propaganda, author and date unknown [c.1958].

145 Tony Shaw, *Eden, Suez and the Mass Media: Propaganda and Persuasion during the Suez Crisis* (London and New York: I.B. Tauris, 1996).

146 Stubbs, 'Making Headlines in a State of Emergency', pp. 76 and 70–71.

147 TNA FCO 141/3727, Draft Note on Propaganda, author and date unknown [c.1958].

148 TNA FCO 141/4186, Governor to War Office, 12/15 October 1955, Red 11, 29, 30; Secret Minute Reddaway, 25 July 1955.

149 TNA FCO 141/4280, 'Information Problems Themes and Organisation in Cyprus, Notes by the Head of Information Department Colonial Office, on a Visit to Cyprus, 22–25 September, 1954', Red 59–55.

150 TNA FCO 141/3727, Draft Note on Propaganda, author and date unknown [c.1958].

151 TNA FCO 141/3727, Draft Note on Propaganda, author and date unknown [c.1958]; SIMAE E 200/7/2 (TNA CO 926/490), Governor to S. of S., 1 December 1956.

152 SIMAE E 206, 'The Church and Terrorism in Cyprus: A Record of the Complicity of the Greek-Orthodox Church of Cyprus in Political Violence', 15 December 1956, p. 33.

153 TNA FCO 141/3727, Draft Note on Propaganda, author and date unknown [c.1958].

154 SIMAE E 209/1/1 (TNA FO 371/123898), Brief on 'Publicity about Cyprus' to S. of S., commenting on Harding's letter of 24 May 1956 (single page, rest of it missing).

155 Thomas, *Fight or Flight*, p. 272.

156 Thomas, *Fight or Flight*, p. 272.

157 *British Documents on the End of Empire, Series A, Volume 4: The Conservative Government and the End of Empire, 1957–1964, Part I: High Policy, Political and Constitutional Change*, ed. by Ronald Hyam and Wm Roger Louis (London: The Stationery Office, 2000).

158 SIMAE E 201/4 (TNA CO 926/546), Governor to S. of S., 23 December 1955.

159 SIMAE E 209/8/1 (TNA FO 371/123899), Peake to Ward, 6 June 1956.

160 SIMAE E 209/8/1 (TNA FO 371/123899).

161 SIMAE E 209/8/1 (TNA FO 371/123899).

162 SIMAE E 209/8/1 (TNA, FO 371/123899).

163 SIMAE E 209/8/1 (TNA, FO 371/123899).

164 SIMAE E 209/8/1 (TNA, FO 371/123899).

165 TNA FO 371/123898, Makins to Governor, 2 June 1956.

166 TNA FO 371/123898.

167 SIMAE E209/8/1 (TNA FO 371/123899), Stewart on Peake's letter, 11 June 1956.

168 SIMAE E209/8/1 (TNA FO 371/123899), Ward to Peake, 19 June 1956.

169 SIMAE E209/8/1 (TNA FO 371/123899).

170 TNA FCO 141/3727, Draft Note on Propaganda, author and date unknown [c.1958].

171 TNA FCO 141/3727, Draft Note on Propaganda, author and date unknown [c.1958].

172 TNA FCO 141/3727.

173 TNA FCO 141/3727.

174 Stubbs, 'Making Headlines in a State of Emergency', p. 77.

175 TNA FO 371/123898, Governor to S. of S., 24 May 1956.

176 George Seferis, 'Salamis in Cyprus', *Poetry Foundation*, 1955 (http://www.poetryfoundation.org/poetrymagazine/browse/105/1#!/20589922/1) [26 March 2019].

177 Demetris Daskalopoulos, *The Age of Bronze*, Back cover (Athens: Hestia Publications, 2012, in Greek). Original Greek text translated to English by M. Hadjiathanasiou.

178 Daskalopoulos, *The Age of Bronze*.

179 Albert Camus, 'L'enfant grec', *L'Express*, 6 December 1955, Manuscript of Albert Camus, *Lekythos Library, University of Cyprus* (http://lekythos.library.ucy.ac.cy/handle/10797/2452) [26 March 2019].

180 Helen O'Shea, *Ireland and the End of the British Empire: The Republic and Its Role in the Cyprus Emergency* (London; New York: I.B. Tauris, 2014).

181 Artemis Cooper, 'Cyprus', in *Patrick Leigh Fermor: An Adventure* (London: John Murray, 2012), p. 288.

182 Cooper, *Patrick Leigh Fermor*, p. 295.

183 Alexandrou, *Propaganda – Counterpropaganda*, p. 8. EOKA leaflets were also published in some previous publications in Greek, such as Spyros Papageorgiou, *Archive of the Illegal Documents of the Cyprus Struggle 1955–1959* (Nicosia: Epifaniou Publications, 1984); Giannis Papadopoulos, *Documents of a Struggle, Illegal Documents of 1955–1959* (Nicosia: Onissilos, 1987); Mihalakis I. Maratheftis and Roulla Ioannidou-Stavrou, *Anthology of the Texts of EOKA Struggle 1955–1959* (Nicosia: Council of the Historical Memory of EOKA Struggle, 1998); Haralambos Alexandrou, 'EOKA Comments on International Diplomacy: Perceptions and Presentation' in *Great Power Politics in Cyprus*, pp. 161–181.

184 Papapolyviou, Foreword to *Propaganda – Counterpropaganda*, p. 8. Original Greek text translated to English by M. Hadjiathanasiou.

185 Papapolyviou, *Propaganda – Counterpropaganda*, p. 9.

186 Papapolyviou, *Propaganda – Counterpropaganda*, p. 9.

187 Papapolyviou, *Propaganda – Counterpropaganda*, p. 9.

188 Alexandrou, Introduction to *Propaganda – Counterpropaganda*, p. 11.

189 Alexandrou, 'EOKA Comments on International Diplomacy: Perceptions and Presentation' in *Great Power Politics in Cyprus*, pp. 161–181.

190 Alexandrou, *Propaganda – Counterpropaganda*, p. 12.

191 Alexandrou, *Propaganda – Counterpropaganda*, p. 12.

192 Maria Hadjiathanasiou, 'The Battle for the Cypriot Mind: The Propaganda Wars of 1950s Cyprus', 8 June 2016, *Hidden Persuaders* (http://www.bbk.ac.uk/hiddenpersuaders/blog/battle-cypriot-mind-propaganda-wars-1950s-cyprus/) [26 March 2019].

193 SIMAE E 205 (TNA CO 926/459), 'The Nature of PEKA, a New Cypriot Subversive Organisation', Secret Telegram from Governor to S. of S., 15 September 1956.

194 Alexandrou, *Propaganda – Counterpropaganda*, p. 14.

195 TNA CO 926/413, Sabotage and other incidents in Cyprus [1955].

196 Alexandrou, *Propaganda – Counterpropaganda*, p. 15.

197 Grivas, *Memoirs*, pp. 129–130.

198 Grivas, *Memoirs*, p. 17.

199 Montis, *Closed Doors*, p. 26.

200 Alexandrou, *Propaganda – Counterpropaganda*. Original Greek text translated to English by M. Hadjiathanasiou.

201 Mark Twain, 'The Chronicle of Young Satan', *Mysterious Stranger Manuscripts*, 1916 (http://www.twainquotes.com/Laughter.html) [26 March 2019].

202 Grivas, *Memoirs*, p. 90.

203 SIMAE E 200, PEKA leaflet 'Thankfulness', 14 October 1956. Original Greek text translated to English by M. Hadjiathanasiou.

204 Alexandrou, 'EOKA Comments on International Diplomacy: Perceptions and Presentation', p. 178.

205 Andrekos Varnava, 'Reinterpreting Macmillan's Cyprus Policy, 1957–1960', *Cyprus Review*, 32:1, 2010, 79–106. TNA FCO 141/4168, Secret report by Special Branch, Police Headquarters, Nicosia, 'EOKA Boycott of British Goods', 28 January 1959.

206 TNA 141/4165 Cyprus: Psychological Warfare; Leaflets.

207 TNA FCO 141/4168, Glass, 'Practicabilities for Psychological Warfare in Cyprus – January, 1959'.

208 TNA FCO 141/4165, Stephens to Sykes, 1 August 1955.

209 TNA FCO 141/4165, Stephens to Sykes, 1 August 1955.

210 TNA FCO 141/4165, Stephens to Sykes, 1 August 1955.

211 TNA FCO 141/3719-24 Cyprus: Counter Propaganda; State of Public Opinion [1955–1957].

212 TNA FCO 141/3727, Draft Note on Propaganda, author and date unknown [c.1958].

213 TNA FCO 141/4168, Glass, 'Practicabilities for Psychological Warfare in Cyprus – January 1959'.

214 Friedman and Paschalidis, 'Cyprus 1954–1959'.

215 Alexandrou, *Propaganda – Counterpropaganda*, EOKA 9/295, PEKA leaflet, p. 224. Original Greek text translated to English by M. Hadjiathanasiou.

216 Alexandrou, *Propaganda – Counterpropaganda*, p. 17.

217 In their article 'Cyprus 1954–1959' Friedman and Paschalidis presented fascinating primary and secondary material on psychological warfare during the Cyprus Emergency. In online correspondence between SGM Friedman (himself an expert on psychological operations) and the author of this book, he explained that the article is being updated with new information since its first publication in 2007. British soldiers who had served in Cyprus during the revolt contact him and provide him with unpublished material from their personal archives. This material consists of testimonies, photographs, correspondence, propaganda leaflets and memorabilia that they kept from their service in the island.

218 Friedman and Paschalidis, 'Cyprus 1954–1959'.

219 Friedman and Paschalidis, 'Cyprus 1954–1959'.

220 Foley, *Island in Revolt*.

221 SIMAE E 205 (TNA CO 926/459), PEKA leaflet, 2 September 1956.

222 TNA FCO 141/3719-22 Cyprus: Counter Propaganda; State of Public Opinion [1955–1957].

223 Grivas, *Memoirs*, p. 111.

224 TNA FCO 141/3727, Reddaway to Brigadier B. Fergusson, Allied Forces H.Q., letter about cartoonists and cartoons produced by Psychological Warfare, 16 November 1956.

225 TNA FCO 141/4165, Cyprus: Psychological Warfare; Leaflets.

226 Vicky, Weisz, Victor (1913–1966) entry, *The Political Cartoon Gallery* http://www. original-political-cartoon.com/cartoon-gallery/artists/vicky-weisz-victor-1913-1966/) [26 August 2019].

227 Cyprus Press and Information Office Archive, 'This Man Vicky: In His Wit … A Magic That Transforms the Pretentious into the Ridiculous', *Cyprus Mail*, 16 November 1958, p. 2.

228 TNA FCO 141/4165, Cyprus: Psychological Warfare; Leaflets.

229 TNA FCO 141/4165, Cyprus: Psychological Warfare; Leaflets.

230 TNA FCO 141/3727, Reddaway to Brigadier B. Fergusson, 16 November 1956.

231 TNA FCO 141/4165, Governor's Office to Colonial Secretary, 24 September 1955.

232 Ian Aitken, *The British Official Film in South-east Asia: Malaya/Malaysia, Singapore and Hong Kong* (London: Palgrave Macmillan, 2016), p. 197.

233 Aitken, *The British Official Film in South-east Asia*, p. 197.

234 Aitken, *The British Official Film in South-east Asia*, pp. 198–199.

235 Elihu Katz and Eberhard George Wedell, *Broadcasting in the Third World: Promise and Performance* (Cambridge: Harvard University Press, 1977), p. 82. A third source, a 2016 article by Nikolaos Stelya called 'The Short-lived Bi-communal Cyprus Broadcasting Corporation' focuses on the bi-communal Cyprus Broadcasting Corporation (CYBC) established in 1960, soon after Cyprus became a Republic, and lasting until 1963, and therefore falls outside this study's time frame. Nikolaos Stelya, 'The Short-lived Bi-communal Cyprus Broadcasting Corporation', *Media History*, 22:2 (2016), 217–231 (p. 217). A new book titled *Films for the Colonies: Cinema and the Preservation of the British Empire* is to be published in October 2019 (University of California Press) and seems to include some information on the Cyprus Broadcasting Television Service; however this is currently unavailable.

236 TNA FCO 141/3297, 'Development of Television in Cyprus', July 1957, Red 161–158.

237 TNA FCO 141/3297, Governor to S. of S., repeated Athens, Ankara, New York, 11 October 1957, Red 167–166.

238 Katz and Wedell, *Broadcasting in the Third World*, p. 82.

239 CSA E 1/527, Horace White, Public Information Officer to Colonial Secretary, 16 October 1950, Red 88–87.

240 CSA E 1/527.

241 Lawrence Durrell mentioned these 'aged film vans' in his *Bitter Lemons*, p. 158.

242 TNA FCO 141/3297 Proposed Television Service in Cyprus, 1955–1960. 'Where There Is No Vision, the People Perish', January 1952.

243 TNA FCO 141/3297.

244 TNA FCO 141/3297.

245 TNA FCO 141/3297 Proposed Television Service in Cyprus, 1955–1960. 'Where There Is No Vision, the People Perish', January 1952.

246 TNA FCO 141/3297, Proud to Sykes, 2 June 1955, Red 2–1.

247 TNA FCO 141/3297, Proud to Sykes, 22 August 1955, Red 7–3.

248 TNA FCO 141/3297.

249 TNA FCO 141/3297.

250 TNA FCO 141/3297, Proud to Sykes, 22 August 1955, Red 7–3.

251 TNA FCO 141/3727, Reddaway to Evans, 25 October 1955.

252 TNA FCO 141/3727.

253 Potter, *Broadcasting Empire*.

254 TNA CO 1027/80, Television Service in Cyprus, 25 October 1955, Red 20.

255 Potter, *Broadcasting Empire*.

256 TNA FCO 141/4343, McCall's Report to Governor, 'Television for Cyprus', 20 October 1955.

257 TNA FCO 141/3297, 'Report of the Working Party Appointed by the British Broadcasting Corporation to Study the Problems Arising from a Television Service in Cyprus', 30 November 1955, Red 51 booklet; Governor to S. of S. 'Television', 16 January 1956, Red 64.

258 TNA FCO 141/3297, Governor to S. of S. 'Television', 16 January 1956, Red 64; From Harding, 15 October 1955, Red 17.

259 TNA FCO 141/3297, Governor to Colonial Office, 16 March 1956, Red 72; Proud to Colonial Office, 21 April 1956, Red 84–83.

260 TNA FCO 141/3297, Proud to Sykes, 2 June 1955, Red 2–1.

261 TNA FCO 141/3297, 'Development of Television in Cyprus', July 1957, Red 161–158.

262 TNA FCO 141/3297, 'Development of Television in Cyprus', July 1957, Red 161–158.

263 Harding, Imperial War Museum Interview, Reel 38-39/50 [16:20].

264 TNA FCO 141/3297, Proud to Colonial Office, 21 April 1956, Red 84–83, 21 April 1956.

265 TNA FCO 141/3297, Author unknown, July 1957, Red 93–92; Red 161–158.

266 TNA FCO 141/3297.

267 TNA FCO 141/4343, McCall to Governor, Report 'Television for Cyprus', 20 October 1955.

268 TNA FCO 141/4343.

269 TNA FCO 141/3297, Governor to Colonial Office, 13 November 1956, Red 93–92; FCO 141/4343, McCall to Governor, Report 'Television for Cyprus', 20 October 1955.

270 TNA FCO 141/3297, S. of S. to Governor, December 1956, Red 115.

271 TNA FCO 141/3297, Governor to Colonial Office, 7 February 1957, Red 123.

272 TNA FCO 141/4343, Governor's inauguration speech for the opening of the Cyprus Television Service, 15 October 1957.

273 TNA FCO 141/4343.

274 TNA FCO 141/3297, Proud to Financial Secretary, 'Television Estimates 1958', 8 November 1957, Red 173–172.

275 TNA FCO 141/3297.

276 TNA FCO 141/3297, Proud to Financial Secretary, 'Television Estimates 1958', 19 February 1958, Red 181.

277 TNA FCO 141/3297, Proud to Financial Secretary, 'Television Estimates 1958', 19 February 1958, Red 181.

278 TNA FCO 141/3297, Minute by D. F. S. 'Future of Television', 11 June 1958, Red 215.

279 TNA FCO 141/3297, Reddaway to Higham, Colonial Office, 10 March 1958, Red 199.

280 TNA FCO 141/3297.

281 TNA CO 1027/316, H. D. Winther's conversation with Hedley Chambers, Controller of Cyprus Television, 12 November 1958, Red 68.

282 TNA FCO 141/3297, Eric Bessborough to S. of S. on the marketing of Pye television receivers in Cyprus, 24 January 1958, Red 185.

283 TNA CO 1027/316, Winther, 12 November 1958, Red 68.

284 TNA FCO 141/3297, Proud's comments on the Pye proposal, 21 February 1958, Red 189.

285 TNA CO 1027/316, Winther, 12 November 1958, Red 68.

286 Alexandrou, *Propaganda – Counterpropaganda*.

287 Alexandrou, *Propaganda – Counterpropaganda*, EOKA 9/167 – PEKA leaflet 'Cyprus Television Service', p. 194. Original Greek text translated to English by M. Hadjiathanasiou.

288 Alexandrou, *Propaganda – Counterpropaganda*, EOKA 9/589 – PEKA leaflet 'Television', p. 284. Original Greek text translated to English by M. Hadjiathanasiou.

289 TNA FCO 141/3794, Durrell to Reddaway, 10 November 1955.

290 Alexandrou, *Propaganda – Counterpropaganda*, EOKA 9/16 – PEKA leaflet 'Faulty Luxury', p. 159. Original Greek text translated to English by M. Hadjiathanasiou.

291 Alexandrou, *Propaganda – Counterpropaganda*, EOKA 9/16 – PEKA leaflet 'Faulty Luxury', p. 159. Original Greek text translated to English by M. Hadjiathanasiou.

292 TNA FCO 141/4343, Governor's inauguration speech, 15 October 1957.

293 Alexandrou, *Propaganda-Counterpropaganda*, EOKA 9/16 – PEKA leaflet 'Faulty Luxury', p. 159. Original Greek text translated to English by M. Hadjiathanasiou.

294 TNA FCO 141/3297, Letter from H. Constantinou, 67 Lynette Ave., London, SW4, 17 March 1957, Red 128; T. J. Lennard, Administrative Secretary's Office, Draft reply refuting Constantinou accusations, 29 March 1957, Red 130.

295 TNA FCO 141/3297, Extract from the Commissioner of Troodos' report for June 1957, Red 164.

296 TNA FCO 141/3297.

297 TNA FCO 141/3297, T. J. Lennard for Administrative Secretary to Chief Secretary, Government of Malta, 5 January 1960, Red 219.

Chapter 5

1   Hugh Foot, *Encyclopaedia Britannica* (https://www.britannica.com/biography/Hugh-Foot) [26 March 2019].

2   British Movietone, *Cyprus – Bone of Contention,* 17 February 1964, *AP Archive* (http://www.aparchive.com/metadata/youtube/54b7b39616364eb0abe7ee470 9f95344) [26 March 2019].

3   Hugh Mackintosh Foot, Entry in *Oxford Dictionary of National Biography* (http://www.oxforddnb.com/view/article/40197?docPos=1) [26 March 2019].

4   Dimitrakis, 'The Special Operations Executive and Cyprus in the Second World War', p. 321.

5   Durrell, 'This Magnetic, Bedevilled Island That Tugs at My Heart', *Daily Mail,* 22 August 1974, p. 6.

6   TNA FCO 141/4168, Secret report by Special Branch 'EOKA Boycott of British Goods', 28 January 1959.

7   TNA CAB 129/54/9, 'Overseas Information Services', 24 July 1952, point 9.

8   Grivas, *Memoirs*, p. 168.

9   Alexandrou, *Propaganda – Counterpropaganda*, p. 13.

10 Grivas, *Memoirs*, p. 133.

11 TNA FCO 141/4168, 'EOKA Boycott of British Goods', 28 January 1959.

12 TNA FCO 141/4168.

13 SIMAE E 203/1 (TNA CO 926/932).

14 TNA FCO 141/4168, 'EOKA Boycott of British Goods', 28 January 1959.

15 Grivas, *Memoirs;* TNA FCO 141/4168, 'EOKA Boycott of British Goods', 28 January 1959.

16 TNA FCO 141/4168, 'EOKA Boycott of British Goods', 28 January 1959.

17 SIMAE E 200/4 (TNA CO 926/932), Foot to S. of S. on EOKA activities in schools, 6 December 1958.

18 SIMAE E 200/4 (TNA, CO 926/932), Foot to S. of S., 6 December 1958.

19 SIMAE E 200/4 (TNA, CO 926/932).

20 TNA FCO 141/4168, 'EOKA Boycott of British Goods', 28 January 1959.

21 TNA FCO 141/4168.

22 TNA FCO 141/4168.

23 TNA FCO 141/4168, Glass, 'Practicabilities for Psychological Warfare in Cyprus – January, 1959'.

24 TNA FCO 141/3727, Lt. General Bower, Commander-in-Chief-Office, GHQ MELF to Foot, 28 May 1958, Red 48–50.

25 TNA FCO 141/3727.

26 TNA FCO 141/3727.

27 TNA FCO 141/3727, Bower to Foot, 28 May 1958, Red 48–50.

28 TNA FCO 141/4168, Glass, 'Practicabilities for Psychological Warfare in Cyprus – January, 1959'.

29 TNA FCO 141/4168.

30 TNA FCO 141/3727, Minute by Cyprus's Deputy Governor to Reddaway, 30 May 1958, Red 48–50.

31 TNA FCO 141/3727.

32 TNA FCO 141/3727.

33 Application No. 176/56 by the Government of the Kingdom of Greece lodged against the Government of the United Kingdom of Great Britain and Northern Ireland, Application of the convention for the protection of human rights and fundamental freedoms to the island of Cyprus, Report of the European Commission of Human Rights volume II. Hatzivassiliou, *Greece and the Cold War: Front Line State, 1952–1967* (London: Routledge, 2006), p. 14; Faustmann, 'The UN and the Internationalization of the Cyprus Conflict, 1949–58', in *The Work of the UN in Cyprus: Promoting Peace and Development*, ed. by Oliver P. Richmond and James Ker-Lindsay (Hampshire & New York: Palgrave, 2001), pp. 3–49 (p. 3); TNA CO 968/690, Brigadier G. H. Baker, 'A Review of the Cyprus Emergency: April 1955–March 1958', March 1958, Red 34; A. W. Brian Simpson, *Human Rights and the End of Empire: Britain and the End of Genesis of the European Convention* (Oxford and New York: Oxford University Press, 2001).

34 Corum, *Training Indigenous Forces*, p. 34; Nancy Crawshaw, *The Cyprus Revolt* (Boston: G. Allen & Unwin, 1978), p. 274; As a parenthesis here it is worth mentioning that after Cyprus's Independence, General Grivas in his memoirs continued talking about the 'Nazi ways' of the British, likening detention centres in Cyprus to Nazi concentration camps, reminding his reader or listener of the tortured EOKA fighters (Grivas, *Memoirs*, p. 61). Even more recently, EOKA fighters have been working on a legal case against the British Government, regarding their alleged mistreatment and torture during their incarceration and interrogation during the Emergency. Very much like the example set by the Mau Mau trial in 2012, where the British government finally compensated the victims. Also see Drohan, 'A Lawyer's War: Emergency Legislation and the Cyprus Bar Council' in *Brutality in an Age of Human Rights*, pp. 16–46.

35 Carruthers, *Hearts and Minds*, p. 239.

36 SIMAE E 200/4 (TNA FO 371/136401), Neale to Aldridge, Colonial Office, 26 February 1958.

37 SIMAE E 200/4 (TNA FO 371/136401).

38 SIMAE E 200/4 (TNA FO 371/136401), Aldridge to Vallat, 27 February 1958.

39 SIMAE E 200/4 (TNA FO 371/136401).

40 TNA FCO 141/4218, Act. Governor to Colonial Office, 7 May 1958.

41 TNA FCO 141/4218.

42 TNA FCO 141/4218, Minute by Act. Governor, copies to Director of Operations and Attorney-General, 6 May 1958.

43 TNA FCO 141/4218, Telegram from Cyprus Governor to Colonial Office. This included the 28 September 1958 message sent to British Forces, 29 September 1958.

44 TNA FCO 141/4218.

45 TNA FCO 141/4168, Glass, 'Practicabilities for Psychological Warfare in Cyprus – January, 1959'.

46 TNA FCO 141/4168.

47 Thomas and Richard Toye, 'Arguing about Intervention: A Comparison of British and French Rhetoric Surrounding the 1882 and 1956 Invasions of Egypt', *The Historical Journal*, 58:4 (2015), 1081–1113; Hyam, *Britain's Declining Empire: The Road to Decolonisation 1918–1968*; W. David McIntyre, *Winding Up the British Empire in the Pacific Islands* (Oxford; New York: Oxford University Press, 2014).

48 TNA FCO 141/3727, 31 May 1958, Red 48–50.

49 TNA FCO 141/3727.

50 SIMAE E 205/2 (TNA CO 926/1075), George Sinclair, Deputy Governor of Cyprus (1955–1960) to Higham, Colonial Office, 26 March 1959.

51 Drohan, *Brutality in an Age of Human Rights*, p. 61.

52 TNA CO 926/1075, Report on the Special Investigations Group in Cyprus, 1959.

53 TNA CO 926/1075, Report on the Special Investigations Group in Cyprus, 1959.

54 TNA CO 926/1075.

55 TNA CO 926/1075.

56 TNA CO 926/1075.

57 TNA CO 926/1075.

58 TNA CO 926/1075, Report on the Special Investigations Group in Cyprus, 1959.

59 TNA CO 926/1075.

60 Holland, *Britain and the Revolt in Cyprus*, p. 503; Karyos, 'Britain and Cyprus, 1955–1959', p. 48.

61 Grivas, *Memoirs*, p. 102.

62 Holland, *Britain and the Revolt in Cyprus*, p. 504.

63 Karyos, 'Britain and Cyprus, 1955–1959', p. 48.

64 Drohan, *Brutality in an Age of Human Rights*, p. 63.

65 TNA CO 926/1075, Report on the Special Investigations Group in Cyprus, 1959.

66 SIMAE E 205/2 (TNA CO 926/1075), Sinclair to Higham, 26 March 1959.

67 SIMAE E 205/2 (TNA CO 926/1075), Sinclair to Higham, 26 March 1959.

68 TNA CO 926/1075, Report on the Special Investigations Group in Cyprus, 1959.

69 Friedman and Paschalidis, 'Cyprus 1954–1959'; also Martin Bell in his book *The End of Empire, The Cyprus Emergency: A Soldier's Story* (p. 36) claims that the organization originally called itself AKOE; however, it allegedly changed its name to anti-EOKA when it discovered that AKOE also stood for the Greek Homosexual Liberation Movement. This is factually wrong as AKOE in Greece was founded in the late 1970s.

70 Michalis Stavri, '"We want to group together all the haters of E.O.K.A.": The British groups of "Cromwell" and "AKOE"', presentation at the History and Literature Regarding the 1955–1959 Struggle Conference, 20–22 November 2015, Nicosia, Cyprus [in Greek]; Michalis Stavri, '"Cromwell" and "AKOE": Aspects of the British counteraction towards EOKA's struggle 1955–1959', *Phileleftheros* newspaper, 2 April 2018 [in Greek].

71 Grivas, *Memoirs*.

72 French, *Fighting EOKA*, p. 229.

73 Foley and Scobie, *The Struggle for Cyprus*, p. 146.

74 TNA FCO 141/4168, Glass, 'Practicabilities for Psychological Warfare in Cyprus – January, 1959'; 'Clandestine Propaganda' subsection.

75 Dimitrakis, 'The Special Operations Executive and Cyprus in the Second World War', pp. 315–328.

76 TNA FCO 141/4168, Glass, 'Practicabilities for Psychological Warfare in Cyprus – January, 1959'.

77 TNA FCO 141/4168, Glass, 'Practicabilities for Psychological Warfare in Cyprus – January, 1959'.

78 TNA CO 127/180, S. of S. to Foot, 17 November 1958.

79 TNA FCO 141/3727, Foot to Colonial Office, 19 November 1958, Red 58.

80 TNA CO 127/180; FCO 141/3727, Foot to S. of S., 19 November 1958.

81 Dimitrakis, 'The Special Operations Executive and Cyprus in the Second World War', pp. 315–328 and p. 321; TNA CO 127/180; FCO 141/3727, Foot to S. of S., 19 November 1958.

82 TNA CO 127/180; FCO 141/3727, Foot to S. of S., 19 November 1958.

83 TNA FCO 141/4168, Glass, 'Practicabilities for Psychological Warfare in Cyprus – January, 1959'.

84 TNA FCO 141/4168, Foot to E. Melville, Colonial Office, 21 April 1959.

85 TNA FCO 141/4168, Foot to Melville, 21 April 1959.

86 French, *Fighting EOKA*, p. 276.

87 French, *Fighting EOKA*.

88 TNA FCO 141/4168, Glass, 'Practicabilities for Psychological Warfare in Cyprus – January, 1959'.

89 TNA FCO 141/4168, Glass, 'Practicabilities for Psychological Warfare in Cyprus – January, 1959'.

90 TNA FCO 141/4168.

91 TNA FCO 141/4168, Foot to Melville, 21 April 1959.

92 TNA FCO 141/4168, Glass, 'Practicabilities for Psychological Warfare in Cyprus – January, 1959'.

93 TNA FCO 141/3727, Colonel Davy, Director of Operations to U.S., 'Psychological Support – Clarification', 3 December 1958, Red 61.

94 TNA FCO 141/3727, Colonel Davy, Director of Operations to U.S., 'Psychological Support – Clarification', 3 December 1958, Red 61.

95 TNA FCO 141/3727.

96 TNA FCO 141/3727.

97 TNA FCO 141/4168, Glass, 'Practicabilities for Psychological Warfare in Cyprus – January, 1959'.

98 TNA FCO 141/3727, Colonel Davy, Director of Operations to U.S., 'Psychological Support – Clarification', 3 December 1958, Red 61.

Chapter 6

1 TNA FCO 141/3794, Durrell to Reddaway, 10 November 1955.

2 TNA FCO 141/3794, Durrell to Reddaway, 10 November 1955.

3 SIMAE E 205/2 (TNA CO 926/1076), K. J. Neale Secretary for the Interior and Local Government, to Witney, MacDonald, Evans, W. A. Morris and Melville, 3 January 1957.

4 SIMAE E 205/2 (TNA CO 926/1076), A. M. MacDonald to K. J. Neale, 4 April 1957.

5 SIMAE E 205/2 (TNA CO 926/1076), Neale to Witney, MacDonald, Evans, W. A. Morris and Melville, 3 January 1957.

6 SIMAE E 205/2 (TNA CO 926/1076), MacDonald to Neale, 4 April 1957.

7 SIMAE E 201/4 (TNA CO 926/546), Governor to S. of S., 23 December 1955; Harding, Imperial War Museum Interview, Reel 39/50 [12:32].

8 TNA FCO 141/3727, Draft Note on Propaganda, author and date unknown [c.1958].

9 TNA FCO 141/3727.

10 TNA FCO 141/3727.

11 TNA FCO 141/3727.

12 Grivas, *Memoirs*, p. 10.

13 French, 'Nasty Not Nice', p. 756.

14 Thomas, 'Insurgent Intelligence: Information Gathering and Anti-colonial Rebellion', *Intelligence and National Security*, 22:1 (2007), 155–163.

15 Karl Hack, 'Everyone Lived in Fear: Malaya and the British Way of Counter-insurgency', *Small Wars & Insurgencies*, 23:4–5 (2012) 671–699; Hack, 'The Malayan Emergency as Counter-insurgency Paradigm', *Journal of Strategic Studies*, 32:3 (2009), 383–414; Hack, '"Iron Claws on Malaya": The Historiography of the Malayan Emergency', *Journal of Southeast Asian Studies*, 30:1 (March 1999), 99–125; Hack, 'British Intelligence and Counter-insurgency in the Era of Decolonisation: The Example of Malaya', *Intelligence and National Security*, 14:2 (1999), 124–155.

16 TNA FCO 141/3727, Draft Note on Propaganda, author and date unknown [c.1958].

17 TNA FCO 141/3727.

18 TNA FCO 141/3727, Draft Note on Propaganda, author and date unknown [c.1958].

19 Paschalis M. Kitromilides, Opening speech, 'Visions and Realities: Cypriot Experience in the Transition from Empire: A Conference in Honour of Professor Robert Holland', London, King's College London, London, 4 December 2015.

20 See for example Simon J. Potter and Jonathan Saha, 'Global History, Imperial History and Connected Histories of Empire', *Journal of Colonialism and Colonial History*, 16:1 (Spring 2015).

Bibliography

Primary sources

Archival

Archive of the Council for the Historical Memory of the Struggle (SIMAE, Nicosia)
  Part of SIMAE's collection is copies of primary colonial material stored at the
  National Archives in London. For this research several files were accessed at SIMAE
  and referenced in this book using SIMAE's reference codes (i.e. E 200; E 201; E 203;
  E 205; E 206; E 209). Where possible these reference codes were cross-referenced
  with TNA's referencing system. This can be found in the footnotes, for example:
  'SIMAE E 200/7/2 (TNA CO 926/490)'.
Cyprus Press and Information Office Archive (Nicosia)
  'This Man Vicky: In His Wit … A Magic That Transforms the Pretentious into the
  Ridiculous', *Cyprus Mail*, 16 November 1958.
Cyprus State Archive (Nicosia)
  Secretariat Archives (SA).
Hansard HC Vol. 552 cols. 1653–750, 14 May 1956 (http://hansard.millbanksystems.
  com/commons/1956/may/14/cyprus) [18 June 2017].
Hansard HC Vol. 582 col. 153, 19 February 1958 (https://hansard.parliament.
  uk/commons/1958-02-19/debates/9762ffe0-2720-49b4-a4fa-33c148abc72f/
  RadioAthens(Jamming)) [26 August 2019].
Lekythos Library, University of Cyprus
  Albert Camus, 'L'enfant grec', *L'Express*, 6 December 1955, Manuscript of Albert
  Camus (http://lekythos.library.ucy.ac.cy/handle/10797/2452) [20 March 2017].
Limassol Historical Archive (Limassol)
  Author unknown, 'Simple Simon: A Social Scrapbook of the Week', *Times of Cyprus*,
  24 March 1957.
The National Archives (London)
  British Council records (BW); Cabinet Office records (CAB); Colonial Office records
  (CO); Foreign and Commonwealth Office records (FCO); Foreign Office records
  (FO).
National Library of Scotland (Edinburgh)
  Patrick Leigh Fermor Archive.

The Spectator Archive

Author unknown, 'Compromise on Cyprus', 18 August 1955 (http://archive.spectator.
co.uk/article/19th-august-1955/3/compromise-on-cyprus) [6 March 2017].

Audio

John Harding, Oral History Interview, 1984, *Imperial War Museum*, Online Collections
(http://www.iwm.org.uk/collections/item/object/80008532) [9 September 2015].

Films

Cyprus – Bone of Contention, 17 February 1964, *British Movietone – AP Archive* (http://
www.aparchive.com/metadata/youtube/54b7b39616364eb0abe7ee4709f95344)
[10 March 2017].

Published

Alexandrou, Charis, ed., *Propaganda – Counterpropaganda: Liberation Struggle,
1955–1959* (Nicosia: Cyprus State Archive, 2013, Catalogue in Greek).

Barker, Dudley, *Grivas: Portrait of a Terrorist* (London: The Cresset Press, 1959).

Bell, Martin, *The End of Empire, The Cyprus Emergency: A Soldier's Story* (South
Yorkshire: Pen & Sword Military, 2015).

Cardiff, Maurice, *Friends Abroad: Memories of Patrick Leigh-Fermor, Lawrence
Durrell, Peggy Gugenheim, Freya Stark and Others* (London; New York: Radcliffe
Press, 1997).

Crawshaw, Nancy, *The Cyprus Revolt* (Boston: G. Allen & Unwin, 1978).

Durrell, Lawrence, *Lawrence Durrell: Conversations*, ed. by Earl G. Ingersoll (New Jersey:
Fairleigh Dickinson University Press, 1998.

Durrell, Lawrence, 'Letters of Lawrence Durrell to Austen Harrison', ed. by David
Roessel, *Deus Loci magazine*, NS3 (1994).

Durrell, Lawrence, 'This Magnetic, Bedevilled Island That Tugs at My Heart', *Daily Mail*,
22 August 1974, p. 6.

Durrell, Lawrence, *Bitter Lemons of Cyprus* (London: Faber & Faber, 1957).

Foley, Charles and W. I. Scobie, *The Struggle for Cyprus* (Stanford, CA: Hoover
Institution Press, 1975).

Foley, Charles, *Legacy of Strife: Cyprus from Rebellion to Civil War* (London: Penguin
Special, 1964).

Foley, Charles, *Island in Revolt* (London: Longmans, 1962).

Foot, Sylvia, *Emergency Exit* (London: Chatto and Windus, 1960).

Glass, Leslie, *The Changing of Kings: Memories of Burma 1934–1949* (London: Peter Owen Publishers, 1985).

Grivas, General George, 'Preparatory General Plan', *Cyprus Conflict* (http://www.cyprus-conflict.org/materials/generalplan.html) [14 June 2017] in Greek.

Grivas, General George, *The Memoirs of General Grivas*, ed. by Charles Foley (London: Longmans, 1964).

Hyam, Ronald and Wm Roger Louis, eds., *British Documents on the End of Empire, Series A, Volume 4: The Conservative Government and the End of Empire, 1957–1964, Part I: High Policy, Political and Constitutional Change* (London: The Stationery Office, 2000).

Luke, Harry, *Cyprus: A Portrait and an Appreciation* (London: Roy Publishers, 1957).

Maratheftis, Mihalakis I., and Roulla Ioannidou-Stavrou, *Anthology of the Texts of EOKA Struggle 1955–1959* (Nicosia: Council of the Historical Memory of EOKA Struggle, 1998, in Greek).

Montis, Costas, *Closed Doors* (Nicosia: Cypriot National Youth Board, 1964, in Greek).

Papadopoulos, Giannis, *Documents of a Struggle, Illegal Documents of 1955–1959* (Nicosia: Onissilos, 1987, in Greek).

Papageorgiou, Spyros, *Archive of the Illegal Documents of the Cyprus Struggle 1955–1959* (Nicosia: Epifaniou Publications, 1984, in Greek).

Reddaway, John, *Burdened with Cyprus: The British Connection* (London; Nicosia; Istanbul: Weidenfeld & Nicolson, 1986).

Seferis, George, 'Salamis in Cyprus', 1955, *Poetry Foundation* (http://www.poetryfoundation.org/poetrymagazine/browse/105/1#!/20589922/1) [3 December 2015] in Greek.

Stark, Freya, *Letters. Vol. 7 Some Talk of Alexander, 1952–1959*, ed. by Caroline Moorehead (Salisbury: Michael Russell, 1982).

Thomas, Alan G., ed., *Spirit of Place: Letters and Essays on Travel* (London: Faber and Faber Ltd., 1969).

Tremayne, Penelope, *Below the Tide* (Boston; Cambridge: Houghton Mifflin Company, BOS/The Riverside Press, CAM, 1959).

Twain, Mark, 'The Chronicle of Young Satan', *Mysterious Stranger Manuscripts*, 1916, *Twain Quotes* (http://www.twainquotes.com/Laughter.html) [14 September 2016].

Unknown author, *British Opinion on Cyprus* (Washington: Royal Greek Embassy, Information Service, 1956).

Varnava, Andreas, *A History of the Liberation Struggle of EOKA (1955–1959)*, Series A': Sources and References to the EOKA Struggle, No. 5, translated to English by Philippos Stylianou (Nicosia: Foundation of the EOKA Liberation Struggle 1955–1959, 2004).

Vasileiou, Efthymios – Mimis, *Walking to Freedom EOKA 1955–1959: Its Foundation and Daily Action* (Nicosia: SIMAE publication, 2009, Chronology of the events in Greek).

Secondary sources

Aitken, Ian, *The British Official Film in South-East Asia: Malaya/Malaysia, Singapore and Hong Kong* (London: Palgrave Macmillan, 2016).

Aldrich, Richard J., *The Hidden Hand: Britain, America, and Cold War Secret Intelligence* (London: John Murray, 2002).

Anderson, David M., *Histories of the Hanged: Britain's Dirty War in Kenya and the End of Empire* (London: Weidenfeld & Nicolson, 2005).

Anderson, David M., 'Policing and Communal Conflict: The Cyprus Emergency, 1954–60', in *Emergencies and Disorder in the European Empires after 1945*, ed. by Robert Holland (Oxford: Frank Cass, 1994), 177–207.

Andrew, Christopher and Simona Tobia, eds., *Interrogation in War and Conflict: A Comparative and Interdisciplinary Analysis* (London and New York: Routledge, 2014).

Assos, Demetris, 'Conspiracy Theories and the Decolonisation of Cyprus under the Weight of Historical Evidence, 1955–1959', *The Cyprus Review*, 23:2 (2011), 109–125.

Assos, Demetris, *Makarios: A Study of Anti-colonial Nationalist Leadership, 1950–1959* (PhD thesis, Institute of Commonwealth Studies, University of London, 2009).

Badger, Anthony, 'Historians, a Legacy of Suspicion and the "Migrated Archives"', *Small Wars and Insurgencies*, 23:4–5 (September 2012), 799–807.

Barros, Andrew and Martin Thomas, eds., *The Civilization of War: The Changing Civil-military Divide, 1914–2014* (London: Cambridge University Press, 2018).

Briggs, Asa, *The History of Broadcasting in the United Kingdom: Volume 5: Competition 1955–1974* (London: Oxford University Press, 1961–1995).

British Cyprus Memorial Trust, 'Sgt Reginald George Hammond', 9 July 2009, *Friends and Relations* (http://www.friendsandrelations.com/html/detail.php/id/3227/relations/reginald_george_hammond.html) [13 May 2017].

Bryant, Rebecca, 'An Aesthetics of Self: Moral Remaking and Cypriot Education', *Comparative Studies in Society and History*, 41:3 (2001), 583–614.

Bryant, Rebecca, 'Disciplining Ethnicity and Citizenship in Colonial Cyprus', in *Manufacturing Citizenship: Education and Nationalism in Europe, South Asia and China*, ed. by Véronique Benei (Oxford: Routledge, 2005), pp. 104–126.

Bryant, Rebecca, 'Justice or Respect? A Comparative Perspective on Politics in Cyprus Ethnic and Racial Studies', *Ethnic and Racial Studies*, 24:6 (2001), 892–924.

Bryant, Rebecca and Yiannis Papadakis, *Cyprus and the Politics of Memory: History, Community and Conflict* (London; New York: I.B. Tauris, 2012).

Calotychos, Vangelis, *Modern Greece: A Cultural Poetics* (Oxford & New York: Berg, 2003).

Carruthers, Susan L., *The Media at War: Communication and Conflict in the Twentieth Century* (Basingstoke: Palgrave Macmillan, 2000).

Carruthers, Susan L., *Winning Hearts and Minds: British Governments, the Media and Colonial Counter-insurgency 1944–1960* (London and New York: Leicester University Press, 1995).

Chrysanthou, Chrysanthos, 'Broadcasting (Cyprus)', in *Encyclopedia of Post-colonial Literatures in English*, ed. by Eugene Benson and L. W. Conolly (London: Routledge, 2004, Revised edition), 155–156.

Cobain, Ian, 'Britain's Secret Wars', *The Guardian*, 8 September 2016 (https://www.theguardian.com/uk-news/2016/sep/08/britains-secret-wars-oman) [27 March 2017].

Cobain, Ian, *The History Thieves: Secrets, Lies and the Shaping of a Modern Nation* (London: Portobello Books, 2016).

Cooper, Artemis, *Patrick Leigh Fermor: An Adventure* (London: John Murray, 2012).

Cormac, Rory, *Disrupt and Deny: Spies, Special Forces, and the Secret Pursuit of British Foreign Policy* (Oxford: Oxford University Press, 2018).

Cormac, Rory, *Confronting the Colonies: British Intelligence and Counterinsurgency* (London: Hurst Publishers, 2013).

Cormac, Rory, 'Organizing Intelligence: An Introduction to the 1955 Report on Colonial Security', *Intelligence and National Security*, 25:6 (2010), 800–822.

Corum, James S., *Training Indigenous Forces in Counterinsurgency: A Tale of Two Insurgencies* (Carlisle, PA: Strategic Studies Institute U. S. Army War College, 2006).

Crawshaw, Michael, *The Evolution of British COIN by Colonel (retd) Michael Crawshaw* (London: Ministry of Defence and Joint Doctrine Publication, 21 December 2012) (https://www.gov.uk/government/publications/the-evolution-of-british-coin) [15 September 2016].

Defty, Andrew, *Britain, America and Anti-Communist Propaganda 1945–53: The Information Research Department* (London: Routledge, 2013).

Dimitrakis, Panagiotis, *Military Intelligence in Cyprus: From the Great War to Middle East Crises* (London: Tauris Academic Studies, 2010).

Dimitrakis, Panagiotis, 'The Special Operations Executive and Cyprus in the Second World War', *Middle Eastern Studies*, 45:2 (2009), 315–328.

Dimitrakis, Panagiotis, 'British Intelligence and the Cyprus Insurgency, 1955–1959', *International Journal of Intelligence and Counter Intelligence*, 21:2 (2008), 375–394.

Drohan, Brian, *Brutality in an Age of Human Rights: Activism and Counterinsurgency at the End of the British Empire* (New York: Cornell University Press, 2018).

Edwards, Aaron, *Defending the Realm: The Politics of Britain's Small Wars since 1945* (Oxford: Oxford University Press, 2012).

Elkins, Caroline, *Britain's Gulag: The Brutal End of Empire in Kenya* (London: Jonathan Cape, 2005).

Faustmann, Hubert, 'The UN and the Internationalization of the Cyprus Conflict, 1949–58', in *The Work of the UN in Cyprus: Promoting Peace and Development*, ed. by Oliver P. Richmond and James Ker-Lindsay (Hampshire & New York: Palgrave, 2001), pp. 3–49.

Faustmann, Hubert, *Divide and Quit? British Colonial Policy in Cyprus 1878–1960. Including a Special Survey of the Transitional Period: February 1959–August 1960* (Mannheim: Mateo, 1999).

Faustmann, Hubert and Nicos Peristianis, eds., *Britain in Cyprus: Colonialism and Post-colonialism 1878–2006* (Mannheim and Mohnesee, GER: Bibliopolis, 2006).

Frakking, Roel, '*Collaboration Is a Very Delicate Concept': Alliance-formation and the Colonial Defence of Indonesia and Malaysia, 1945–1957* (PhD thesis, European University Institute, Florence, 2017).

French, David, 'British Intelligence and the Origins of the EOKA Insurgency', *British Journal for Military History*, 1:2 (2015), 84–100.

French, David, *Fighting EOKA: The British Counter-insurgency Campaign on Cyprus, 1955–1959* (Oxford: Oxford University Press, 2015).

French David, *The British Way in Counter-insurgency, 1945–1967* (Oxford; New York: Oxford University Press, January 2011).

French, David, 'Nasty Not Nice: British Counter-insurgency Doctrine and Practice, 1945–1967', *Small Wars & Insurgencies*, 23:4–5 (October–December 2012), 744–761.

Friedman (Ret.), SGM Herbert A., and Brigadier General Ioannis Paschalidis, 'Cyprus 1954–1959' (http://www.psywarrior.com/cyprus.html) [3 April 2017].

Hack, Karl, 'Everyone Lived in Fear: Malaya and the British Way of Counter-insurgency', *Small Wars & Insurgencies*, 23:4–5 (2012), 671–699.

Hack, Karl, 'The Malayan Emergency as Counter-insurgency Paradigm', *Journal of Strategic Studies*, 32:3 (2009), 383–414.

Hack, Karl, '"Iron Claws on Malaya": The Historiography of the Malayan Emergency', *Journal of Southeast Asian Studies*, 30:1 (March 1999), 99–125.

Hack, Karl, 'British Intelligence and Counter-insurgency in the Era of Decolonisation: The Example of Malaya', *Intelligence and National Security*, 14:2 (1999), 124–155.

Hadjiathanasiou, Maria, 'The Battle for the Cypriot Mind: The Propaganda Wars of 1950s Cyprus', 8 June 2016, *Hidden Persuaders* (http://www.bbk.ac.uk/hiddenpersuaders/blog/battle-cypriot-mind-propaganda-wars-1950s-cyprus/) [20 June 2017].

Hansen, Peter, 'Dame Freya Madeline Stark', *Oxford Dictionary of National Biography* (http://www.oxforddnb.com/view/article/38280) [19 June 2017].

Hatzivassiliou, Evanthis, 'Cold War Pressures, Regional Strategies, and Relative Decline: British Military and Strategic Planning for Cyprus, 1950–1960', *The Journal of Military History*, 73:4 (October 2009), 1143–1166.

Hatzivassiliou, Evanthis, *Greece and the Cold War: Front Line State, 1952–1967* (London: Routledge, 2006).

Hatzivassiliou, Evanthis, *Strategies of the Cyprus Struggle: The 1950s* (Athens: Patakis, 2004, in Greek).

Hatzivassiliou, Evanthis, *The Cyprus Question, 1878–1960: The Constitutional Aspect* (Minneapolis: Minnesota Mediterranean and East European Monographs, 2002).

Hatzivassiliou, Evanthis, *Britain and the International Status of Cyprus, 1955–59* (Minneapolis: Minnesota Mediterranean and East European Monographs, 1997).

Hatzivassiliou, Evanthis, 'Blocking Enosis: Britain and the Cyprus Question, March–December 1956', *The Journal of Imperial and Commonwealth History*, 19:2 (1991), 247–263.

Heraclidou, Antigone, 'Politics of Education and Language in Cyprus and Malta during the Inter-war Years', *Journal of Mediterranean Studies*, 23:1 (2014), 75–89.

Hitchens, Christopher, *Hostage to History: Cyprus from the Ottomans to Kissinger* (London, New York: Verso, 1997).

Holland, Robert, 'Patterns of Anglo-Hellenism: A "Colonial" Connection?' *The Journal of Imperial and Commonwealth History*, 36:3 (2008), 383–396.

Holland, Robert, 'Reviewing *Cyprus: A Modern History*. By William Mallinson', *International Affairs*, 81:5 (October 2005), 1152–1153.

Holland, Robert, *Britain and the Revolt in Cyprus, 1954–1959* (Oxford: Oxford University Press, 1998).

Holland, Robert, ed., *Emergencies and Disorder in the European Empires after 1945* (Oxford: Frank Cass, 1994).

Holland, Robert, 'Never, Never Land: British Colonial Policy and the Roots of Violence in Cyprus, 1950-54', *Journal of Imperial and Commonwealth History*, 21 (1993), 148–175.

Holland, Robert, and Diana Markides, *The British and the Hellenes: Struggles for Mastery in the Eastern Mediterranean 1850–1960* (Oxford: Oxford University Press, 2006).

Holland, Robert, and Hubert Faustmann, 'Independence Day through the Colonial Eye: A View from the British Archive', *The Cyprus Review*, 22:2 (Fall 2010), 49–60.

Holland, Robert, Carl Bridge and H. V. Brasted, 'Counsels of Despair or Withdrawals with Honour?: Partitioning in Ireland, India, Palestine and Cyprus, 1920–1960', *The Round Table: The Commonwealth Journal of International Affairs*, 86:342 (1997), 257–268.

Horten, Gerd, *Radio Goes to War: The Cultural Politics of Propaganda during World War II* (Berkeley, CA; London: University of California Press, 2002).

Hunt, David, 'John [Allan Francis] Harding', *Oxford Dictionary of National Biography* (http://www.oxforddnb.com/view/article/40129) [27 June 2016].

Hyam, Ronald, *Britain's Declining Empire: The Road to Decolonisation 1918–1968* (Cambridge: Cambridge University Press, 2006).

Jeger, Lena M., 'Hugh Mackintosh Foot', *Oxford Dictionary of National Biography* (http://www.oxforddnb.com/view/article/40197?docPos=1) [30 September 2016].

Karyos, Andreas, 'Britain and Policing of the Revolt in Cyprus, April 1955–March 1956' ('*H Vrettania kai h astynomeush ths Epanastasis sthn Kypro, Aprilios 1955-Martios 1956: To Prooimio ths Klimakwshs tou Kypriakou Agwna*'), *National Guard & History* (*Ethniki Froura & Istoria*), 33 (January–June 2014), 34–51, in Greek.

Karyos, Andreas, 'The Political Committee of the Cypriot Struggle (PEKA), 1956–1959: An Introductory Approach' ('*H Politikh Epitroph Kypriakou Agwna (PEKA), 1956-1959: Mia Eisagwgikh Proseggish*'), *National Guard & History* (*Ethniki Froura & Istoria*), 34 (July–December 2014), 66–77, in Greek.

Karyos, Andreas, 'British Archival Sources and Individual Aspects of the Cypriot Struggle: The Case of Markos Drakos' ('*Oi Vretanikes Arxeiakes Phges kai oi Epi Merous Ptuxes tou Kypriakou Agwna: H Periptwsh tou Markou Drakou*'), *National*

Guard & History (*Ethniki Froura & Istoria*), 31 (January–June 2013), 74–85, in Greek.

Karyos, Andreas, *EOKA 1955–59: A Study of the Military Aspects of the Cyprus Revolt* (PhD thesis, Institute of Commonwealth Studies, University of London, 2011).

Katz, Elihu, and Eberhard George Wedell, *Broadcasting in the Third World: Promise and Performance* (Cambridge: Harvard University Press, 1977).

Kennedy, Greg and Christopher Tuck, eds., *British Propaganda and Wars of Empire: Influencing Friend and Foe 1900–2010* (Surrey, UK; Burlington, USA: Ashgate, 2014).

Kontos, Michalis, Nikos Panayiotides and Haralambos Alexandrou, eds., *Great Power Politics in Cyprus: Foreign Interventions and Domestic Perceptions* (Cambridge: Cambridge Scholars Publishing, 2014).

Liera, Maria G. Flores, 'The Writer – British Crown Spy', *Mignatiou.com* (http://mignatiou.com/2014/09/osingrafeaskataskopostouvretanikoustemmatos/) [28 January 2015] in Greek.

Linstrum, Erik, *Ruling Minds: Psychology in the British Empire* (Cambridge, MA; London: Harvard University Press, 2016).

Linstrum, Erik, 'The Politics of Psychology in the British Empire, 1898–1960', *Past and Present*, 215 (May 2012), 195–233.

MacKenzie, John M., *Propaganda and Empire: The Manipulation of British Public Opinion 1880–1960* (Manchester: Manchester University Press, 1984).

Mallinson, William, 'Spies, Jolly Hockeysticks and Imperialism in Cyprus', *Journal of Balkan and Near Eastern Studies*, 3:2 (2011), 263–268.

Mallinson, William, *Cyprus, A Modern History* (London: I.B. Tauris, 2005).

Markides, Diana, *Cyprus 1957–1963: From Colonial Conflict to Constitutional Crisis: The Key Role of the Municipal Issue* (Minneapolis, MN: University of Minnesota, 2001).

Markides, Diana, 'Britain's "New Look" Policy for Cyprus and the Makarios-Harding Talks, January 1955–March 1956', *The Journal of Imperial and Commonwealth History*, 23:3 (1995), 479–502.

McIntyre, W. David, *Winding Up the British Empire in the Pacific Islands* (Oxford; New York: Oxford University Press, 2014).

Mumford, Andrew, *The Counter-insurgency Myth: The British Experience of Irregular Warfare* (Milton Park, Abingdon, OX; New York: Routledge, 2012).

Mumford, Andrew, *Puncturing the Counterinsurgency Myth: Britain and Irregular Warfare in the Past, Present, and Future* (Carlisle, PA: Strategic Studies Institute, U.S. Army War College, 2011).

Novo, Andrew R., 'The God Dilemma: Faith, the Church, and Political Violence in Cyprus', *Journal of Modern Greek Studies*, 31:2 (October 2013), 193–215.

Novo, Andrew R., 'Friend or Foe? The Cyprus Police Force and the EOKA Insurgency', *Small Wars & Insurgencies*, 23:3 (2012), 414–431.

Novo, Andrew R., *On All Fronts: EOKA and the Cyprus Insurgency, 1955–1959* (PhD thesis, Oxford University, 2010).

O'Shea, Helen, *Ireland and the End of the British Empire: The Republic and Its Role in the Cyprus Emergency* (London: I.B. Tauris, 2014).

Papadopoullos, Theodore, 'Orthodox Church and Civil Authority', *Journal of Contemporary History*, 2:201 (1967), 201–209.

Parry, Marc, 'Uncovering the Brutal Truth about the British Empire', *The Guardian*, 18 August 2016 (https://www.theguardian.com/news/2016/aug/18/uncovering-truth-british-empire-caroline-elkins-mau-mau) [30 September 2016].

Paulu, Burton, *Radio and Television Broadcasting on the European Continent* (Minneapolis: University of Minnesota Press, 1967).

Persianis, Panayiotis, 'British Colonial Higher Education Policy-making in the 1930s: The Case of a Plan to Establish a University in Cyprus', *Compare: A Journal of Comparative and International Education*, 33:3 (2003), 351–368.

Persianis, Panayiotis, 'The British Colonial Education "Lending" Policy in Cyprus (1878–1960): An Intriguing Example of an Elusive "Adapted Education" Policy', *Comparative Education*, 32:1 (1996), 45–68.

Potter, Simon J., 'Propaganda and Empire', in *The Encyclopedia of Empire*, ed. by John M. MacKenzie (John Wiley & Sons, Ltd., 2016), 1–6 (p. 5) (http://onlinelibrary.wiley.com/doi/10.1002/9781118455074.wbeoe086/full) [16 March 2016].

Potter, Simon J., *Broadcasting Empire: The BBC and the British World, 1922–1970* (Oxford: Oxford University Press, 2012).

Potter, Simon J., 'Webs, Networks, and Systems: Globalization and the Mass Media in the Nineteenth- and Twentieth-Century British Empire', *The Journal of British Studies*, 46:3 (July 2007), 621–646.

Potter, Simon J., 'Strengthening the Bonds of the Commonwealth: The Imperial Relations Trust and Australian, New Zealand and Canadian Broadcasting Personnel in Britain, 1946–1952', *Media History*, 11:3 (2005), 193–205.

Potter, Simon J. and Jonathan Saha, 'Global History, Imperial History and Connected Histories of Empire', *Journal of Colonialism and Colonial History*, 16:1 (Spring 2015).

Ramakrishna, Kumar, *Emergency Propaganda: The Winning of Malayan Hearts and Minds 1948–1958* (London: Routledge, 2013 edition).

Rappas, Alexis, 'The Transnational Formation of Imperial Rule on the Margins of Europe: British Cyprus and the Italian Dodecanese in the Interwar Period', *European History Quarterly*, 45:3 (2015), 467–505.

Rappas, Alexis, 'Greeks under European Colonial Rule: National Allegiance and Imperial Loyalty', *Byzantine and Modern Greek Studies*, 34:2 (2010), 201–218.

Rappas, Alexis, 'The Elusive Polity: Imagining and Contesting Colonial Authority in Cyprus during the 1930s', *Journal of Modern Greek Studies* 26:2 (October 2008), 363–397.

Rice, Tom, *Films for the Colonies: Cinema and the Preservation of the British Empire* (Berkeley, California: University of California Press, 2019).

Schmid, Alex P. and Albert J. Jongman, *Political Terrorism: A New Guide to Actors, Authors, Concepts, Data Bases, Theories, and Literature* (New Brunswick; London: Transaction Publishers, 1988).

Severis, Rita, *'Although to Sight Lost, to Memory Dear': Representations of Cyprus by Foreign Travellers/Artists 1700–1955*, Vol. 1 (PhD thesis, University of Bristol, 1999).

Shaw, Tony, *Eden, Suez and the Mass Media: Propaganda and Persuasion during the Suez Crisis* (London; New York: I.B. Tauris, 1996).

Simpson, A. W. Brian, *Human Rights and the End of Empire: Britain and the End of Genesis of the European Convention* (Oxford and New York: Oxford University Press, 2001).

Stavri, Michalis, '"Cromwell" and "AKOE": Aspects of the British Counteraction towards EOKA's Struggle 1955-1959', *Phileleftheros* newspaper, 2 April 2018.

Stavri, Michalis, '"We Want to Group Together All the Haters of E.O.K.A.": The British groups of "Cromwell" and "AKOE"', presentation at the History and Literature Regarding the 1955-1959 Struggle conference, 20-22 November 2015, Nicosia, Cyprus, in Greek.

Stelya, Nikolaos, 'The Short-lived Bi-communal Cyprus Broadcasting Corporation', *Media History*, 22:2 (2016), 217-231.

Stubbs, Jonathan, 'Making Headlines in a State of Emergency: The Case of the Times of Cyprus, 1955-1960', *The Journal of Imperial and Commonwealth History*, 45:1 (2017), 70-92.

Stubbs, Jonathan, 'Lawrence Durrell and the Information Services Department in Cyprus', *Deus Loci: The Lawrence Durrell Journal*, 14 (2015), 173-179.

Stubbs, Jonathan and Bahar Taşeli, 'Newspapers, Nationalism and Empire', *Media History*, 20:3 (2014), 284-301.

Thomas, Martin, *Fight or Flight: Britain, France, and Their Roads from Empire* (Oxford: Oxford University Press, 2014).

Thomas, Martin, 'Insurgent Intelligence: Information Gathering and Anti-colonial Rebellion', *Intelligence and National Security*, 22:1 (2007), 155-163.

Thomas, Martin and Gareth Curless, *Decolonization and Conflict Colonial Comparisons and Legacies* (London: Bloomsbury Academic, 2017).

Thomas, Martin and Richard Toye, 'Arguing about Intervention: A Comparison of British and French Rhetoric Surrounding the 1882 and 1956 Invasions of Egypt', *The Historical Journal*, 58:4 (2015), 1081-1113.

Trenear-Harvey, Glenmore S., *Historical Dictionary of Intelligence Failures* (Lanham; Boulder; New York; London: Rowman & Littlefield, 2014).

Unknown author, 'Hugh Foot', *Encyclopaedia Britannica* (https://www.britannica.com/biography/Hugh-Foot) [22 March 2017].

Unknown author, 'What Was EOKA; on April 1st, 1955 Her Liberation Struggle Begins' ('*Poia itan i EOKA; 1 Apriliou 1955 xekina o apeleftherotikos agonas tis*'), 1 April 2015, *On Alert* (http://www.onalert.gr/stories/poa-itan-eoka/23832) [9 September 2015] in Greek.

Vanezis, P. N., *Makarios: Life and Leadership* (London: Abelard-Schuman, 1979).

Vanezis, P. N., *Makarios: Pragmatism v. Idealism* (London: Abelard-Schuman, 1974).

Vanezis, P. N., *Makarios: Faith and Power* (London: Abelard-Schuman, 1971).

Varnava, Andrekos, 'Reinterpreting Macmillan's Cyprus Policy, 1957–1960', *Cyprus Review*, 32:1 (2010), 79–106.

Varnava, Andrekos and Michalis N. Michael, eds., *The Archbishops of Cyprus in the Modern Age: The Changing Role of the Archbishop-Ethnarch, Their Identities and Politics* (Newcastle upon Tyne: Cambridge Scholars Publishing, 2013).

Index

9 780755 637546